A Preface to Action

Interpretations of Politics in America

A Preface to Action

Interpretations of Politics in America

Kenneth Smorsten

Goodyear Publishing Company, Inc.

Pacific Palisades, California

Library of Congress Cataloging in Publication Data

Smorsten, Kenneth.
A Preface to action.

Includes index.
1. Political participation—United States. I. Title.
JK1764.S56   320.9'73   75-30236
ISBN 0-87620-700-X

Library of Congress Catalog Card Number: 75-30236
ISBN: 0-87620-700-X
Y-700X-1
Current Printing (last number): 10 9 8 7 6 5 4 3 2 1
Printed in the United States of America

Supervising production editor, Sally Kostal
Copy editor, Tom Moule
Designer: Design Office/Peter Martin
Photo editor, Barbara Hodder.

Photo Acknowledgments

Page x Eileen Christelow, Jeroboam, Inc.
Page 150 © Alex Webb, Magnum Photos
Page 270 Mark Godfrey, Magnum Photos

To Sherry

Contents

Preface

In the wake of Watergate, the war in Southeast Asia, and myriad other shocks to the American psyche, the question of whether to engage in or retreat from political action looms as a major issue of our time. It is a question that perplexes students with high ideals and great ambitions who now feel frustrated by their own inconclusive attempts at achieving reform. It is a question that confounds members of Congress, state legislators, and other governmental officials who, despite noble intentions, sometimes feel lost in the bureaucracy of the modern political state. And it is a question that challenges those people generally who, with various amounts of political ambition, still strive to have some impact on the political life of this country.

Much controversy has accompanied this question—controversy over whether this nation's political system truly offers meaningful opportunities for citizen participation. While some cling optimistically to the view that the United States remains an open and accessible society, others see an ever-expanding dominance by rich and powerful elites hell-bent on muting the voices of those who challenge their authority.

This book offers a unique look at the nature of citizen politics and its accompanying controversies. It presents, for the student's inspection, several popular interpretations of the political power structure and their implications for individual participation. The issues relating to participation have been largely ignored in introductory books on American politics. Rarely has consideration been given to how the nature of American politics affects the opportunities for political action—by ordinary citizens, members of Congress, even Presidents. In part, at least, this oversight may explain why many students find political science courses irrelevant or dissatisfying.

Also, the majority of texts espouse a certainty about the nature of political "reality" in the United States, offering readers few tools with which to evaluate and challenge their conclusions. My feeling is that political reality in this country is what one sees it to be. It is merely the sum total of our diverse perspectives, theories, and models. Depending on where we stand in society— as rich man, poor man, baker, or thief—we will form our own unique vision of the political landscape.

Understanding that, I have tried as fairly as possible (given my own biases) to present alternative perspectives and theories, encouraging the reader to form a systematic view of American politics that most comfortably conforms with his or her own experiences. While this book offers much of the information traditionally covered in introductory government courses, my central goal has been to draw the student into the great controversies and debates concerning the relationship between people and government. To this end, I have tried to maintain a lucid, easy-to-read style of writing—one that I hope will stimulate, rather than inhibit, creative thinking by the student. Topics such as bureaucracy, constitutional foundations, and civil liberties that are usually placed in separate chapters have been woven throughout this volume and discussed in the contexts that give them special meaning. And I have purposely kept the book short for those instructors, who, in these inflationary times, still wish to use supplemental paperbacks to explore further the social and political issues they find compelling.

Acknowledgements

Like most books, this one owes its existence to the combined efforts of many people. Perceptive reviewers, supportive friends, and helpful colleagues, as well as an excellent editorial and production staff at Goodyear Publishing Company all played a significant part in the creation of this book. I am especially grateful to David Grady, Sally Kostal, Peter Martin, Jane Hellesoe-Henon Barbara Hodder, Dana Floyd, and Richard Harris Smith for their creative advice and contributions. And, without the talented assistance of my wife, Sherry, it is doubtful this book could ever have been written; my debts to her are incalculable. Finally, I owe much to my mother, Jenny, without whom this book definitely would not exist. My thanks to all.

Kenneth Smorsten

Dilemmas of Citizen Participation

1 The Political Experience

*A*n introductory course in American politics offers a won-
derous opportunity—the chance to see everyday news items dis-
sected, classified, and occasionally made inexplicable. Concepts
like "power" and "democracy" suddenly lose their simplicity,
turning into solemn and obscure topics for all-night essays.

Perhaps this is inevitable. Studying politics at a distance—
whether in the classroom or on television—somehow changes the
nature of political experience, making it seem more detached,
more abstract, than what we may remember about door-to-door
campaigning, demonstrating, or inking in a ballot. Regardless of
whether we have engaged in such activities, we still sense that
studying politics in the classroom is only part of our education,
a step on the way to whatever political experiences are in store
for us. At least we can hope that by reading and talking with
others we will acquire new perspectives from which to perceive
those experiences.

To ease the reader into the subjects at hand, this chapter reviews
how some Americans see politics in the 1970s, and how they feel
about voicing their concerns. It also presents a brief look at a
few definitions of politics, and, for those curious about the discipline, a peek at political science itself.

The Despair and Cynicism of Politics

In contrast to many other countries, such as England, where politics is still regarded as a totally respectable profession, in the United States we often view the political world with suspicion, conjuring up images of shady conduct and under-the-table dealings by astute politicians striving for personal gain. To praise those in public life is to proclaim them as being "above politics."

This jaundiced view is extremely widespread, and has been nurtured even by those active in government. Ronald Reagan, for instance, often remarked during his first campaign for Governor of California in 1966 that it was time to save the state from "politicians," time to elect someone like him who had not been tainted by contact with professional politics. When Martha Mitchell fled Washington in the summer of 1972, dragging her husband, John, along with her, she paused to condemn "all those dirty things that go on."

The disillusionment with politics is, of course, not a new phenomenon; it did not spring entirely from such recent scandals as Watergate. In looking back through the years of polling public attitudes, one finds that politics in this country rarely has been regarded as a respectable occupation. As Table 1-1 shows, 68 percent of Americans back in 1945 said they would not want their child to take up a political career. In June 1973, at the height of the Watergate scandal, negative responses stood at 64 percent. The reasons people most commonly gave for not recommending the political life to the young were that politics made it "hard to be honest," that it involved "too much pressure," and that it was "too crooked/corrupt."

One clear effect of the Watergate scandal, however, has been to magnify the public's concern over political corruption. Prior to Watergate, Gallup surveys found only a few instances where people considered corruption in government to be among the most pressing issues facing the country. But by May of 1973, political corruption was surpassed only by inflation, crime, and drugs as the most important national problem. Moreover, Harris polls found that whereas 46 percent of Americans in 1967 believed that "most politicians are in politics to make money for themselves," in 1973 more than 63 percent believed this to be the case.

Whether politics in the United States actually suffers from more corruption today than it has in the past remains debatable. But it is certain that the evidence of corruption and misuse of governmental power has been presented so persuasively by the news media as to make cynicism and distrust of politicians practically

Table 1-1. Son into Politics? June 22–25, 1973

Question: "If you had a son, would you like to see him go into politics as a life's work?"

National	Yes 23%	No 64%	No Opinion 13%
Sex			
Male	29	57	14
Female	19	69	12
Race			
White	23	65	12
Non-white	29	52	19
Education			
College	31	56	13
High School	22	65	13
Grade School	18	69	13
Occupation			
Prof. & Bus.	30	55	15
White Collar	23	64	13
Farmers	12	77	11
Manual	24	64	12
Age			
18–29 years	24	61	15
30–49 years	27	61	12
50 & over	19	69	12
Religion			
Protestant	22	67	11
Catholic	26	59	15
Jewish	X	X	X
Politics			
Republican	23	68	9
Democrat	24	83	13
Independent	24	61	15
Region			
East	25	60	15
Midwest	23	64	13
South	21	65	14
West	26	65	9
Income			
$15,000 & over	30	58	12
$10,000–$14,999	26	59	15
$ 7,000–$ 9,999	21	70	9
$ 5,000–$ 6,999	22	67	11
$ 3,000–$ 4,999	18	69	14
Under $3,000	17	69	14
Community Size			
1,000,000 & over	25	59	16
500,000–999,999	30	52	18
50,000–499,999	27	64	9
2,500–49,999	19	72	9
Under 2,500, Rural	19	68	13
The Trend			
1945	21	68	11
1953	20	70	10
1955	27	60	13
1965	36	54	10
1973	23	64	13

Source: *Gallup Opinion Index*, July 1973.

Ken Smorsten

epidemic. Indeed, the revelations of governmental improprieties during the past few years have been extraordinary. The revelations began to surface with increasing rapidity in the early 1970s when, as a result of the publication of the *Pentagon Papers*, Americans learned of the deceit by top governmental and military officials intent on prolonging and justifying U.S. military actions in Southeast Asia. Then came the story of ITT's collusion with the CIA to stage a coup in Chile, the Watergate burglary, and a whole series of federal indictments of former presidential aides and Cabinet officers. By early 1975, close to forty of Richard Nixon's White House associates had gone before the courts to face Watergate-related charges. And, if that was not enough to dispel public confidence and trust, Americans witnessed the successive resignations of a Vice-President convicted of tax evasion and a President implicated in the Watergate cover-up. Unlike previous scandals and crises in government, such as the Teapot Dome affair under Warren Harding, news of the more recent scandals was brought "live" into American homes by television, making each viewer feel almost like a participant in the unfolding drama.

Some insist that television and other communications media have helped reinforce feelings of political distrust and alienation not only by disclosing scandals but by commenting on the magnitude of public disenchantment with government. The media daily

"Once upon a time there lived a little green elf in an old oak tree which had been condemned to make way for Interstate 95. The old oak tree stood by contaminated waters that ran along the edge of the strip mine just twenty-five miles from the heavily polluted air of the city. In spite of his emphysema he was a fairly happy elf . . ."

remind the individual that with apathy and cynicism spreading across the land, he or she is not alone in harboring feelings of disenchantment. Natural suspicions of politicians and government are reinforced and given credence by the media's revealing similar doubts in others.

Indeed, in recent years Americans have engaged in a great deal of introspection about the character of life in the United States. Magazine articles, books, television news specials, and college seminars have abounded with analyses and explanations of the violence, alienation, and polarization afflicting American society. Vance Packard, for example, has insisted in his book *A Nation of Strangers*[1] that the increasing mobility of Americans—one-fifth of whom change their address at least once a year—has reduced trust, has fragmented communities, and has increased indiffer-

Figure 1–1. Do You Make a Difference?

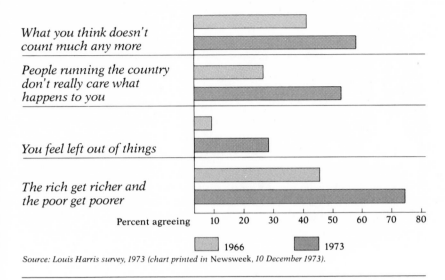

What you think doesn't
count much any more

People running the country
don't really care what
happens to you

You feel left out of things

The rich get richer and
the poor get poorer

Percent agreeing   10   20   30   40   50   60   70   80

☐ 1966   ▨ 1973

Source: Louis Harris survey, 1973 (chart printed in Newsweek, 10 December 1973).

ence to crime. Such commentaries have made many formerly popular interpretations of American culture seem dated and out-worn. Whereas the society was once described as a huge "melting pot," it is now seen as a "pressure cooker." Whereas it had once been said that most Americans were optimistic about the future, the national mood now seems pessimistic. Instead of public confidence in government, a general political malaise (again, brought on only partly by Watergate) has been said to be enveloping the country. Many Americans, notes Packard, "feel unconnected to either people or place and throughout much of the nation there is a breakdown in community living. . . . We are confronted with a society that is coming apart at the seams."[2]

However, this is not to downplay the tremendous outpouring of commentary on the promise of America and its political institutions. Many observers have viewed the long ordeal of Watergate as a reaffirmation, not an undermining, of the political system's basic strengths. Although the White House may temporarily have sunk into the mud, the judicial branch, the press, some independent prosecutors, and even Congress performed their jobs. These observers see the United States, embroiled in a crisis of epic proportions, emerging with its political institutions alive and well.

Still, whatever the communications media's impact on people's general attitudes toward politics (for more on this, see Chapter Five), a large share of the population views its relationship to government in anything but glowing terms. One of the most dramatic crises presently facing the country is the overwhelming lack of public confidence in government's responsiveness to the individual. As we will see later, many Americans have come to believe not that they can regulate or control government but that government regulates and controls them. They sense that policy making has fallen into the hands of corrupt and self-serving scoundrels who pursue their own selfish interests without regard for the welfare of the nation as a whole. According to an opinion survey conducted by pollster Louis Harris for a Senate subcommittee in 1973, public confidence in the country's political institutions has been falling off dramatically since 1966. As Figure 1-1 shows, a growing number of people take a disheartened view of both the American political process and their own role in it. "America looks to the top of the governmental structure for inspiration," Harris concluded, "and finds it missing. In that unhappy verdict is summed up the broad loss of confidence, the pervasive sense of discontent and the most serious reasons for concern about the future course of the American democracy."[3]

Ironically, the two-hundredth anniversary celebration of the American Revolution brings such expressions of discontent into clearer focus by pointing up the underlying similarities between the dissatisfactions of Americans who lived two centuries ago and those of the present generation. Like many of the early colonists, a large number of contemporary Americans are concerned about individual rights and their control over their own future. Although no longer pitted against a foreign king, they find themselves fearing similar forms of impersonal and arbitrary power—now being exercised by corporations, bureaucrats, and politicians.

It would be difficult to overstate the degree of dissatisfaction and frustration evoked by the feeling of powerlessness in society today. As student protesters found during the Vietnam War, efforts to dissent, petition, and demonstrate against the determination and resources of national government usually result in little change in policy. The important political decisions of life and death continue to be rendered by those far removed from the experiences and desires of ordinary citizens on the street. In this context, the rise of a "New Left," the growing support for self-proclaimed "Populists" like George Wallace, the demands of black militants, even the refusal of a large portion of the electorate to vote, can all be interpreted as protests against the current practices of national politics.

To Be or Not To Be in Politics

Many Americans, it is true, still dream of exercising some measure of influence on their political environment. To them, the idea of making a mark in a world they did not create remains vivid and compelling. The desire for that elusive ingredient called "power"—which we will examine more closely later—can be one of the most common of human aspirations. It can be a source of ambition as potent and persistent as the quest for security or love. In this society people are often judged, and awarded prestige, on the basis of their ability to influence the behavior of others, to affect or determine the outcome of events. Obviously the motivations underlying the pursuit of political power may vary enormously from one person to another. Some people, for example, may envision themselves as potentially great reformers who wish to improve human welfare or reverse the decay of society. Others may seek merely to augment their own self-importance or gratify a lifelong lust for economic gain. Whatever the basic motivation for political power, the political arena seems to many an exciting place in which to shape human events, to make something—anything—happen.

Yet few Americans who dream of exerting a profound influence on the course of political events ever manage to see their dreams fulfilled. In a country with a population exceeding 210 million, it is difficult for any individual—especially one lacking exceptional wealth or political savvy—to be more than just another face in the crowd. A person may vote in every election, join a prominent interest group, write erudite and seething letters to the President, even run for office and still wonder whether he or she will ever be able to exercise significant political clout.

The reaction of many Americans is simply to stop trying, to forget about politics and avoid the frustrations. They may continue to daydream of personal power, wishing they could change the course of events; but their incentives to action remain weak. As we will see later, the actual proportion of those who become involved in any kind of political activity apart from voting is small. Only a tiny fraction of the voting-age population write letters to their representatives, join in political campaigns, become active in lobbying, or run for political office. Although a hundred reasons may account for the inaction—including just a basic lack of interest in politics—many people abstain out of a deep sense of futility, out of the belief that their involvement makes no significant difference. They feel that, as only one voice among millions, they are incapable of making government responsive to their desires.

In short, they simply do not wish to imitate the proverbial optimist who sits all day long on the pier pushing hard with his feet against the hull of a docked ship, only to find himself, and not the ship, moving under the strain.

Yet despite the frustrations and discouragements, many Americans continue to try their hand at politics. In newspapers and on television screens we see public school teachers parading in front of state capitols, and students protesting in the streets. We hear about lobbyists courting legislators while prison inmates or secluded kidnappers negotiate with authorities for changes in the established order. We follow the progress of hard-working reformers, of environmentalists, and of anticommunist crusaders. And for every American we see struggling to change the status quo, we see another seeking to conserve it. All these active participants maintain an optimism that their efforts are worthwhile, that while their success may be modest, it is still worth striving for.

In a sense, those of us who do not participate actively in politics still remain involved in the political drama. Even the so-called spectators among us find the views and actions of politicians, reformers, and revolutionaries, portrayed so vividly by the news media, intruding on our consciousness. The indignations of Ralph Nader or the surprise revelations by a congressional committee of corruption in industry and government often find their way into our opinions and attitudes. Even personal views expressed in the presence of close friends—or on bumper stickers, or as graffiti on walls—can be seen as a response to, and a participation in, the politics of the times.

"Politics" and Some Views of "Power"

What, then, is "politics"? While some would argue that "politics" refers simply to the activities of government, others view it more broadly as the totality of everyday experience. In activist Abbie Hoffman's opinion, politics is "the way you live your life." In fact a major problem faced by political scientists is how to determine what politics is and what, therefore, they should study. The concept has become so ambiguous and controversial that no universal definition of it exists. As a result of the ambiguity, political scientists have been ridiculed for "riding off in many directions, evidently on the assumption that if you don't know where you are going, any road will take you there."[4]

But, assuming one wants to define and narrow the focus of political study to make it more comprehensible, how may a "political" act or event be distinguished from other kinds of acts or events? How may one determine when labor union bosses or corporation presidents are engaged in "politics" and when they are not? Although disagreement is rampant among political scientists, many view politics as the means of settling conflict and distributing scarce benefits. They point out that in most societies, controversy rages over who should receive the lion's share of whatever happens to be of value—whether it be material possessions such as money and land or intangibles such as prestige and power. People tend to want their own needs and desires satisfied, craving benefits that are in short supply and great demand. As often happens, unless they receive these benefits (or become convinced they cannot have them), disorder and even violence will ensue. Consequently, many political scientists see politics as the means of deciding how wealth, power, and other values are to be distributed and how conflicts and disagreements are to be managed. As Harold Lasswell succinctly put it, politics is the process of choosing "who gets what, when, and how."

This means that even many associations not usually regarded as "political"—such as schools, private clubs, and churches—may become embroiled in internal political conflicts resulting from disputes among rival factions. Casually speaking, even families may become engaged in "politics," as when a mother has to resolve a dispute between her children over which television program to watch, in effect deciding who will receive this "benefit" and who will not. Political scientists do not usually study such family quarrels, however, on the grounds that the outcome does not dramatically affect society as a whole.

It has been said that only when disputes over "who gets what" no longer exist in a society can there be an absence of politics. If benefits could be allocated totally without conflict—without anyone protesting they had "been had"—then even governmental decisions would become merely routine and administrative. Karl Marx, for instance, insisted that in a true "communist" society, where all class and labor distinctions have been erased and where each individual receives "according to his need," there would no longer be a basis for conflict and hence no need for political machinery to settle it. "Government over persons," he declared, would be replaced by a simple "administration of things."

In a sense, then, as long as conflict exists it hardly matters how a decision is made in order for that decision to be "political." Whether the distribution of wealth and power is decided by a

European dictator using strong-arm tactics, by a congressional committee compromising on a trade bill, or by citizens voting in a special referendum, a political process is under way to resolve conflict and distribute society's benefits. What is common to most (if not all) political systems, however, is a process of unequal distribution. The "rules of the game" rarely are unbiased; some groups get more of what there is to have, while others get less or nothing at all. When the cake is being sliced, some can expect a larger piece while others remain outside with their noses pressed against the window.

Thus, we can see why "power" is such an integral part of the study of politics. So long as conflict continues over "who gets what, when, and how," there will also be a struggle to see who gets to make this decision. If "power" is considered the ability to influence the behavior of others (see Chapter Two), then "political power" is the ability to decide how benefits will be distributed and disputes settled—to determine, for example, whether major oil companies will receive special tax breaks, whether the elderly will enjoy an increase in social security benefits, or whether environmentalists will win out over oil refineries in disputes over pollution control. In short, the study of politics leads to an analysis of how power is pursued, achieved, used, and lost. It leads to an examination of political campaigns, back room deals, voting, manipulation and propaganda, the link between corporate wealth and governmental policy, and even personal motivations and drives—the processes, in other words, that determine who will make the major political decisions affecting society's welfare. As we will see later, the analysis of "power" has resulted in sharply conflicting views of how important political decisions are made in the United States, and of who makes them.

DOONESBURY   **by Garry Trudeau**

The Tribulations of Studying Politics

Many political scientists, after having dealt with their subject a number of years, experience a letdown—a depression—about politics similar to that felt by many other people. As with history and sociology, the study of politics involves examining human behavior, with all its recurring brutality, selfishness, miseries, and injustices. There are probably few political scientists who have not at some time given thought to pursuing some other subject, such as art history or astronomy. There is a certain appeal to contemplating a Rembrandt painting or sitting alone in a mountaintop observatory viewing stars through a telescope, feeling removed in spirit from the daily turmoil of human events.

Moreover, some students continuing in the discipline complain that the study of politics does not offer the same "thrills of discovery" found in disciplines like physics, chemistry, or biology. For them, it does not appear that examining political behavior and philosophy will yield dramatic new information comparable to the discovery of a new subatomic particle, theory of creation, or animal species. In a sense they are probably right. As the oldest social science, political science continues to inspect many of the same fundamental problems that have confounded political thinkers for three thousand years. And with perhaps only a few notable exceptions, not many new and startling visions have occurred. Over the years the methods and approaches have become more sophisticated, and there certainly has been a proliferation of eager professionals devoted to political research, but the majority of subjects and concepts remain substantially unchanged. It is as if the superstructure of political study has exploded into a thousand little particles, with dozens of academics clumped around each particle, endlessly dissecting it.

This does not imply that new knowledge of political behavior and organization is not being sought. A number of inventive political scientists have been working to expand the discipline, seeking contact with scholars in biology, psychology, mathematics, anthropology, and ethology. In fact, some political scientists see no outer limits to their research; they are constantly involved with the progress and findings of other areas of study, regardless of labels. As one scholar has concluded, "A political scientist cannot close any doors. He must use the historian's evidence of past human experience; the economist's analysis of wealth, value, and distribution; the sociologist's explanation of status and group interrelations; the geographer's comparative data on natural resources; the psychologist's insights and findings about human behavior;

and the philosopher's analysis of political ends."[5]

There is also considerable controversy within the discipline over its true "scientific" capabilities. While some political scientists deeply feel that the study of politics can be both objective and empirical, others insist that politics—whether studied or practiced—cannot, and should not, be divorced from personal values.

The controversy will probably never be resolved, because the nature of "science" is primarily a matter of definition. If science is regarded simply as a way of gathering information through careful and deliberate observation—treating the subject matter with only as much precision as it allows—then perhaps political science can rightly be thought of as a "science." But if "science" implies instead an ability to submit the subject matter to controlled experiments that other scholars can duplicate and test under the same conditions, as well as the ability to produce general laws capable of yielding accurate predictions about future behavior, then the label may be less precise.

What we can say for certain is that political science must struggle with its own inherent limitations. Not only do personal values and biases often surface in treatises on politics (and perhaps should not be disguised), but in addition, people tend to be very unpredictable subjects of analysis who do not readily adapt to precise laboratory conditions. In fact, there is little overall agreement in political science about the meaning of even the most basic terms—such as *power, legitimacy,* or *democracy.* A scholar may select a topic for study and carefully gather data, only to discover that the findings have to be explained using concepts other political scientists do not accept.

We are therefore likely to find in political science a relative paucity of simple and established conclusions. Although political scientists may generally feel comfortable describing certain features of the political scene—such as the number of people voting in an election or the rules of a committee in Congress—they will have to be a great deal more tentative in offering explanations—such as *why* people vote in a certain way or *how* committee members reach their decisions. As we will discover throughout this volume, political scientists are rarely in harmonious agreement on the major questions of politics, especially on how a citizen may fit into the political scheme of things. We will find that to arrive at some definite conclusions about our own role in the politics of this country, ultimately we will have to furnish our own explanations.

Lasswell, Harold D. *Politics: Who Gets What, When, How*. New York: McGraw-Hill, 1958.

Murphy, Robert E. *The Style and Study of Political Science*. Glenview, Ill.: Scott, Foresman, 1970.

Safire, William. *The New Language of Politics: A Dictionary of Catchwords, Slogans, and Political Usage*, 2d ed. New York: Collier Books, 1972.

Schuman, David. *Preface to Politics*. Boston: D. C. Heath, 1973.

Sherrill, Robert. *Why They Call It Politics*, 2d ed. New York: Harcourt Brace Jovanovitch, 1974.

Sorauf, Frank J. *Political Science: An Informal Overview*. Columbus, Ohio: Charles E. Merrill, 1965.

Wasby, Stephen L. *Political Science: The Discipline and Its Dimensions*. New York: Charles Scribner's Sons, 1970.

Recommended Reading

1. Vance Packard, *A Nation of Strangers* (New York: David McKay, 1972). Used with permission of David McKay Company, Inc.

2. Ibid., pp. 1–2. Used with permission of David McKay Company, Inc.

3. U.S. Senate, Committee on Government Operations, "Confidence and Concern: Citizens View American Government, A Survey of Public Attitudes," pt. 1 (Washington, D.C.: U.S. Government Printing Office, 1973). See also *Newsweek*, 10 December 1973, pp. 39–48.

4. Heinz Eulau, "Political Science," in Berthold F. Hoselitz, ed., *A Reader's Guide to the Social Sciences* (New York: Free Press, 1959), p. 91.

5. Robert E. Murphy, *The Style and Study of Political Science* (Glenview, Ill.: Scott, Foresman, 1970), p. 7.

Notes

2 Political Elites:

Who Governs in America?

The question of who really governs in the United States has probably haunted most of us at one time or another, and when the issue is raised it usually stirs a flurry of strong opinion. Political scientists have been especially caught up in the controversy and have spent years trying to resolve several pertinent questions: Who makes most of the important political decisions? How widely is political power shared? What impact do economic and other elites have on governmental policies? How accountable are these elites to the general public?

The answers to these questions are obviously crucial to those of us who wonder how we fit into the political system. Clearly our ability to accomplish anything meaningful in the political system depends enormously on how power is distributed and how difficult or easy it is to gain access to that power. Since we will be assessing some popular strategies for influencing policy in Chapter Nine, we should first look at some opposing theories of "who governs" relevant to citizen action.

Although there has been much debate over the question of how power is distributed, the dispute has been essentially narrowed to two currently popular alternatives: the "ruling-elite" theory and the "pluralist" theory. Briefly stated, the ruling-elite theory holds that power is concentrated in the hands of a small group of people subject to little or no control by the rest of society, while the pluralist theory states that power is more widely dispersed among many separate groups held in check by the public and by each other. As we will see, depending on which of these two theories is more plausible, certain implications concerning our own participation and influence become apparent. If the pluralist view is correct, it would seem that most of us can gain meaningful access to and influence over decision making. But, if the ruling-elite view comes closer to the truth, then the opportunity for effective action becomes more limited. As we examine these two conflicting theories, each of us ultimately must decide which one better describes the conditions of American politics and what are its full implications for individual action.

Before proceeding, we should keep in mind that few political scientists accept all the tenets of either complex theory. Nor does either theory necessarily refute point for point all the assumptions of the other. Each is unique in several of its interpretations of the American political scene and should be evaluated on its own merits. And, one should not be surprised to discover that disagreements about "who governs" will continue to arise—no matter how persuasive one theory may seem. Despite the elaborate evidence supporting each theory, the problems inherent in defining key terms like *elite* and *power,* and in circumventing the long-standing prejudices on each side, probably will continue to prevent either theory from being universally accepted.

The concept of "elite" remains especially troublesome, in spite of the many good definitions that have been proposed. Perhaps the most widely accepted definition today of an elite is the few who have the most of anything valued in society—whether that happens to be money, fame, status, or power. In political terms, an elite includes those who have the most control over the major decisions affecting other people's lives, who determine how scarce and desirable goods and values (like money, security, and even influence) will be distributed. This means that a political elite may comprise not only high governmental officials like the President and members of Congress, but also corporation executives and labor union bosses. We have seen that the decisions of oil companies to raise their prices and unions to strike can affect the distribution of benefits as greatly as can any single governmental policy.

A similar problem of definition arises with the central concept of "power." At best we can say that power is always *relational:* Power is not something that can be possessed in a vacuum or stored, but arises only in relations among people. Thus, social scientists often assert that "power" is the ability to affect the behavior of others, to compel them to do something they might otherwise not do. This means that as President of the United States or as corporation executive, a person can compel others to support a particular policy he or she advocates. It should be understood, of course, that it may be extremely difficult to determine exactly how that individual is able to get his or her own way. After all, power can assume many different forms. For example, a person may succeed in securing compliance from someone by relying on "authority" (where "power" is regarded as legitimate and right, as in the case of a mother to her son), by resorting to "force" (such as putting a gun to another person's head), by using "influence" (such as gentle, reasoned persuasion), or even by relying on "manipulation" (where subtle, underhanded methods leave the subject unaware of what is taking place). And a person's success in the matter may depend as much on his or her position as on any personal talents or attributes. Consequently, in view of the many varieties of "power," it is often difficult to pin down precisely not only *who* wields the power to make major political decisions in America but also *how* that power is exercised.[1]

The Ruling-Elite Theory

One of the most popular views of "who governs" in America today is the ruling-elite theory, which holds that power is concentrated in the hands of a small, fairly cohesive, group.[2] This theory appeals to those who believe the country is run by a "military-industrial complex," an "establishment," a "ruling class," or a behind-the-scenes "political machine." As one scholar remarked, "This kind of view . . . is simple, compelling, dramatic, 'realistic.' It gives one standing as an inside-dopester. For individuals with a strong strain of frustrated idealism, it has just the right touch of hard-boiled cynicism."[3] Although the ruling-elite theory has several different strains, a number of general conclusions about the structure of American political power are offered.

Single Elite

First, the ruling-elite theory holds that only a relatively small number of people dominate policy making in American society.

Figure 2–1. Ruling Elite Pyramid of Power

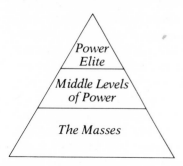

According to the late C. Wright Mills, a sociologist and leading proponent of the ruling-elite view, the basic pattern of power in the United States takes the shape of a pyramid. (See Figure 2-1.) At the apex of this pyramid stand the "power elite," a triumvirate consisting of top corporation executives, military officers in the Joint Chiefs of Staff, and high-ranking politicians like the President and his advisors. Together these three groups control most of the wealth, weapons, and other political resources that underlie the "important" decisions in government and the economy— whether to plunge the nation into war, recognize or trade with other countries, or overhaul current economic policies. The power elite wield this enormous power not because they have seized command by design but primarily because they occupy positions in great and powerful institutions. They get their own way mainly because they serve as chief of staff of the army, president of General Motors, Secretary of Agriculture, or chairman of the Chase Manhattan Bank.

Beneath this powerful triumvirate is a second layer consisting of judges, interest groups, members of Congress, and media executives who constitute what Mills terms the "middle levels of power." Although they exert a great deal of influence on policies, they cannot usually match the influence of the top elite. At best they can muster limited veto power (for example, through congressional committees) that may temporarily thwart policies of the top elite. But they lack the capacity to initiate and implement major new policies or to permanently block programs enthusiastically favored by the President, large corporations, and the military, especially in economic and foreign affairs.

Finally, at the bottom of the pyramid sit the rest of the population—the "mass society"—who not only have little say on policy, but are controlled and dominated from above. They have no direct access to the decision-making levels of government—except perhaps through elections, which are manipulated anyway by the elite. "The bottom of this society," Mills concluded, "is politically fragmented, and even as a passive fact, increasingly powerless: at the bottom there is emerging a mass society."[4]

Cohesive Power Elite

A second contention of the ruling-elite view is that an interlocking relationship exists among the top leadership in the United States. Although a balance of power may prevail among interest groups, members of Congress, and judges at the "middle levels of power," the "power elite" at the top—the President, corporation executives, and the military brass—have been drawn together into a fairly cohesive group who know one another and who usually get what they want by pooling their resources. In other words, the top elite are not only more powerful than other groups but they also interlock in several important respects.

In the first place, the career patterns of the top elite frequently overlap. Many former military and governmental officials, for example, eventually join major industries as executives and lobbyists, helping their firms win lucrative government contracts, price supports, and other political favors. Senator William Proxmire noted that in 1969, more than two thousand retired military officers with the rank of colonel or higher were on the payrolls of the top hundred military defense contractors.[5] In addition, many top corporation executives move into important appointive positions in government. Among those who held cabinet posts during the Nixon administration, for example, were George Romney, former president of American Motors; David Kennedy, chairman of the board of the Continental Illinois National Bank and Trust Company; David Packard, president of Hewlett-Packard Corporation; and Bryce Harlow, vice-president of Procter & Gamble.

In the second place, a basic overlapping of interests prevails among the military and many large corporations, especially those seeking defense contracts. As Table 2-1 shows, a sizable number of major companies—including Lockheed, McDonnell Douglas, and Newport News Shipbuilding—depend on military contracts for a significant portion of their business. In the year ending in

June 1973, the Pentagon awarded military contracts totalling more than $31 billion to major U.S. industries.[6] Lockheed alone accounted for 5.3 percent of all defense contracts, doing more than 80 percent of its business with the Pentagon. Among its military products were the S3A antisubmarine plane, the C5A airbus, and the *Poseidon* and *Trident* submarine-launched ballistic missiles. Ac-

Table 2-1. *Prime Military Contracts Awards 1960–1967 to U.S. Companies, for firms totaling more than $1 billion in this seven-year period (amounts in millions of dollars)*

Fiscal Year	1961	1962	1963	1964	1965	1966	1967	7-yr. Total	Percent of Total Sales
1. Lockheed Aircraft	1,175	1,419	1,517	1,455	1,715	1,531	1,807	10,619	88%
2. General Dynamics	1,460	1,197	1,033	987	1,179	1,136	1,832	8,824	67
3. McDonnell Douglas	527	779	863	1,360	1,026	1,001	2,125	7,681	75
4. Boeing Co.	920	1,133	1,356	1,365	583	914	912	7,183	54
5. General Electric	875	976	1,021	893	824	1,187	1,290	7,066	19
6. No. American Rockwell	1,197	1,032	1,062	1,019	746	520	689	6,265	57
7. United Aircraft	625	663	530	625	632	1,139	1,097	5,311	57
8. American Tel. & Tel.	551	468	579	636	588	672	673	4,167	9
9. Martin-Marietta	692	803	767	476	316	338	290	3,682	62
10. Sperry-Rand	408	466	446	374	318	427	484	2,923	35
11. General Motors	282	449	444	256	254	508	625	2,818	2
12. Grumman Aircraft	238	304	390	396	353	323	488	2,492	67
13. General Tire	290	366	425	364	302	327	273	2,347	37
14. Raytheon	305	407	295	253	293	368	403	2,324	55
15. AVCO	251	323	253	279	234	506	449	2,295	75
16. Hughes	331	234	312	289	278	337	419	2,200	u
17. Westinghouse Electric	308	246	323	237	261	349	453	2,177	13
18. Ford (Philco)	200	269	228	211	312	440	404	2,064	3
19. RCA	392	340	329	234	214	242	268	2,019	16
20. Bendix	269	286	290	257	235	282	296	1,915	42
21. Textron	66	117	151	216	196	555	497	1,798	36
22. Ling-Temco-Vought	47	133	206	247	265	311	535	1,744	70
23. Internat. Tel. & Tel.	202	244	266	256	207	220	255	1,650	19
24. I.B.M.	330	155	203	332	186	182	195	1,583	7
25. Raymond International ·	46	61	84	196	71	548	462	1,568	u
26. Newport News Shipbuilding	290	185	221	400	185	51	188	1,520	90 +
27. Northrop	156	152	223	165	256	276	306	1,434	61
28. Thiokol	210	178	239	254	136	111	173	1,301	96
29. Std. Oil of N.J.	168	180	155	161	164	214	235	1,277	2
30. Kaiser Industries	—	87	49	152	219	441	306	1,255	45
31. Honeywell	86	127	170	107	82	251	306	1,129	24
32. General Tel.	61	116	162	229	232	196	138	1,124	25
33. Collins Radio	94	150	144	129	141	245	202	1,105	65
34. Chrysler	158	181	186	170	81	150	165	1,091	4
35. Litton	—	88	198	210	190	219	180	1,085	25
36. Pan. Am. World Air.	127	147	155	164	158	170	115	1,046	44
37. F.M.C.	88	160	199	141	124	163	170	1,045	21
38. Hercules	117	182	183	137	101	120	195	1,035	31

u—unavailable. · Includes Morrison-Knudsen, Brown & Root, and J. A. Jones Construction Co.

Source: Ralph E. Lapp, *The Weapons Culture* (New York: W. W. Norton, 1968), pp. 186–87. (Data from Dept. of Defense, Directorate for Statistical Services.)

cording to the ruling-elite interpretation, because a major corporation like Lockheed wants lucrative military contracts and the Pentagon needs the equipment the corporation produces, each strives to maintain a high degree of cooperation with the other. Thus, it should be no surprise that the Nixon administration would offer a $250-million loan to Lockheed in 1971. Even though Lockheed's financial troubles stemmed in part from its $2-billion cost-overrun on the C5A cargo plane, the mutual benefits to the Pentagon and the company were given as justification for providing governmental relief.

But the close partnership between the government and corporations, according to the ruling-elite view, is not based solely on defense contracting. There is a shared conviction that policies benefiting major industries like General Motors and Exxon will equally benefit the government and the economy as a whole. The Nixon administration, for example, openly declared itself a "business administration"—a label more than justified, it seemed, by its cozy relationship with International Telephone and Telegraph, its support of the dairy industry in raising milk prices, its backing of oil interests in the Alaskan pipeline (strengthened by the so-called energy crisis), and its efforts to push the development of the supersonic transport (SST).

One explanation commonly given for this overlapping of interests between big business and government is that corporations contribute heavily to political campaign funds. Although corporations are prohibited by law from giving money directly to candidates, they have continued to do so. As the Watergate investigations revealed, a number of the biggest corporations in America— including Gulf Oil, American Airlines, and Greyhound—admitted to illegally scratching up large sums of money for Richard Nixon's 1972 reelection campaign. Another explanation is that no administration can afford to ignore the views and interests of industry leaders, whose decisions may create jobs and augment income that make an administration look good in the eyes of the public. As a result, from one administration to another, industries involved in such activities as shipping, oil, sugar production, mining, and agriculture reap subsidies and special tax breaks in the billions of dollars to enhance their profits and reduce their losses— constituting a blatant form of "welfare for the rich."

For these reasons, according to the ruling-elite view, the ties between government and business are hardly confined to Republican administrations. Corporations will exert a great deal of influence on government regardless of which party controls the White House. As labor boss John L. Lewis once complained, "The only

Table 2-2. Income Distribution Among American Families, 1947–1972

Year	Lowest 5th (Under $5,600)	Second 5th (Under $9,300)	Third 5th (Under $12,900)	Fourth 5th (Under $17,800)	Highest 5th ($17,800 and more)
1972	5.4%	11.9%	17.5%	23.9%	41.4%
1971	5.5	12.0	17.6	23.8	41.1
1970	5.4	12.2	17.6	23.8	40.9
1969	5.6	12.4	17.7	23.7	40.6
1968	5.6	12.4	17.7	23.7	40.5
1966	5.6	12.4	17.8	23.8	40.5
1960	4.8	12.2	17.8	24.0	41.3
1950	4.5	11.9	17.4	23.6	42.7
1947	5.1	11.8	16.7	23.2	43.3

Source: U.S. Bureau of the Census, 1972.

difference between Republicans and Democrats is that the Republicans stay bought. Democrats keep coming back for more."

Many people even interpreted the 1974 "energy crisis" according to the ruling-elite view. The fuel shortage during the winter of that year created suspicions that the energy crisis was fabricated by the oil companies, in collusion with the Nixon regime. A number of outspoken critics, including Ralph Nader, U.S. Senator John Tunney, and ecologist Barry Commoner, contended that the energy crisis may have been primarily an excuse used by the oil industry to boost the price of gasoline, quell environmentalists' criticisms, and increase profits. (Indeed, Exxon reported a 39-percent profit rise for the first quarter of 1974; Texaco reported a whopping 123-percent rise in profits.) Christopher T. Rand, former Middle East specialist for Standard Oil of California, even insisted that the White House helped manufacture the crisis because it "wanted some way to take the public's mind off Watergate, and also wanted to create a recession to stop inflation."[7]

Concentration of Economic Resources

Complementing the view of a closely knit power elite then is the argument that economics and politics are inevitably intertwined. Wealth provides the means to gain access to elected officials as well as to sustain the lobbyists, lawyers, and experts needed to promote one's special interests. In the opinion of one scholar, "Wealth . . . is doubly powerful, not only for what it can purchase

Table 2-3. The 50 Largest Industrial Corporations (ranked by sales)

Rank '74	Rank '73	Company	Sales ($000)	Assets ($000)	Rank	Net Income ($000)	Rank
1	2	Exxon (New York)	42,061,336	31,332,440	1	3,142,192	1
2	1	General Motors (Detroit)	31,549,546	20,468,100	2	950,069	8
3	3	Ford Motor (Dearborn, Mich.)	23,620,600	14,173,600	4	360,900	20
4	6	Texaco (New York)	23,255,497	17,176,121	3	1,586,441	3
5	7	Mobil Oil (New York) ROCKEFELLER	18,929,033	14,074,290	5	1,047,446	5
6	11	Standard Oil of California ROCKEFELLER (San Francisco)	17,191,186	11,639,996	8	970,018	7
7	10	Gulf Oil (Pittsburgh)	16,458,000	12,503,000	7	1,065,000	4
8	5	General Electric (Fairfield, Conn.)	13,413,100	9,369,100	10	608,100	12
9	8	International Business Machines (Armonk, N.Y.)	12,675,292	14,027,108	6	1,837,639	2
10	9	International Tel. & Tel. (New York)	11,154,401	10,696,544	9	451,070	16
11	4	Chrysler (Highland Park, Mich.)	10,971,416	6,732,756	13	(52,094)	493
12	13	U.S. Steel (New York)	9,186,403	7,717,493	12	634,858	9
13	15	Standard Oil (Ind.)(Chicago) ROCKEFELLER	9,085,415	8,915,190	11	970,266	6
14	18	Shell Oil (Houston)	7,633,455	6,128,884	16	620,539	11
15	12	Western Electric (New York)	7,381,728	5,239,551	18	310,633	28
16	21	Continental Oil (Stamford, Conn.)	7,041,423	4,673,434	22	327,609	23
17	16	E.I. du Pont de Nemours (Wilmington, Del.)	6,910,100	5,980,300	17	403,500	17
18	26	Atlantic Richfield (Los Angeles)	6,739,682	6,151,608	15	474,600	15
19	14	Westinghouse Electric (Pittsburgh)	6,466,112	4,301,804	24	28,132	277
20	36	Occidental Petroleum (Los Angeles)	5,719,369	3,325,471	32	280,677	32
21	24	Bethlehem Steel (Bethlehem, Pa.)	5,380,963	4,512,617	23	342,034	21
22	28	Union Carbide (New York)	5,320,123	4,882,800	20	530,058	14
23	19	Goodyear Tire & Rubber (Akron, Ohio)	5,256,247	4,241,626	25	157,461	54
24	29	Tenneco (Houston)	5,001,474	6,401,557	14	321,468	25
25	40	Phillips Petroleum (Bartlesville, Okla.)	4,980,704	4,028,112	28	402,138	18
26	22	International Harvester (Chicago)	4,965,916	3,326,962	31	124,053	72
27	38	Dow Chemical (Midland, Mich.)	4,938,483	5,114,314	19	557,457	13
28	30	Procter & Gamble (Cincinnati)	4,912,279	3,071,322	35	316,695	26
29	23	LTV (Dallas)	4,768,010	2,030,722	65	111,692	87
30	27	Esmark (Chicago)	4,615,715	1,266,143	124	68,066	154
31	20	RCA (New York)	4,594,300	3,646,600	29	113,300	83
32	25	Eastman Kodak (Rochester, N.Y.)	4,583,629	4,703,293	21	629,519	10
33	31	Kraftco (Glenview, Ill.)	4,471,427	1,710,438	84	94,627	108
34	49	Union Oil of California (Los Angeles)	4,419,049	3,458,650	30	288,003	30
35	35	Rockwell International (Pittsburgh)	4,408,500	3,043,000	36	130,300	68
36	34	Caterpillar Tractor (Peoria, Ill.)	4,082,127	2,933,940	40	229,181	36
37	60	Sun Oil (St. Davids, Pa.)	3,799,581	4,063,278	27	377,727	19
38	80	Amerada Hess (New York)	3,744,521	2,255,256	54	201,858	42
39	33	Boeing (Seattle)	3,730,667	1,746,314	82	72,432	144
40	37	Firestone Tire & Rubber (Akron, Ohio)	3,674,890	2,997,938	38	154,025	57
41	41	Xerox (Stamford, Conn.)	3,576,442	4,090,055	26	331,083	22
42	43	Beatrice Foods (Chicago)	3,541,216	1,419,424	105	116,991	80
43	45	Monsanto (St. Louis)	3,497,900	2,938,000	39	323,200	24
44	42	W.R. Grace (New York)	3,472,291	2,476,239	50	130,558	67
45	32	Greyhound (Phoenix)	3,458,336	1,357,328	110	57,955	169
46	59	United Aircraft (East Hartford, Conn.)	3,321,106	1,820,112	76	104,705	95
47	48	Borden (New York)	3,264,502	1,659,263	90	83,845	127
48	56	R.J. Reynolds Industries (Winston-Salem, N.C.)	3,229,668	3,126,074	34	310,698	27
49	44	Lockheed Aircraft (Burbank, Calif.)	3,222,000	N.A.		N.A.	
50	75	Ashland Oil (Russell, Ky.)	3,215,667	1,715,761	83	113,004	84

Source: *Fortune* magazine, May 1975.

now but for what it can buy in the future. In this double sense wealth negates, or at least frustrates, other more fleeting power factors that unquestionably are dispersed—ethnic popularity, ingenuity, luck, and others. Men of wealth can afford to wait, to bide their time while maintaining continual pressure on behalf of their interests."[8]

For this reason, advocates of the ruling-elite theory consider it significant that the structure of economic power and resources in America also assumes the shape of a pyramid. As illustrated in Table 2-2, the 1972 census shows that the richest 20 percent of the families in the United States received 41.4 percent of the total private income in the country, while the poorest 20 percent received only 5.4 percent—a distribution that has not changed substantially since the 1940s. In fact, when measured in terms of accumulated wealth instead of just annual income, the economic scales are weighted even more unevenly. According to recent estimates, the top 1 percent of wealthy adults in the United States lay claim to roughly 25 percent of all personal property and financial assets in the country.[9] They own at least 51 percent of all the stock and collect almost 47 percent of all the dividends.[10]

A similar concentration of resources prevails among major corporations. In 1974, the 500 largest industrial corporations, representing less than 0.5 percent of all industrials, accounted for approximately 66 percent of the sales of all U.S. industrial companies and 72 percent of the total profits (see Table 2-3).[11] Many of these corporations even interlocked as a result of having some of the same people sitting on their boards of directors. Moreover, according to a report issued by two Senate Government Operations subcommittees in January 1974, "A few institutional investors, principally six superbanks headquartered in New York," held enough stock in competing corporations to influence entire industries. Of these six, the report stated that the Chase Manhattan Bank, headed by David Rockefeller (brother of Nelson Rockefeller), was the biggest bank stockholder in twenty major corporations. Chase Manhattan held more than 5 percent of the stocks of four airlines and was a substantial stockholder in the firms that own the three major television networks. Altogether the banks held 38.1 percent of the stock of Columbia Broadcasting System, 34.8 percent of the American Broadcasting System, and 6.7 percent of RCA Corporation, parent of the National Broadcasting Corporation. The report concluded that control of even small blocks of stock "by a single or few like-minded financial institutions provides them with disproportionately large powers."[12]

Elites Share Consensus

According to the ruling-elite interpretation, the top corporate, political, and military elite are fairly united, not only because they share common economic interests but because they subscribe to a number of similar values: a commitment to private property and capitalism, a willingness to compromise, and a conservative attitude toward change. Though members of the top elite do disagree over politics from time to time, and even compete for power, they agree on the basic "rules of the game," on preserving the capitalist "system" and their privileged positions within it.

This sharing of values filters down even to the "middle levels of power" among, for example, the Democratic and Republican party leadership. Although the two major parties may have somewhat different ideological perspectives, their policies and programs usually are similar and moderate. While Democrats and Republicans disagree, for example, over the extent to which government should regulate the economy, neither advocates a total nationalization of industry. If either party offered radical policy alternatives, ruling-elite theorists proclaim, it would only alienate voters and undermine the consensus of values shared by prominent leaders of both parties and by other elites. As a result, the Democratic and Republican parties offer voters only a narrow range of policy alternatives—a range confined to the interests and values of the elite themselves.

This naturally raises an important question. If a small, cohesive elite with shared values actually govern, why then do significant changes in policy ever see the light of day? Why do policies emerge—such as minimum wage laws, collective bargaining, and environmental restrictions on industry—that appear to conflict with elite interests? Part of the answer, according to the ruling-elite view, is that the elite themselves sponsor and support such changes. Dramatic new policies are occasionally enacted by the elite—as in the 1930s under Franklin Roosevelt's New Deal—when a major crisis like the Great Depression threatens the very essence of the economic system. By remaining somewhat flexible—by tolerating some regulation of commerce and industry, social security programs, and fair labor practices—the elite can incorporate policy changes to satisfy public demands while still preserving the system's basic features and their control of it.

Elites Unrepresentative

Supporters of the ruling-elite theory also are quick to point out that the top corporate and governmental elite, including the second layer of elites such as members of Congress, are not representative of the rest of the population. In addition to possessing considerably greater wealth, the elite are drawn disproportionately from a certain social background: white, male, Anglo-Saxon, Protestant. Neither the House nor the Senate, for example, truly reflects a cross section of the American public. As noted in Chapter Seven, most of the seats in Congress are filled by lawyers, bankers, or businessmen who belong to the white upper-middle class, and are mostly male. Many other groups—the poor, ethnic and racial minorities, and women—have a great deal less representation in Congress than would be expected from their percentages in society. Similarly, almost all Presidents, Vice-Presidents, Supreme Court Justices, and Cabinet officials have been white, male, Anglo-Saxon Protestants. Many like Lyndon Johnson and Nelson Rockefeller have also laid claim to considerable wealth.

In fact, the confirmation in late 1974 of multimillionaire Rockefeller as Vice-President troubled many observers who worried about the potential conflicts between his enormous wealth and his public responsibilities. As a spokesman for the Americans for Democratic Action lamented, "In a nation of over 200 million people, President Ford has chosen the person who will have more conflicts of interest . . . than any other person he might have chosen." A study of the Rockefeller family business connections made by G. William Domhoff and Charles L. Schwartz, presented to Congress in 1974, revealed that fifteen members of the Rockefeller family were directors of forty corporations with total assets of $70 billion. The study showed also that the boards on which the Rockefellers sat had interlocking directorates with ninety-one major U.S. corporations having combined assets of $640 billion.

Although some argue that certain unrepresentative qualities— such as high levels of education and considerable wealth—are prerequisites for holding public office in this country, advocates of the ruling-elite theory remain unconvinced. They fear that a government and economy dominated by wealthy white males simply cannot be responsive to the needs of most members of society.

Access Not Open

Supporters of the ruling-elite theory further contend that it is difficult for most people ever to move into the ranks of the elite. Although persons without enormous wealth and proper social connections sometimes can reach positions of significant political

and economic power, the occasions are rare. They cite a number of sociological studies indicating that the rate of social mobility in the United States remains slight for most people, especially for those from the poorest classes. As one study revealed, most upward mobility occurs within the middle range of society; at the extremes of the richest and poorest classes, sons and daughters tend to remain at the same level as their parents.[13] In other words, those who possess few financial and political resources will not likely be admitted to the ruling elite.

And even if they should acquire these resources, only those subscribing to the values of the present elite and willing to play by the "rules of the game"—to accept compromise, go slowly, and submerge their individuality—will be accepted. "Personal relations," argues Mills, "have become part of 'public relations,' a sacrifice of selfhood on a personality market, to the sole end of individual success in the corporate way of life . . . the elite careerist must continually persuade others and himself as well that he is the opposite of what he actually is."[14]

Elites Not Accountable

Finally, supporters of the ruling-elite view strongly criticize the present distribution of political and economic power. They charge that elites are subject to little control by the rest of society and, as the investigations of the Watergate break-in revealed, are fre-

Jeffrey Blankfort/BBM

quently corrupt and irresponsible. "The men of the higher circles," C. Wright Mills concluded years ago, "are not representative men; their high position is not a result of moral virtue; their fabulous success is not firmly connected with meritorious ability. Those who sit in the seats of the high and mighty are selected and formed by the means of power, the sources of wealth, the mechanics of celebrity, which prevail in their society."[15] Although power is supposed to reside ultimately in the people and their elected representatives, in reality it rests with those who control the corporations, bureaucracies, and military. It rests with those who are neither elected by the people nor morally responsible to them.

Indeed, ruling-elite theorists charge, not even elected officials like the President and members of Congress are truly accountable. Although voters are able to choose among alternative party candidates at election time, their choices are narrow and their power is limited almost exclusively to the act of voting itself. Because only a small proportion of the American public participate in other kinds of political activity besides voting or even know what their elected representatives are doing, politicians tend to cater to the wishes and interests of those few influentials who keep informed and voice their demands. "Policy questions of government," Dye and Ziegler insist, "are seldom decided by the masses through elections or through the presentation of policy alternatives by political parties. For the most part, these 'democratic' institutions—elections and parties—are important only for their symbolic value. They help tie the masses to the political system by giving them a role to play on election day and a political party with which they can identify."[16]

In fact, according to the ruling-elite view, elites not only are unaccountable to the general public but influence the public more than the public influences them. Corporation leaders and politicians, for instance, employ television, radio, and the press to manipulate public attitudes through sophisticated advertising and slick public relations techniques. Because the elite dominate the major communications media—and the Madison Avenue advertising firms that use them—the public has few opportunities to get radically different points of view or to voice their own views and opinions. In fact, the views and opinions of most Americans probably have been conditioned to a significant degree by the media, anyway. As a result, governmental policies and social values do not ultimately reflect the needs and interests of the public as much as they mirror those of the power elite.

Implications for Action

In summary, the ruling-elite theory sees little opportunity for most of us to work effectively within the existing political system—at least not for any significant reform. Although we may believe we can play a major role in the political system (through such tools as elections), our participation remains more symbolic than real. The true source of power rests with a small, fairly cohesive elite drawn from top economic, military, and governmental circles. These elite share interlocking relationships based on mutual self-interest, overlapping careers, and a commitment to the same basic values. They not only are unrepresentative of the rest of society but restrict access to all those who lack wealth, proper social connections, and a world view similar to their own. And instead of being controlled by public opinion, they usually are in the position to dominate and manipulate that opinion. They, not the public, mark the boundaries of political activity for the majority of society.

One other implication is clear. The ruling-elite theory implies that to achieve significant political change, it may become necessary to engage in actions more extreme or radical than would be necessary in an open political system. If the system remains closed to large segments of society, justification is offered for resorting to direct action and even violence. It is not just coincidental that groups favoring radical means of political action—such as the Weather underground—view the system as hopelessly controlled by an establishment bent on thwarting any kind of major reform. Ironically, however, the ruling-elite theory also offers justification for those deciding not to engage in any political action at all. Those who might ordinarily be motivated to work for political change possess the excuse that such actions remain futile in the face of an indomitable elite.

The Pluralist Theory

Despite widespread support for the ruling-elite theory, many political scientists do not accept all its tenets. While they agree that elites exist, they believe ruling-elite theorists greatly exaggerate the concentration of political power in the United States.[17] Perhaps the leading critic of the ruling-elite view is political scientist Robert Dahl, who views political power in this country as "pluralistic"—that is, widely dispersed among many separate elites kept in check by numerous social and political forces. The underlying assumption of Dahl and other pluralists is that any theory of who governs must be examined "scientifically" and supported by hard evidence. It must not be assumed that simply because persons occupy important positions of power, they constitute a single, cohesive "ruling-elite" whose decisions usually prevail. According to one scholar, "Only if it can be shown that such a group is a cohesive one with a sense of group identity, and that it has a grip on the governmental power in that community approaching a monopoly, can it be argued that it constitutes a 'ruling-elite.' "[18] Nor must it be assumed that those with considerable economic or military resources actually employ these resources to exert great power. Even though the military controls the armaments, for example, it does not employ them to impose a military dictatorship.[19] In other words, one must study the actual decisions made in society and not simply assume that persons in high positions or possessing great wealth actually constitute a single, powerful, ruling group.

In effect, pluralists contend that their examinations of political power are more careful and objective than those of ruling-elite theorists (a view not shared, of course, by the latter), and that their studies paint a considerably more realistic picture of who governs in America. Although, as with the ruling-elite theory, the pluralist theory embraces several different interpretations, certain basic assumptions stand out.

Multiple Elites

First, pluralists reject the idea that a single ruling elite makes most of the "important" decisions in America. Although they agree with ruling-elitists that powerful groups exist, they contend that the power structure is too decentralized and complex to permit such groups to act together in a common design. Whereas ruling-elite proponents see the power structure as a single pyramid dominated by a unified power elite at the top, pluralists see it as a range of pyramids, with different groups controlling separate areas of policy making. They do not find that the same military, corporate, and governmental leaders determine most major policies but rather that different groups exercise power in different spheres.

Figure 2–2. Pluralist Pyramids of Power

| Education | Military | Industry |

In studying community power in New Haven, Connecticut, Dahl found that those making the major decisions in the area of urban renewal were not the same as those making the major decisions in education. "Leaders in redevelopment," he reflected, "are with a few exceptions officially, professionally, or financially involved in its fate. Most of the leaders in the public schools have a professional connection of some kind with education . . . a leader in one issue-area is not likely to be influential in another."[20] Part of the reason for this dispersal of power, Dahl and other pluralists contend, is that many different resources of power exist in our society. Whereas ruling-elite theorists assume that economic resources are the key to power, pluralists find that power is based on a variety of attributes—wealth, expertise, access to the media, prestige, position in a major institution—each of which may be decisive in different areas. That is, although pluralists do not dispute the fact that economic resources remain in the hands of a small percentage of society, they do insist that other resources may be equally, if not more, consequential in determining who wields influence. Further, although these other resources may not be equally distributed among the population, no one individual or group can claim a monopoly over any of them.

Competition Among Elites

Adding still more fire to the controversy, most pluralists insist that a great deal of competition prevails among elites. Whereas ruling-elite proponents believe the top elite are unified and mutually supportive—with squabbles occurring mainly at the "middle levels of power," such as among interest groups and members of Congress—pluralists see evidence of competition at all levels. They see power spread widely among many different "veto groups," which balance one another; that is, the ambitions of one group are tamed by the conflicting ambitions of another. Industry, the government, and the military are all fragmented by numerous subgroups having opposing interests and policy goals.

Thus, among top corporations one finds vigorous competition not only between businesses operating within a similar field (such as in transportation) but also between those having different interests regarding governmental policies. Whereas legal restrictions on air freight, for example, may be applauded by one industry, they may be condemned as disastrous by another. Even the Vietnam War (which many considered to be economically inspired) revealed a considerable division within industry. While some companies clearly benefited from the defense contracts, other companies suffered, especially those geared to a peacetime, consumer-oriented economy. (Indeed, it may be significant that the *Wall Street Journal* and *Business Week* were among the first publications to take an editorial stance against the war.)

Similarly, as the evening news keeps demonstrating, conflict frequently erupts among the various branches of government. The President, members of Congress, and the officials of each of the fifty states represent diverse constituencies and do not necessarily share the same policy goals. Indeed, pluralists argue, the competition that occurs in government often thwarts powerful elite interests, as when Congress succeeds in blocking presidential initiatives. In 1970, for example, Congress halted the development of the supersonic transport, which both President Nixon and major corporations like Boeing Aircraft desperately wanted. Although Congress was under great pressure to support the program, it eventually succumbed to the outcries of scientists and environmental groups (such as Friends of the Earth and the Sierra Club), who argued that the plane posed an environmental hazard. As Figure 2-3 shows, presidential success in pushing desired policies through Congress has fluctuated wildly during the past twenty years, reaching a new low point with Richard Nixon after investigations into the Watergate burglary.

Figure 2–3. Presidential Success on Votes, 1953–1974

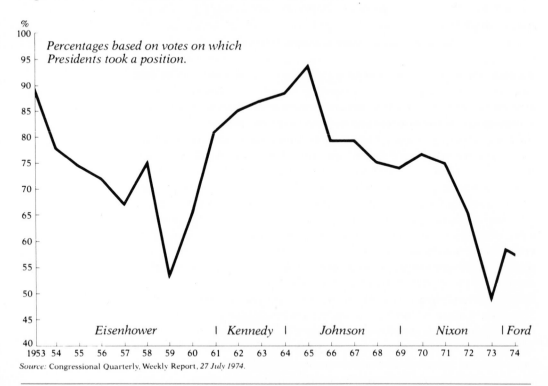

Source: Congressional Quarterly, Weekly Report, 27 July 1974.

Even more dramatically, Congress and the federal courts eventually pressured Nixon into resigning from the White House following repeated probes into the Watergate scandal. Although supporters of the ruling-elite theory point to the scandal as evidence of elite conspiracy and corruption—and, in fact, insist Nixon's demise was hastened by other elites who never fully accepted him—the head-on collision between Nixon and Congress revealed, to pluralists, the presence of true institutional pluralism. Only in a decentralized power structure, they argue, could one find a President compelled to resign his office, and top Cabinet officials and White House aides being carted off to prison. In other words, when viewed in historical perspective, Presidents have not been able perpetually to strong-arm either Congress or the courts, nor to force unpopular issues and behavior on the American people.

What makes this competitive situation valuable, according to pluralists, is that as long as governmental and corporate elites hold each other in check, average citizens have some protection from abuse. As long as corporations must compete for consumers' dollars, and as long as Presidents and members of Congress must vie for voters' support, people's interests can neither be ignored nor ultimately repressed.

Distinction Between Elites and Masses Blurred

Pluralists also find the distinction between "elites" and "masses" not as clear as the ruling-elite theory suggests. How is it possible, they ask, to draw precise lines between an "elite" and a "nonelite" when groups with wide public membership such as labor unions wield such enormous influence on policy? Not only do unions threaten major industries with strikes but they flex their muscles in Congress and contribute money and organizational skills to political campaigns. It may be significant, for example, that in 1972 both Richard Nixon and George McGovern worked hard to court labor's support. And it may testify to the clout of labor that, according to a 1968 Gallup survey, more Americans said they feared big labor than feared big business.[21]

In addition, pluralists suggest that there is really little difference between the social and economic values of elites and those of most other Americans. Although business and governmental leaders may not be truly representative of the total population in terms of education, wealth, and social composition, elites and nonelites alike tend to subscribe to similar values: private property, capitalism, a belief in compromise, and a conservative attitude toward change. These shared values in effect restrain business and governmental leaders, forcing them to act within the boundaries of society's overall expectations. "How leaders act," Dahl concludes, "what they advocate, what they are likely to believe, are all constrained by the wide adherence to the creed that exists throughout the community."[22]

Access Is Open

Pluralists, furthermore, toss out the ruling-elite thesis that access to decision making is blocked for most members of society. They point out that many persons from relatively poor families and with diverse racial and ethnic backgrounds have successfully reached positions of political and economic power. Contrary to the ruling-elite interpretation of sociological studies, pluralists argue that upward mobility has been steadily increasing during the past several decades. According to one study, for example, the proportion of high-level executives who actually "started at the top"—taking into account the board chairmen, presidents, and vice-presidents of the 600 largest industrial corporations in the United States—has steadily declined, until it is now down to only about 3 percent. Most of the other 97 percent rose through the ranks after twenty or twenty-five years of service to the company; very few of them had any family connections in the firm they now head.[23] In fact, pluralists feel that access to elite positions probably will continue to improve, especially as more women and members of minorities are elected to public office and work their way into higher positions in industry and finance. Although women and minority groups are still underrepresented in Congress and the executive branch, they are making significant inroads in other areas. Large cities like Detroit, Los Angeles, Washington, D.C., and Atlanta, for example, have been headed in recent years by black mayors; and in 1974 Connecticut elected the first woman to become governor in her own right, while North Carolina elected the first woman to be state supreme court chief justice.

In any case, continues the argument, if access to elite positions is restricted, society itself is to blame, not just the elites. The widespread prejudices and low level of popular support for equal opportunity have set up the roadblocks preventing certain groups from reaching positions of power. The fact that individuals must support certain values and codes to join the ranks of the elite reflects the prevailing ideas of society as a whole, not just those of the elite.

Elites Are Accountable

The proposition that economic and other elites are unaccountable to the rest of society is similarly rejected by pluralists. While they agree that important political decisions are passed down by non-elected, frequently invisible, corporate heads, military brass, and civil servants, they believe these elites can be kept in check by elected governmental representatives who are subject to public scrutiny. After all, they contend, elected governmental officials ultimately hold the most powerful positions in America. Only they possess the authority, and have access to the legitimate use of physical force (such as the armed forces and the Justice Department), to make and enforce decisions affecting the whole society. Only the President and members of Congress have the authority to establish the limits of the military budget, set up new regulatory agencies, and (together with the courts) break up monopolistic enterprises. All of this, according to the pluralist view, means that ordinary Americans ultimately can exert a great deal of power. Citizen influence can be felt through elected officials who must remain alert to public reaction at the polls. Although corporate and military elites are not directly accountable to the public, their independence is curtailed by governmental elites who are accountable through elections. Presidents and members of Congress often must initiate policies that do not favor prominent corporate executives or military brass—or run the risk of losing public office. Even though Presidents and most members of Congress share backgrounds similar to those of other powerful elites, the institutional imperatives of their office—their public reputations and need of voter support—compel them to respond to other influences besides corporate wealth or military pressure. The necessity of responding to a wider public interest, pluralists argue, accounts for the succession of laws in American history protecting the individual citizen and consumer: truth-in-labeling laws, statutes curbing deceptive advertising, antitrust laws, and regulation of labor practices. Admittedly such protections often are only poorly enforced or minimally applied, but their existence is nonetheless a testament to the frequently opposing interests of corporate and governmental elites.

The very fact, therefore, that top elites occasionally must "walk the line" to preserve their privileged positions (as ruling-elite theorists also contend) signifies a degree of latent power among the citizenry. Although only a relatively small number of citizens actually throw themselves into the political fray, the voice of the majority is still heard because politicians must remain attentive to opinion polls, votes, and the views of influential community leaders. As Dahl has put it, "The leaders who directly control the decisions of political associations are themselves influenced in their own choices of policies by their assumption as to what the voting populace wants."[24]

Elites and Democratic Values

Perhaps the final important area where pluralists and ruling-elitists tangle is in their views of public apathy. As we shall discuss later, many Americans turn their backs to politics and are poorly informed about even the most rudimentary facts of government. While these findings disturb ruling-elite theorists—who fear that nonparticipation and apathy give elites even greater freedom to ignore public needs—a number of pluralists (although certainly not all) conclude that nonparticipation may, to some degree, be beneficial to the political system. First, those who are politically uninformed and apathetic often have a low commitment to such principles as freedom of speech. It might be a mistake, some pluralists warn, to call for greater participation from people who are relatively uninformed and who reject many of the nation's basic political values. Such people are likely to ignore society's best interests and are the most susceptible to entreaties of silver-tongued demagogues. Further, a more politically active populace might only interfere with the work of elected representatives chosen to create policy. A highly active electorate marked by extreme ideological differences might only lead to increased fragmentation of the political system. As one writer exclaimed, "Apathy is probably good for the political system in that it is conducive to overall stability."[25]

In any case, the argument goes, it is the elites, not the general public, who protect and safeguard the American political system. Research on political opinion reveals that leaders in government, education, and industry—those with higher education, social prestige, and positions of power—generally show greater support for freedom of speech, freedom of the press, and equality of opportunity than do most other Americans. (Of course, there may be a distinction between what people say and how they actually feel. Persons in high positions may be under greater pressure to appear more tolerant than those not in the limelight.)[26] Thus, both apathy and rule by elites are regarded, not as a malfunction of the political system, but as a necessary condition for preserving American political values. As long as governmental elites remain accountable to the public through periodic elections, as long as the people possess freedoms of speech and choice, pluralists contend that a political system responsive to the interests of most Americans will prevail.

Implications for Action

We may conclude from this brief view of the pluralist theory that those of us who accept this interpretation of American politics might be considerably more optimistic about the opportunities for effective citizen action than those of us who adopt the ruling-elite view. According to the pluralist interpretation, the political system in the United States offers a number of ways for persons with motivation and skill to gain access to positions of power and consequently to mold public policy. Because there are many different resources of power besides wealth and social position, it would follow that a variety of groups and individuals can play major roles in the policy-making process. Under existing conditions no single power elite can continually restrict access to positions of power. The system is too decentralized and complex for any cohesive group to act in a common design. Rather, many different groups exercise power in separate policy spheres. These groups not only tend to balance one another but are kept in check by a variety of social and political forces.

This does not necessarily imply that political access is wide open under the pluralist interpretation. Obviously, racial and sexual prejudices—not to mention the ever-present obstacles facing the poor—continue to prevent many groups from achieving their political goals. The main difference, however, between the pluralist and ruling-elite views is that pluralists regard the system as considerably more flexible and capable of responding to internal pressures for needed social and political reforms.

Evaluation: The Two Theories

Reviewing the differences between the ruling-elite and pluralist theories gives one the distinct impression that advocates of the two theories do not really speak the same language. Although both groups refer to hierarchy in American society, they disagree about the nature of the hierarchy and how it affects the chances of ordinary citizens to influence the political process. Although they occasionally depend on the same data and statistics (as when evaluating different groups' degree of access to elite positions), they arrive at entirely different conclusions. Part of the reason for this difference is that each group employs a different research methodology. Whereas those who find a ruling-elitism stress the social backgrounds and institutional positions of elites, those who find a pluralist situation emphasize the difficulties inherent in decision making.

It is clear, too, that each theory represents an overview of the entire political system in the United States. Each is essentially an ideal or abstract model that attempts to diagram and explain the distribution of political power. Indeed, most texts on American government tend to view political institutions and behavior from the vantage point of one of these two overarching theories. Many conclusions reached in various chapters of this text, for example, reflect assumptions about the distribution and exercise of power that other observers do not accept. Whereas advocates of the pluralist theory probably would feel uneasy about our discussion in Chapter Nine of the frustrations faced by ordinary citizens trying to voice their concerns, supporters of the ruling-elite theory would probably feel just as uneasy about our discussion in Chapter Six of the pitfalls and frustrations of presidential power.

Actually, both theories are persuasive in some respects. This is particularly the case at the community level, where the amounts of pluralism and ruling-elitism seem to vary considerably from one city to another.[27] In addition, it is possible to accept one proposition of a theory without necessarily accepting all its other propositions. Even if one adopts the pluralist view, for instance, that separate elites dominate in different policy areas, one need not agree that these elites are restrained by competition among themselves or that they are responsive to the wishes of most people.[28]

Advocates of the two theories even agree on some points— perhaps most importantly on the inequality of access. While differing over the true potentials for citizen action, both groups acknowledge that the ideal of American democracy, in which most citizens wield equal influence over policy making, hardly prevails. Not only are there elites who exert considerably greater influence on government than do most people, but it is also true that many citizens become only minimally involved in the political fabric of society. Many people remain pessimistic about their chances to affect the political process and do not especially care whether a single cohesive elite or a plurality of elites actually govern.

A Third Theory: The Politics of Bureaucracy

It should be pointed out, finally, that a third, and increasingly popular, theory of power in America holds that ultimately *no one* is in charge. It states that the political system in the United States has become so enveloped in the tentacles of bureaucracy, so divided by a system of internal checks and balances, and so beset by a growing complexity of problems and solutions that effective control over policy making by any group has become virtually impossible. The reason many people feel powerless is due neither to the concentration of power in the hands of a few remote, unfeeling individuals nor to the dispersal of power among a large number of competing institutions. Rather it is due to the fact that no one ultimately has responsibility for policy. The "system" is running by itself, out of control, with no group capable of controlling it.

Some of us probably have suspected as much for quite some time. There is something compelling about this theory, especially in light of the growing use of computers that tolerate no back talk, the pervasive reliance of government and industry on those long, forgettable numbers marking our credit cards, bank accounts, and driver's licenses, and the proliferation of faceless bureaucrats who refuse to budge from "the rules."

Although this theory embraces a variety of concepts and concerns, it is ultimately a response to the seemingly pervasive bureaucratization of American society. In government, especially, bureaucracy seems to be everywhere, comprising a powerful and independent "fourth branch" elected by, and accountable to, no one. The federal labyrinth of bureaus, commissions, and independent agencies is so vast that neither the President, Congress, nor even those working within it can fully comprehend its scope. According to a report issued by the Library of Congress, "The Federal Government now spends nearly four billion dollars annually on research and development in its laboratories, but it does not know exactly how many laboratories it now has, where they are, what kind of people work in them, or what they are doing." Some critics suggest that the bureaucracy merely feeds upon itself, swelling under its own internal momentum, as a perfect illustration of Parkinson's Law: "Work expands so as to fill the time available for its completion."[29]

Perhaps the most alarming aspect of this sprawling and incomprehensible bureaucracy is the power it exerts over the individual. With its army of obedient officials it reaches into every corner of society, creating and enforcing rules that often bear little relation to reason or justice. It has this immense power because it possesses discretionary authority. Although bureaucratic agencies like the Federal Communications Commission (FCC) and the Internal Revenue Service (IRS) administer policy decisions made by Congress and the President, policies rarely are so specific that these agencies cannot use discretion in carrying them out. For instance in 1962, when Congress stipulated that new drugs on the market had to be safe and effective, the Food and Drug Administration (FDA) was handed the power to establish actual standards of safety and effectiveness—a power that sometimes has been exercised carelessly and with more concern for drug companies than for consumers.

At no time, in fact, has the discretionary authority of federal agencies been more evident than when they have been engaged in the surreptitious surveillance of private citizens. The proliferation of governmental investigators, computer networks, and data banks has made each citizen's private life subject to the prying eyes of countless civil servants. It has been estimated that at least ten separate dossiers exist in governmental files on the average American, detailing his or her medical history, financial status, educational achievements, and political activities. Occasionally the existence of such surveillance is revealed in newspaper headlines, such as when it was disclosed in early 1975 that the post office voluntarily had been turning over private citizens' letters to the Central Intelligence Agency, and that the Federal Bureau of Investigation had been collecting information on the sexual and drinking habits of U.S. Presidents, members of Congress, and other high-ranking federal officials. Attorney General Edward Levi testified before a House subcommittee that 883 entries on Senators and 722 on House members existed among the FBI's general files on 6.5 million Americans.[30]

The question is, who is to be held responsible for such acts? Officials who carry out the surveillance claim merely to be obeying orders of superiors who, in turn, similarly claim to be following instructions "from above." In many instances—especially when publicity does not accompany a bureaucratic policy—the maze of specialized departments and the devotion to secrecy make it virtually impossible for an outsider to trace the source of a decision. Although one could always place responsibility directly on the President's desk, it is unlikely any Chief Executive could possibly maintain effective control over all bureaucratic decisions. As we will see later, Presidents often experience many of the same frustrations as the rest of us in dealing with bureaucratic obstinacy and red tape. Meanwhile, those ultimately responsible for a

policy decision—presuming they even know they are responsible—remain hidden in the impenetrable jungle of federal office
buildings and bureaucratic executive suites.

Thus, in view of the seemingly ubiquitous presence of bureaucracy in the lives of Americans at all levels of the political system,
the alternative theory that ultimately no one can maintain effective control over policy making offers few promises for effective
citizen participation. Indeed, the implications of this theory may
be even more pessimistic for political action than those of the
other two theories we have considered. If no one is in charge—if
no one is in control—then no group can be singled out as the
target for reform. Those of us who are intent upon influencing
the political process will have to wander through a maze of organizations and rules simply trying to locate the pressure points. And
for every policy decision we wish to affect, we will have to seek
an entirely different and obscure locus of power.

Bachrach, Peter. *The Theory of Democratic Elitism*. Boston: Little,
Brown, 1967.

Connolly, William E., ed. *The Bias of Pluralism*. New York: Atherton
Press, 1969.

Dahl, Robert. *Who Governs: Democracy and Power in an American City*.
New Haven: Yale University Press, 1961.

Domhoff, G. William. *Who Rules America?* Englewood Cliffs, N.J.: Prentice-Hall, 1967.

————, and Ballard, Hoyt B., eds. *C. Wright Mills and the Power Elite*.
Boston: Beacon Press, 1968.

Dye, Thomas R., and Zeigler, L. Harmon. *The Irony of Democracy*. Belmont, Cal.: Duxbury Press, 1971.

Hunter, Floyd. *Community Power Structure*. New York: Doubleday, Anchor, 1953.

Lundberg, Ferdinand. *The Rich and the Super-Rich*. New York: Lyle
Stuart, 1968.

Mills, C. Wright. *The Power Elite*. New York: Oxford University Press,
1956.

Parenti, Michael. *Democracy for the Few*. New York: St. Martin's Press,
1974.

Parry, Geraint. *Political Elites*. New York: Praeger, 1969.

Polsby, Nelson. *Community Power and Political Theory*. New Haven: Yale
University Press, 1963.

*Recommended
Reading*

Presthus, Robert. *Men at the Top*. New York: Oxford University Press, 1964.

Prewitt, Kenneth, and Stone, Alan. *The Ruling Elites*. New York: Harper & Row, 1973.

Ricci, David. *Community Power and Democratic Theory*. New York: Random House, 1971.

Rose, Arnold. *The Power Structure*. New York: Oxford University Press, 1967.

Notes

1. For one excellent interpretation of the different forms of power, see Peter Bachrach and Morton S. Baratz, "Two Faces of Power," *American Political Science Review*, December 1962, pp. 947–52.

2. For additional background on the theory, see C. Wright Mills, *The Power Elite* (New York: Oxford University Press, Galaxy, 1959); Floyd Hunter, *Community Power Structure* (New York: Doubleday, 1963); G. William Domhoff, *Who Rules America?* (Englewood Cliffs, N.J.: Prentice-Hall, 1967); Thomas R. Dye and L. Harmon Zeigler, *The Irony of Democracy*, 3rd ed. (Belmont, Cal.: Duxbury Press, 1975).

3. Robert Dahl, "A Critique of the Ruling-Elite Model," *American Political Science Review*, June 1958, pp. 463–69.

4. C. Wright Mills, *The Power Elite* (New York: Oxford University Press, Galaxy, 1959), p. 324.

5. Senator William Proxmire, *Congressional Record*, 24 March 1969.

6. *Congressional Quarterly Weekly Report*, 9 June 1973, p. 1430.

7. Christopher J. Rand, quoted in the Associated Press, January 1974.

8. David M. Ricci, *Community Power and Democratic Theory* (New York: Random House, 1971), pp. 168–69.

9. Cited in *Business Week*, 5 August 1972, pp. 54–56.

10. See *Newsweek*, 23 December 1974, p. 68.

11. *Fortune*, May 1975.

12. *Time*, 21 January 1974, p. 71.

13. Joseph A. Kahl, *The American Class Structure* (New York: Holt, Rinehart and Winston, 1965), p. 272.

14. C. Wright Mills, *The Power Elite* (New York: Oxford University Press, Galaxy, 1959), p. 348.

15. Ibid., p. 361.

16. Thomas R. Dye and L. Harmon Zeigler, *The Irony of Democracy* (Belmont Cal.: Duxbury Press, 1971), p. 5.

17. See, for example, Robert A. Dahl, *Who Governs: Democracy and Power in an American City* (New Haven: Yale University Press, 1961);

Nelson Polsby, *Community Power and Political Theory* (New Haven: Yale University Press, 1967).

18. Carl Friedrich, *Man and His Government* (New York: McGraw-Hill, 1963), p. 326.

19. See Robert Dahl, "A Critique of the Ruling-Elite Model," *American Political Science Review*, June 1958, pp. 463–69.

20. Robert A. Dahl, *Who Governs: Democracy and Power in an American City* (New Haven: Yale University Press, 1961), p. 183.

21. *Gallup Opinion Index*, August 1968.

22. Robert A. Dahl, *Who Governs: Democracy and Power in an American City* (New Haven: Yale University Press, 1961), p. 325.

23. "The Big Business Executive, 1964," *Scientific American*, Lithographed Report, 1965.

24. Robert A. Dahl, *Who Governs: Democracy and Power in an American City* (New Haven: Yale University Press, 1961), p. 101.

25. Lewis A. Froman, *Congressmen and Their Constituencies* (Chicago: Rand McNally, 1963), p. 49.

26. For still another interpretation of this research, see Robert W. Jackman, "Political Elites, Mass Publics, and Support for Democratic Principles," *Journal of Politics*, August 1972, pp. 753–73.

27. See, for example, Robert Presthus, *Men at the Top: A Study in Community Power* (New York: Oxford University Press, 1964).

28. See, for instance, Wallace S. Sayre and Herbert Kaufman, *Governing New York City* (New York: W. W. Norton, 1965).

29. C. Northcote Parkinson, *Parkinson's Law* (Boston: Houghton Mifflin, 1957), p. 2.

30. See *Newsweek*, 10 March 1975, p. 16.

3 Citizen Politics:

Actors and Nonactors

There is no denying that few of us see eye to eye on politics: while some of us adhere loyally to "liberalism," others cling to "conservatism"; while some of us cry loudly for expanded federal regulation of industry, others clearly do not. But *why* do we hold such different views? Why do some of us accept the idea, for example, that powerful elites keep a tight grip on the political system, whereas others see the system as open and unrepressed?

Since the 1920s, political scientists have been investigating how people behave—how they vote, perceive current issues, and communicate their political views. More recently, political scientists have joined with sociologists and psychologists to investigate how and when people acquire their political views. By turning to opinion surveys and personality profiles, they have tried to gain insight into how family upbringing, encounters with friends, and experiences in school, on the job, and in front of the television set mold attitudes and opinions.

Although not all the information collected by political scientists can be considered either provocative or surprising, it does offer a picture of the way many Americans relate to the political system and how they feel about becoming involved in—or avoiding—the political world. Some of the research into the origins of political attitudes and opinions has been especially revealing, suggesting that people's willingness, desire, or refusal to immerse themselves in politics depends enormously on their environment, upbringing, and education. Since we will focus later on the popular strategies for political action, we should look first at the social base and the character of political behavior in this country. After all, strategies for political action will be relevant only if people intend to use them, and that intention will largely depend on how people acquire a "political self."

The Social Base: Learning About Politics

A "political self" is made, not born. Infants do not emerge from the womb with a preconceived view of the political world, no matter how strongly opinionated their mothers may be. They possess no inherent allegiance to one political party over another, no loyalty to any government or ideology. All such things must be acquired and learned. As the authors of one study explain, "Acquiring a political self is a natural corollary to general social maturation. As with all social learning, political learning is gradual and incremental. . . . Each citizen's political views result from lifelong experiences."[1]

Even people's perceptions of the world around them are thought to be the end products of their experiences. What they see—and *how* they see it—reflects what they have learned. Naturally, each of us tends to believe that we are unique, that what we perceive is objectively real and not just subjective. Yet, it is difficult to imagine how any of us can distinguish between our perceptions and any other reality; our own view of the world is the only reality most of us understand.

Let us consider a vivid illustration of this point. Anthropologist Colin Turnbull, in his book *The Forest People*,[2] offers an interesting example of how one's perceptions even of physical dimensions—something most of us take for granted—are affected by upbringing and environment. When a Pygmy friend of his named Kenge was led for the first time to a vast open plain uncluttered by the dense forests in which he had spent his life, he was unable to grasp its immense expanse. Noting a herd of wild buffalo grazing on the plain several miles away, Kenge said he thought they were very unusual looking "insects." His lack of experience with great distances would not allow him to be persuaded that the buffalo appeared small only because they were so far away. His range of vision in the forest had been so restricted that he was unaccustomed to allowing for distance in judging the size of the animals.

We might say that our perceptions of politics are similarly conditioned by our experiences and environment. If we have been taught the virtues of only one ideology or political party, we will not easily be persuaded that our loyalties or values are purely relative. Although the influences on our lives are virtually boundless, political scientists have tried to identify the socializing agents that share the major responsibility for inculcating our political values and opinions. Apart from the overall culture of American society itself (which we will consider briefly later), the first and most fundamental of these agents studied has been the family.

The Family

In both political science and folklore ("As the twig is bent so grows the tree"; "The hand that rocks the cradle. . . ."; "Like father, like son") the family is regarded as an important influence on the development of political attitudes and values. In the nineteenth century, the French writer Alexis de Tocqueville stressed the importance of the family in the early stages of political learning. To understand the mature adult, he said, "We must begin higher up; we must watch the infant in his mother's arms; we must see the first images which the external world casts upon the dark mirror of his mind, the first occurrences which he witnesses; we must hear the first words which awaken the sleeping powers of thought, and stand by his earliest efforts, if we would understand the prejudices, the habits, and the passions which will rule his life."[3]

When most of us first come into contact with the political world it is with a set of social values acquired from our family. Depending on the family we are born into, we are given at birth a race, a religion, and an economic background, all of which may strongly influence our political actions in later life. According to David Wallace, by the time a child enters "kindergarten—where many adults naively think his learning is about to start—this new semisocial being has already acquired the equivalent of 350 college courses, enough for an A.B. degree more than eight times over, in learning the values, customs, and attitudes that are sanctioned by his own unique family."[4]

Although many changes have been taking place in the American family, it continues to play a vital role in the development of political attitudes. One reason is that the family tends to have almost exclusive influence over the child during the early pre-school years, a period many psychologists believe is the most emotionally critical part of a child's life. During this early period, even when parents are not consciously trying to indoctrinate their children with certain values and attitudes, children are picking them up anyway, just as they are picking up their parents' habits and expressions.

Studies have revealed that when both parents support the same political party, a child frequently acquires "an ordering device almost as simple as that of T.V. westerns: he can tell the good guys from the bad guys—not by whether they are clean-shaven or unkempt but by their party labels. As a result, when children are asked how they would vote in an election, a vast majority report the same preference as their parents."[5] One political scientist found in his interviews with fourth-grade children in New Haven that many voiced support for a political party as if it were a family, not a personal, decision. As one ten-year-old girl put it, "All I know is *we're* not Republicans."[6] Only a few of the children said their party preferences differed from those of their parents.

However, if family influences tend to be so exclusive at an early age, how does one explain those individuals—apparently one out of every three—whose party preferences differ from those of their parents? How does one account also for the approximately 34 percent of Americans who now consider themselves Independents?[7] Indeed, how does one account for those "radical" sons and daughters whose conservative parents voted for Richard Nixon in 1972?

As children grow older, they do not remain political carbon copies of their parents. Political scientists normally prefer to distinguish between "opinions" and "attitudes" in terms of their endurance. As one pair of scholars have concluded, "Usually the term 'opinion' refers to more superficial and transitory issues, the term 'attitude' to somewhat deeper and longer-lasting convictions, and the term 'value' or 'belief' to the deepest of all."[8] If one accepts this differentiation, then perhaps one can argue that although fundamental attitudes and values shaped early on by the family (perspectives toward authority, social prejudices, and so on) will endure in some form, specific views and opinions on political issues will change in response to new influences. Thus, one study found that the views of parents and their children toward such issues as school integration and the right of certain unpopular groups to speak were generally less similar than even their party preferences.[9]

To some extent, changes in occupation, education, and residence contribute to this "political generation gap." Many children shun the occupational and educational goals of their parents, and move to areas that expose them to different political viewpoints. Shifting up or down the economic ladder, moving near a university campus or to the suburbs, and assuming family responsibilities are all experiences that can modify political views.

It also should be remembered that for many people the adult years can be, as Dawson and Prewitt express it, "a period of testing reality. If predispositions carried to this point from early life turn out to be inadequate, basic alterations will occur. The political world often fails to operate as the young citizen had expected it to. Cynicism may replace unquestioning trust. Disillusionment may replace naive optimism. Conversely, the young adult may learn the value of political participation, though as a child he was taught its futility."[10]

Thus, although the family usually exerts the first major influence on political attitudes, it does not retain its exclusive role for long. It eventually yields a great deal of its authority to other socializing agents, such as the schools, peer groups, and the mass media.

The School

A seven-year-old child, when asked in school why American Presidents are the most important persons, replied: "They do much more work and they're much importanter."[11]

Similarly, a ten-year-old child, when asked what communism means, answered, "Well, communism is sort of—it's a different way of people; well, sort of like . . . to me it's *bad*."[12]

While other social forces, including the family and the media, also greatly affect political orientations and loyalties, no social institutions are handed as much responsibility for spreading the basic symbols of the political system as are the schools. Most of us probably can recall sitting in elementary school learning about the country's early political heroes and celebrating our national holidays. We can recall solemnly saluting the flag, raising our voices to the chords of the "Star-Spangled Banner," and perhaps identifying with the rowdy young George Washington and his infamous cherry tree. And, as we advanced into junior high and high school, we can remember being herded into American history and civics classes.

Political scientists found in the 1960s that the schools tended to reinforce most children's loyalties to the political system through these political symbols. A study in Boston, for example, revealed that although the curriculum inspired few students to immerse themselves in politics, it did tend to reinforce national-istic feelings and to encourage acceptance of the political values being taught.[13] Similarly, other research disclosed that most school children expressed great esteem for and confidence in such gov-ernmental figures as the President of the United States. Most of the fourth-graders in New Haven, for example, felt a personal attachment to the President, regarding him as wise and worthy of great trust. As one child volunteered, "The President is doing a very good job of making people be safe."[14]

We might wonder, however, what effect the dramatic historical events of the 1970s, such as the Watergate scandal, have had on this idealistic view of the President and the political system. A 1973 study of elementary school children in Boston found that most of the children questioned had come to reject the image

Eileen Christelow, Jeroboam, Inc.

of the President as a benevolent leader.[15] Comparing them with a similar group interviewed in the early 1960s, the study found that the number of children who felt the President was "not one of my favorites" had jumped from 17 percent to 75 percent. Under the impact of Watergate, the study noted, politicians as a group were cynically viewed by the children in 1973 as "more selfish, less intelligent, more dishonest and less likely to keep their promises."

Political scientists were well aware before Watergate, of course, that for many children the lessons in school are undermined by conflicting family and peer attitudes. Children living in city slums, for instance, often find that their own experiences contrast sharply with the idealistic views of society and government touted in the school curriculum. Children whose parents are distrustful and disapproving of the political system often share similar doubts and negative feelings.

One interesting discovery—in light of the discussion of political influence in Chapter Nine—is that many people's perceptions of their place in the political system are greatly affected by the amount of formal education they acquire. As their educational level advances, so does their level of participation and interest in politics. Education appears to have some correlation with their confidence in being able to understand the political world and to play an effective role within it.

But it is not only the amount of education or the formal curriculum that contributes to political learning. The informal learning in the classroom also can teach children certain political values. One social scientist made the following observations about his visit to a third-grade class:

"As I was sitting in the back of the classroom shortly after school started, three boys larger than those in the class came in and asked for Mike Smith. The teacher asked the boys what he had done, and she was told that he had pushed in line. She called Mike to the front, made disapproving sounds, and commanded Mike to leave the room with the boys. The leader of the three placed one monitor in front of Mike and one behind, and, with the leader directing, Mike was marched from the room. As an observer I felt very uneasy and a bit like it must have felt to watch the Gestapo come for an enemy of the state. . . .

"A little later this same morning, after the lesson on current events, which was notable for the vapidity of the items discussed, mass movement began in the class. Soon I discovered that all the boys had—at some unseen signal—lined themselves up on the opposing side of the room from the girls and both groups stood patiently waiting for the teacher to do something. I became alarmed at this bizarre behavior until I realized that they were preparing to march to the bathrooms simultaneously. No one was allowed to remain behind. . . . I found this regimentation as disconcerting as the fact that earlier mere accusation had been enough to establish Mike's guilt in the teacher's mind. Relating the two events, I thought the children were being well trained for a life of regimentation."[16]*

He also concluded from his classroom visit that the accused child "learns that punishment is capricious, not judicious. He learns that it depends on factors over which he has no control and little understanding, that accusation is more important than investigation, and that, in the distribution of punishments, some are privileged, some are not." Consequently, what the school teaches in theory about democracy and justice in the United States may or may not conform with the informal lessons children learn in dealing with teachers, classmates, and school administrators.

Peer Groups

While our initial views on politics may stem from our family environment, these views often are greatly affected later by our peers: friends, classmates, co-workers, and neighbors. Although peers may become influential at almost any time in our lives, they tend to assume special importance during early adolescence when most of us first become involved in activities away from the family. At this early stage, the family rapidly yields its exclusive influence and may become less significant in providing daily political guidance. Certain peers, of course, exert greater influence than others as we grow into adulthood. Those individuals with whom we are most closely associated probably have the greatest effect on our political development; the more personal the relationship, the more forceful it can be in influencing opinion.

It is not difficult to understand the reasons for the potency of peer groups. The opinions and views of people one sees face to face each day are usually harder to ignore than those voiced by distant and formal acquaintances or expressed, as we will see later, through the news and information media. One's spouse, close friends, roommates, and especially those who seem better informed and more articulate than average, enjoy a unique influence not shared by other social forces. Should a close friend or neighbor suddenly launch into a tirade against the evils of Congress, one might find it awkward to slip out of the room or tactfully change the subject.

In fact, if people very close to us voice strong party preferences that are different from those of our parents, they may succeed in drawing us away from our previous partisan loyalties. One study found that, in about 80 percent of the cases examined, a person whose close friends support a party different from that of his family will eventually forsake his family's party.[17]

Although the influence of peers is usually casual and reciprocal, pressures to conform also can augment the importance of peer groups. Psychologists have found that people often will support the views of a group even when those views conflict with their own judgments. This propensity to conform has been most strikingly illustrated by experiments in which people yield to group pressure in their perceptions of inanimate objects and shapes. One experiment, for example, revealed that when a group of college students are told to state incorrectly that one of several unequal lines is shorter (even though it is clearly longer), other, unsuspecting students often will repudiate the evidence before their eyes and echo the group's false response.[18] It has been hypothesized that the students' desire to be accepted by their peers is stronger than the clues supplied by their own senses. They adopt the group's false view because they fear ridicule and rejection if they do not. This suggests that if people willingly respond to group pressure by ignoring their own perceptions of inanimate objects and shapes, they may just as effortlessly conform by altering their views of less concrete political and social issues. Clearly, one's peers can have a strong effect on political opinion—competing with and often surpassing the influences of family and school.

Mass Media

Some scholars contend that the communications media—television, radio, films, newspapers, and magazines—now compete with the family, school, and other institutions in shaping our political opinions and values. It has been estimated, for example, that American families spend an average of six hours a day in front of the television set, and that the set baby-sits for the average child more hours of the week than he or she spends in school. Indeed, many of us continue to pass a great part of our lives tranquilized by television, absorbed in magazines and newspapers, and listening to the radio.

Yet, controversy continues over the degree of the media's influence on political orientations. On the one hand, there appear to be severe limitations in the ability of the media to change political views, especially on controversial issues. Studies indicate that the media tend to reinforce political predispositions acquired from such familiar agents as the family, school, and peers rather than create new ones. Part of the reason given is that most people pay greater attention to those news programs, editorial opinions, and political advertisements that conform to their present views and, conversely, tune out those they may find disagreeable. This does not mean, of course, that people can completely avoid political information that conflicts with their views, any more than they can avoid repetitious television commercials that peddle toothpaste and deodorants. It just means that "the audiences of the mass media," as one scholar reflects, "tend toward a selectivity that supports rather then weakens their pre-existing outlooks."[19]

Moreover, much of the information carried by the communications media goes through a "two-step flow." Rather than persuading people directly, the information is explained by a small number of "opinion leaders" who pass on their interpretations. This means that the television program an individual watches on Monday may have less effect on his opinions than what someone he respects says about the program on Tuesday.

Although it is sometimes difficult to identify an opinion leader, the term usually refers to someone deeply interested in politics who attempts to persuade others and who commands considerable respect. He or she might be a prominent newspaper columnist, a popular television correspondent, a union official, or a religious leader. The opinion leader may even be someone who neither holds an official position nor necessarily is well educated. Thus, a person's opinions on specific issues may be influenced by a fellow worker in the office, a sister, a neighbor, or anyone else whose political views are sought. As with peer groups, the more personal the source of the message, the greater its effect can be on opinion.

Other observers insist, however, that the important question is not whether the media can change political views on controversial issues; rather, it is whether the media offer certain conceptions of the world that indirectly influence political perceptions over the long run. Children may be especially susceptible to the messages of television and other media because their political views are rarely as well developed as those of adults.

Indeed, studies strongly suggest that the communications media teach, or at least reinforce, certain kinds of social values. Children constantly are exposed to lessons of social importance in comic books, television dramas, magazine ads, and films. All these common means of communication promote, sometimes unintentionally, certain social concepts and stereotypes—such as that violence is a simple, masculine way to settle disputes, or that a woman's place is in the kitchen.

Children in school are likely to be assigned books with particular social messages. David Riesman and his colleagues illustrated this point in *The Lonely Crowd*[20] with a once-popular volume in the "Little Golden Books" series called *Tootle the Engine*. In this tale, Tootle is a young locomotive who attends engine school where he learns that, to become a big streamliner, he must obey two important lessons: stop at a red flag and "always stay on the track no matter what." Despite repeated warnings, however, Tootle continues to wander off the track to find flowers in the field. To stop him from doing so, the town in which his school is located finally decides to play a trick on him. The next time Tootle leaves the track, red flags suddenly pop up wherever he goes. He turns and twists but can find no spot of grass on which a red flag does not appear. Confused, he returns to the track where he feels relieved to be able to speed back and forth unhindered. He then promises the town never again to leave the track and to grow up to be a streamliner.

The obvious moral of the tale is that it is bad to leave the track and that, over the long run, success and approval, and even freedom, can be found only by conforming to the expectations of the community. The child reading this tale may apply its lesson to relations with peers: adopt the views and behavior of the group to avoid disapproval. More will be said about television and other media in Chapter Five.

Additional Influences

Ultimately, it is difficult to determine precisely which of the four major influences discussed thus far has the most telling impact on political opinions and ideas, although perhaps the influence of the family remains the most fundamental. Because each person is a unique product of many social forces, no one influence can be said to apply equally to all. For this reason, we must also take into account other potentially significant social forces.

Considering, first, how a job can affect income, place of residence, and exposure to other people, it is conceivable that a person's occupation can significantly influence his or her basic political orientations. Although no universal rule applies to any occupational group, there has been a tendency for well-paid professional people such as doctors and business executives to vote Republican, and for factory workers, union members, and teachers to vote Democratic. Obviously, related factors such as education and family environment also help to influence partisan preferences.

An individual's political orientations may be affected also by whether he or she lives in a large city, a suburb, or a rural area; each is said to have its own unique character and historical salience. Demographic studies show, for instance, that Democratic voters usually have been more numerous in the South and in large cities and that Republican voters have been more abundant in the Midwest and in small towns. It is doubtful, however, whether regional differences in party preference or in political views are as meaningful as they once were. On most issues today (for example, foreign policy and school desegregation), the differences of opinion *within* most regions appear to be greater than the differences between them.

Sometimes, momentous social crises create pressure for adjustments in political thinking. History is made up of major events that have produced dramatic breaks with the past. The Civil War in the 1860s, the Great Depression in the 1930s, the Vietnam War and protest demonstrations during the late 1960s, and the Watergate scandals of the 1970s have all led to alterations in many people's political orientations.

The same can be said for a crisis in the life of an individual, such as the loss of a job or the death of a spouse. One's normal interest in and perspectives on the activities of government can change abruptly in the face of a personal problem or tragedy.

Finally, people's broad political orientations are molded by the social and cultural traditions of the society in which they live. They learn not only the specific values of their families and friends but the general values and ideas that make their culture (or subculture) unique. It is said, for instance, that many people in this country tend to express a general suspicion of authority, a distrust of "the establishment" and the impersonal forces that determine (or, as some have it, undermine) the destiny of America. It is also said that, in contrast to most other nationalities, Americans are inclined to view politics as both a dirty business and a private matter. Many support the idea that political opinions, like religion, should not be discussed openly at the dinner table but instead should be hidden behind the protective curtain of the voting booth. It even has been suggested that, as a group, Americans tend to be exceedingly competitive and materialistic, religion-oriented, and infatuated with violence. Whether or not any of these generalizations is true, American society undoubtedly propagates—with the aid of the schools, the communications media, and the family—its own special kinds of demands, expectations, and traditions that sustain the unique quality of American political life.[21]

A Portrait of the American Voter

Having considered some of the contributing social influences on political opinions and attitudes, we may wonder how such influences ultimately are expressed: how do people in this country vote, view political issues, and feel about some of the underlying principles of American politics? Some classic political writers, like John Locke and John Stuart Mill, thought that the citizens of a democracy probably would sense a responsibility toward their society: they would keep abreast of current social issues; they would participate actively in political affairs; and they would weigh the alternatives carefully before lending their support to

any policy. Similarly, it is commonly believed today that most Americans, although not necessarily highly educated about politics, still try to keep reasonably informed about political issues and carefully consider the facts before stepping into the voting booth.

Yet, studies completed during the past forty years reveal a considerable gulf between this idealization and reality. From these studies, political scientists have discovered that a great number of Americans not only fail to participate in political activities, but also lack an understanding of current issues and even oppose specific applications of freedom of speech and legal justice. Let us consider each of these discoveries in turn.

Low Participation

One remarkable discovery about American political behavior is that a sizable number of adults do not actively participate in politics. The most conspicuous proof of this lack of participation is the low turnout of voters at election time. Even during presidential elections, when voter interest is usually greatest, more than one-third of the voting-age population do not show up at the polls. As Table 3-1 shows, in the presidential elections since 1948, turnout has tended to hover around 60 percent of the voting-age population. In the 1972 election, the number of voters fell to 54.5 percent, the lowest fraction since 1948. This means that out of a potential electorate of about 140 million, only 77 million registered voters marched to the polls to choose between George McGovern, Richard Nixon, and assorted third-party candidates; 63 million others stayed home.

In other elections the turnout is usually even lower. In most off-year congressional elections, when the entire House of Repre-

Table 3-1. Voter Turnout in Presidential Elections, 1948–1952

1948	52%
1952	63
1956	60
1960	64
1964	62
1968	61
1972	54

Source: U.S. Bureau of the Census, *Statistical Abstract of the United States.*

sentatives and one-third of the Senate is chosen, less than one-half
the potential voters show up at the polls. In the six congressional
elections between 1954 and 1974, for example, an average of only
about 43 percent voted. And in statewide and local elections, involving the choosing of governors and mayors, a 35-percent turnout may be considered typical.

These figures compare rather unfavorably with those of many
other countries. Turnout in Italy, Denmark, and Belgium, for example, is commonly about 85 to 90 percent; West Germany usually
has participation levels ranging from 75 to 90 percent; and Nor-
wegian and French turnout is normally 75 to 80 percent. Although
these figures, as we will see, may be somewhat misleading because
turnout is computed differently in each country, they do suggest
a difference in electoral behavior.

Those Americans who go beyond voting to engage in other kinds
of political activity represent an even smaller fraction of the voting-
age population. One political scientist, Lester Milbrath, has
stratified the population into three basic types: "gladiators" (who
become active in party politics or run for office); "spectators"
(who seek information and vote); and "apathetics" (who either
minimally participate or totally abstain). Although such type-
casting may seem arbitrary, those "gladiators" who engage in
one of the more active forms of participation, such as raising
campaign funds, tend to be active in other ways as well. "This
division," Milbrath reflects, "is reminiscent of the roles played
at a Roman gladiatorial contest. A small band of gladiators battle
fiercely to please the spectators, who have the power to decide
their fate. The spectators in the stands cheer, transmit messages of
advice and encouragement, and, at given periods, vote to decide

DOONESBURY by **Garry Trudeau**

who has won a particular battle (election). The apathetics do not bother to come to the stadium to watch the show."[22]

Thus, although most Americans have made at least some effort to vote and express a political opinion, only about 15 percent have written letters to an elected official; less than 5 percent have volunteered their services in a compaign; and only 12 percent have contributed money to a candidate or party.[23] It has been estimated that the number of Americans who have done anything political other than vote is less than those who have participated in amateur stage shows. And, contrary to expectations, relatively few college students ever take an active part in campaigns. After the 1970 congressional elections, a Gallup poll found that 91 percent of the students interviewed had not been involved at all in political campaigning.[24]

Poorly Informed

Many Americans not only shun campaign politics but are poorly informed about even the most rudimentary elements of government. A 1973 Harris survey, conducted for a Senate subcommittee, revealed that only 46 percent of those questioned could correctly name their Representative in Congress, and only 41 percent could identify the Representative's party.[25] Even among those with some college education, only 55 percent could name their Representative, and no more than 49 percent could identify their Representative's party. The survey also found that only 39 percent knew the names of both U.S. Senators from their state, and that 20 percent believed Congress includes the U.S. Supreme Court. Legend even has it that a few years back, voters in one part of Illinois renominated a man for Congress who had died three months before. His name on the ballot apparently was sufficient recommendation for his reelection.

Widespread lack of knowledge also is revealed in surveys of public opinion on current political issues and events. Researchers have discovered repeatedly that while most people enjoy "sounding off" on politics, few support their views with much accurate information. As late as 1964, more than one-fourth of all American adults were still unaware that mainland China was ruled by a "communist" government.[26] Moreover, in 1969, a Gallup poll found that 31 percent of a national sample had not heard about the ABM (Anti-Ballistic Missile) program President Nixon had submitted to Congress, despite extensive media coverage of the controversial issue during the previous year. And when the Supreme Court in 1971 ruled that the *New York Times* and *Wash-*

ington Post could publish articles based on a secret Pentagon study of Vietnam policy, 45 percent admitted they had not heard of the "Pentagon Papers."[27]

An explanation often given for this lack of information is that many people simply lack curiosity about politics. According to a recent Gallup poll, more than one-fourth of those surveyed said they had little or no interest in politics.[28]

However, lack of interest alone cannot account for the dismaying statistics. Some observers insist that much of the public's ignorance of and disinterest in politics can be attributed directly to the social influences discussed earlier, such as the schools and media. For example, many critics blame television for stooping to the trivial and mediocre, for rarely fulfilling its potential to stimulate and educate. Although most people report television to be their main source of news, the actual amount of broadcast time given to public affairs programs is considerably less than that devoted to other programming. Except for coverage of unusual and dramatic events, such as the Watergate scandal, there is little sophisticated presentation of current political and social issues. The nature and quality of programming reflect instead a commercial desire to reach the greatest number of viewers, to offer the lowest common denominator of entertainment. Apart from a few creative mavericks in the industry—notably in public television—most executives strive to sell programs that, as one scholar sarcastically observed, "arouse no controversy, irritate no sensitivity, disturb no gray cell."[29]

The schools also share some responsibility for the public's ignorance of politics, although the level of most people's awareness of and interest in political affairs does correspond to the amount of formal education they have received. Even though in 1973 only 55 percent of those with some college education could correctly name their Representative, this was still considerably higher than the 35 percent of those whose schooling stopped at the eighth grade.[30] Persons with more formal education also are more likely to read newspapers and watch the few public affairs programs on television to become better informed about current events.

The widespread absence of political information may not actually be too remarkable in view of the low levels of political participation. After all, those who are not politically involved frequently have less motivation to keep up with the issues than those who actively participate. Merely expressing an occasional opinion requires less time and energy than does any other kind of political activity and in many instances involves almost no substantive information.

Low Support for Individual Rights

Many people in this country also display little tolerance for individual rights—although evidence does suggest that the tolerance is increasing. While many say they believe in the right of free speech, they do not always endorse the right when applied to specific groups and situations.

In the early 1950s, political scientists began to examine the public's views toward individual rights to find out how many Americans supported or rejected the constitutional "rules of the game." One of the first to undertake such a study was Samuel Stouffer, who found in 1954 that most Americans would not permit certain groups to exercise their right of free speech. He discovered, as Table 3-2 shows, that 60 percent would not permit an individual to speak in their community against churches and religion. He also found that 31 percent would not permit a socialist to speak; 68 percent would not permit a communist to speak; and 21 percent would not allow an individual to speak whose loyalty had only been *questioned* before a congressional committee. The people in this sample were not asked to support any criminal activity; they were asked only whether an individual with generally unpopular beliefs should be allowed to express an opinion.

Stouffer's findings were validated by later studies that revealed a similar lack of support for individual rights. In 1964, Herbert

---

Table 3-2. Free Speech for Whom? (1954)

	Yes	No	Don't Know
If a person wanted to make a speech in your community against churches and religion, should he be allowed to speak, or not?	37%	60%	3%
If a person wanted to make a speech in your community favoring government ownership of all the railroads and big industries, should he be allowed to speak, or not?	58	31	11
Consider a man whose loyalty has been questioned before a congressional committee, but who swears under oath he has never been a communist. Should he be allowed to make a speech in your community, or not?	70	21	9
Suppose an admitted communist wanted to make a speech in your community. Should he be allowed to speak, or not?	27	68	5

Source: Samuel A. Stouffer, *Communism, Conformity, and Civil Liberties* (New York: Doubleday, 1955), pp. 28–41.

Table 3-3. Consistency in Political Values?

	Percent Agreeing
1. No matter what a person's political beliefs are, he is entitled to the same legal rights and protections as anyone else.	94.3
Any person who hides behind the laws when he is questioned about his activities doesn't deserve much consideration.	75.7
2. I believe in free speech for all no matter what their views might be.	88.9
Freedom does not give anyone the right to teach foreign ideas in our schools.	56.7
3. Nobody has a right to tell another person what he should and should not read.	80.7
A book that contains wrong political views cannot be a good book and does not deserve to be published.	50.3

Source: Adapted from Herbert McClosky, "Consensus and Ideology in American Politics," *American Political Science Review*, June 1964, pp. 361–82.

McClosky found that, although a favorable consensus emerged on most general statements concerning civil liberties and procedural justice, the consensus evaporated when specific examples were given. He found, as Table 3-3 indicates, that freedom of speech was generally supported as a concept, but not necessarily when applied by school teachers. Similarly, legal rights were strongly defended in principle, but not always for those who "hide behind the laws" when questioned about their activities.

One interpretation of these findings was that people often react positively to such popular phrases as "free speech" and "legal rights and protections," and negatively to such loaded concepts as "foreign ideas" and "wrong political views." If the persons questioned had a real commitment to the principles of civil liberties and procedural justice, they would have been more consistent in their responses, no matter what emotional phrases were given. In McClosky's view, the evidence clearly indicated that "a large proportion of the electorate has failed to grasp certain of the underlying ideas and principles on which the American political system is based."[31]

More recent studies indicate, interestingly, a significant shift toward greater tolerance of individual rights. In 1973, the National Opinion Research Center at the University of Chicago asked a national sample of Americans the same questions Stouffer had asked in 1954, and obtained quite different results. For instance,

Table 3-4. Free Speech for Whom? (1973)

	Yes	No	Don't Know
If a person wanted to make a speech in your community against churches and religion, should he be allowed to speak, or not?	65%	34%	1%
If a person wanted to make a speech in your community favoring government ownership of all the railroads and big industries, should he be allowed to speak, or not?	77	20	3
Suppose an admitted communist wanted to make a speech in your community. Should he be allowed to speak, or not?	59	38	3

Source: National Opinion Research Center, University of Chicago, 1973.

although in 1954 only 27 percent would allow a communist to speak in their community, at least 59 percent would do so in 1973 (see Table 3-4). Similarly, when asked whether a person who wants "to make a speech in your community against churches and religion should be allowed to speak," 65 percent said yes in 1973, as compared with only 37 percent in 1954. Apparently, either pressures to appear more tolerant toward such persons have increased during the past two decades or more Americans generally feel unthreatened by these persons' views and opinions. Of course, we should remember that even though more people appear to support specific applications of free speech today, a significantly high percentage—at least one-third—still do not in situations involving atheists and communists.

A final illustration also suggests how unwillingness to support individual rights relates to lack of knowledge about our system of government. In Fairfield, California, a few years ago, high school students in an American Studies class made a door-to-door survey in a residential neighborhood to ask support for what they described as "a possible amendment to the Constitution." After reading the proposed amendment, one resident exclaimed it was "unconstitutional"; another said it was "gibberish"; a third was afraid "This would increase the sale of marijuana"; and a fourth sneered, "Sounds like SDS stuff to me." Out of a total of 850 Fairfield residents surveyed, only 290 agreed that the proposed amendment should be added to the Constitution and only 64 (8 percent) recognized it as being, in fact, a verbatim copy of the First Amendment: "Congress shall make no law respecting an establishment of religion, or prohibiting the free exercise thereof; or abridging the freedom of speech, or of the press; or the right of the people peaceably to assemble, and to petition the Government for a redress of grievances."[32]

Obstacles to Participation

Although there has been sustained interest in unraveling the reasons people *do* participate in the political process—that is, respond to "civic duty," try to influence the actions of government, or simply express a desire to be a participant instead of a spectator (see Chapter Nine)—political scientists have also been interested in discovering factors that inhibit participation. Because nonvoting seems to be related to low levels of political awareness and because the act of voting is such an important ritual in American politics, political scientists have tried to explain why millions of people stay home on election day. Even though they do not yet have a definitive answer to this question, a few explanations have been offered.

Demographic

Political scientists have found—although the data are subject to interpretation—that certain groups of people have tended to vote less than others. Women, for example, have been less inclined than men to show up at the polls (although the gap has been narrowing). Similarly, the young and the elderly have tended to vote less than the middle-aged; those with only grade-school education less than those with high school education or college degrees; Democrats less than Republicans; single persons less than married persons; blacks less than whites; southerners less than northerners, and so on. Table 3-5 shows Census Bureau percentages of those reporting they voted in 1972 and 1968.

These statistics do not necessarily mean, of course, that people fail to vote *because* of their age, sex, religion, race, or occupation.

Table 3-5. Voter Turnout by Group and Region, 1972 and 1968

	1972	1968
College-educated	82.3%	83.1%
White-collar	76.4	81.6
$10,000 and above	74.3	80.4
North and west	66.4	71.0
High school-educated	65.4	72.5
White	64.5	69.1
Metropolitan area	64.3	68.0
Male	64.1	69.8
65 years and over	63.5	65.8
Female	62.0	66.0
Nonmetropolitan area	59.4	67.3
South	55.4	60.1
Grade school–educated	55.2	62.4
Manual worker	54.2	64.7
Black	52.1	57.6
21–24 years	50.7	51.1
$3,000 and under	45.7	55.0

Source: U.S. Bureau of the Census, *Current Population Reports.*

Rather, these factors often coincide with a variety of other social conditions that may explain the nonvoting. Women, for instance, may have tended to vote less than men partly because of social prejudices about the role of women; that is, many women as well as many men have regarded politics as principally a "man's game." Similarly, those under twenty-four years of age probably have been less likely to vote than those of middle age, in part because of their greater mobility and lack of exposure to political stimuli. And it has been suggested that turnout in the South has tended to be lower than in other regions partly because of the usual absence of strong two-party competition and the relatively high proportion of persons in the South who have been poor. One can argue, in fact, that persons under twenty-four years of age struggling at jobs paying less than $3,000 a year may suffer special hardships and disillusionments that will dampen their political interest.

Legal and Mechanical Obstacles

These demographic factors aside, the low turnout of voters may be partially explained by state residence and registration requirements. Surveys indicate that as many as 40 percent of eligible voters claim not to have voted because they failed to register.[33]

State laws usually require voters to register in person and to renew their eligibility whenever they move or miss a major election. Sometimes these registration procedures are awkward or burdensome for potential voters or they are too far removed from the election itself; someone who normally is interested in the outcome of an election may not feel sufficiently excited a month before it to register. Thus, if the various states and localities could make it easier for new voters to register, turnout might be significantly boosted. In many European countries, for example, voters are registered automatically when they come of age and are thus spared having to take the extra step in order to vote.

Furthermore, in a country where an estimated twenty million people move each year, residence requirements discourage or prevent many Americans from going to the polls—especially those under thirty years of age who tend to be the most mobile and are more likely to be unregistered. Most states and counties now require voters to be residents at least a month before they register—which is quite a change from several years ago when states normally required residence of at least a year. These requirements can be justified, of course, for protecting against such fraudulent practices as casting ballots for fictitious or deceased persons or for keeping persons from voting who have not resided in an area long enough to know the major issues and candidates. However, it may be difficult to justify a residence requirement of even one month if this discourages persons from voting who happened to move across town a few weeks before the election.

In addition to residence and registration requirements, other legal and mechanical obstacles contribute to nonvoting. Several million people are disqualified due to lack of American citizenship, confinement to a mental hospital, or conviction for a criminal act. In 1972, at least 10 percent of those interviewed failed to vote because they were sick or disabled, while many others could not leave their jobs, or were away from home.[34] If these people could have been added to the voting numbers, the percentage of those voting in 1972 might have been substantially greater than the 55 percent cited above. Or, to put it another way, out of the approximately ninety-five million people who *did* register that year, 80 to 85 percent actually voted—a turnout percentage roughly equal to that in most European countries.

Still, even after considering these legal and mechanical impediments to voting, we find that at least twenty million other eligible voters did not turn out in 1972; and a much larger number ignored other kinds of political activity. To account for these nonparticipants, we must consider some additional reasons.

Absence of Stimulation and Time

Certainly one common reason for nonparticipation is that many people are too absorbed in their own affairs to become more than marginally involved in politics. While the political world may be looked upon with some interest, it still remains distant from the more immediate needs and worries of day-to-day living. A harried factory worker with four children, for example, may spend more time worrying about automobile repairs, the high cost of meat for his family, and how to enjoy an inexpensive weekend than worrying about whether the United States will solve its balance of payments problems or will sever its diplomatic relations with Spain.

Some regard such behavior as nothing more than apathy or complacency, believing that each person ultimately decides how involved he or she wants to be in the political world. While this assumption certainly applies to some people, others simply feel too imprisoned by circumstance and personal responsibilities to devote much time to politics. Becoming informed about and active in politics today takes a significant commitment in time. Those whose energies are devoted to securing the necessities of life, who perhaps moonlight to support their families, often will have little time and energy left over to ring doorbells, write letters to the editor, or go to political meetings.

It is common also for some people to be discouraged by the absence of any personal invitation to participate. Even though they may ordinarily have the time to be politically active, they have not been recruited by friends or party officials. In one study on political apathy, a person remarked that "Many of my friends were asked to help—ring doorbells, stamp envelopes, and things like that. But I wasn't asked to do anything. Had I been asked, I would have been glad to help."[35]

Perhaps as important as the lack of time or the absence of stimulation is the extent to which people remain uninvolved in politics by observing the apathy of others. Those who initially harbor some guilt about their inactivity lose it when they find how common apathy is among their friends, neighbors, and the rest of the community. "Whatever guilt they feel," Rosenberg suggests, "may be assuaged by the observation that others (including the most respectable) are equally apathetic."[36] Once again, the behavior of other people often serves as a guide for individual behavior. Those who have little interest in politics sometimes rationalize their inactivity by seizing upon any potential excuse, whereas those who are highly motivated experience little difficulty in surmounting even major obstacles.

Social Conflicts

Although most Americans are taught in school that it is their civic duty to vote, some find politics socially distasteful. They carry images of themselves as agreeable, likeable persons who do not wish to create conflicts with their bosses, friends, or families by having political disagreements—at the dinner table or anywhere else. As a result, they will impose a self-censorship on their political expressions. One person admitted she does not discuss politics with her husband "because when we do, we are likely to disagree violently. Right now I want to avoid friction—we were just married last June—so we try not to get into political discussions." Another said she wanted to avoid conflict with her friends and neighbors: "We don't discuss politics much. I think it's sort of like religion. It's personal, and I don't like to get into arguments—When politics comes up in conversation, I always say—'Let's talk about something else.' "[37]

The consequences are sometimes similar when people are subject to "cross-pressures." An individual may have close friends who support a party different from that of his parents. Friends may try to persuade him to vote for the Democratic candidate for President, whereas since childhood he has been taught to vote a straight Republican ticket. In a situation where he cannot resolve the dissonant stimuli coming from the two groups, he may defer the decision on how to vote until the last minute, or may not vote at all.

Views of the Parties

Certain features of American political parties also can discourage participation. Many who ordinarily have time for and interest in politics do not vote because they are disgusted by the lack of meaningful choice between the parties. They do not care which party wins and thus feel less motivated to vote than those who care deeply about the outcome of the election. Quite a number of people abstain from voting as a form of political expression. This includes those who scorn politics because it appears to be dishonest and self-serving. We might sympathize with the little old lady who, when asked which candidates she was going to vote for, replied, "I never vote. It only encourages 'em."[38]

Also in cases where one party has no more than a slim chance of defeating the other, feelings of futility may halt further political involvement. Some people decide that, even with their participation, their party's candidate will fail at the polls anyway (or, conversely, that their candidate will coast to an easy victory and does not require their additional support). This kind of situation often prevails in regions, such as the South and some areas of the Midwest, where one party traditionally dominates statewide and congressional elections (see Chapter Four). Persons who favor the minority party may prefer to stay at home rather than experience again the frustrations of defeat.

Feelings of Impotency

But perhaps the most telling reason given for nonparticipation is a feeling of futility that reaches beyond the outcome of any single election. Many people are deterred from participating in politics by the belief that their involvement would not make a significant difference. The air around them is being poisoned,

Andy Mercado, Photographer

Table 3-6. Political Influentials vs. the Electorate: Responses to Items Expressing a Sense of Political Futility

Items	Political Influentials (N= 3020)	General Electorate (N= 1484)
	% Agree	
It's no use worrying my head about public affairs; I can't do anything about them anyhow.	2.3	20.5
The people who really "run" the country do not even get known to the voters.	40.2	60.5
I feel that my political leaders hardly care what people like myself think or want.	10.9	39.0
Nothing I ever do seems to have any effect upon what happens in politics.	8.4	61.5
Political parties are so big that the average member hasn't got much to say about what goes on.	37.8	67.5
There doesn't seem to be much connection between what I want and what my representative does.	24.0	43.7
It seems to me that whoever you vote for, things go on pretty much the same.	21.1	51.3

Source: Herbert McClosky, "Consensus and Ideology in American Politics," *American Political Science Review*, June 1964, pp. 361–82.

prices continue to rise unchecked, and their neighborhoods seem unsafe and increasingly wrought with violence. Yet they feel lost among the millions of other voters and sense that those who make the major political decisions—politicians, interest groups, and corporations—will not pay any attention. As we will discuss further in Chapter Nine, many even accept the ruling-elite view that elections are primarily just "rituals" anyway, which do not communicate people's real wants or needs. Consequently, they see little point in doing anything, least of all voting.

A feeling of powerlessness may derive to some degree, of course, from the sheer size and complexity of modern America. In a large society where power can frequently seem remote and unreachable, people may see little chance of personally influencing the decision-making process. According to some studies, there is a pervasive pessimism that the actions of ordinary citizens are ineffective against the wishes of powerful and often anonymous elites. As Table 3-6 shows, approximately half the people queried in a survey more than a decade ago believed even their elected public officials were unresponsive to their needs and wishes.

It is not surprising that such feelings of personal inefficacy are most pronounced among the poor, the less-educated, the aged, and the members of racial minorities—although they are spreading to the young and the middle class as well. Such people most often express estrangement from the political system and are likely to feel they have little control over their political environment. It is not simply that the relatively poor and uneducated tend to be isolated from political stimulation or have little access to sources of information. Rather, it is that they lack the confidence and resources to deal effectively with the political structure.

Nor is such pessimism necessarily unrealistic. Many of these people have been served badly by the political system; they have experienced a long history of futility in trying to draw some kind of governmental response to their needs. American political institutions have been notable for their failure to heed the cries of the elderly and the poor—people who, for the most part, have lacked organization and meaningful representation of their interests. If one accepts the ruling-elite view that "money talks" in politics, then one can understand why a poor person may feel that his or her political actions would be futile.

We may ask, therefore, whether apathy and political disinterest are not in some ways understandable responses to frustration in dealing with the political system. In view of the fact that government often seems remote and unresponsive, the desire to remove oneself from the disappointments of politics may be a necessary psychological defense. Similarly, the decision to shelter oneself from public issues and the news may stem from a reluctance to be overly informed, a desire to veil oneself from the oppressive horrors of public events. Through the news media, the outside world can impose a despairing reality on people—murders, kidnappings, plane crashes, and scandals—over which they have no control. Although awareness of political events may be a positive goal, it may be absurd to expect people to feel guilty about screening out events that augment a sense of helplessness.

Still, some earnestly hope that such withdrawal does not proceed too far, that the political world never becomes so oppressive and foreign as to force most of us into a permanent cocoon of apathy. As anthropologist Margaret Mead warned many years ago, "We must never see *the government* as something other than ourselves, for then automatically we become children; and not real honest children, but adults dwarfed to childhood again in weakness and ineffectiveness."[39]

Evaluation: Political Inaction

The argument sometimes is advanced that the failure of so many people to become actively involved in politics may account for major difficulties in the way the political system has been operating. Indeed, how serious are the low levels of participation and awareness? Do they suggest a fundamental impairment of the political system?

Participation and Control

Many of us assume that if public opinion and periodic elections are to control politicians, most citizens must be aware of what these characters are doing—if only to decide at election time whether to keep them in office or throw them out. Although, as we saw in the preceding chapter, there are different interpretations of the relationship between people and government, it is widely believed that public opinion and elections serve, as one writer has put it, "as means by which consent is given or taken away and rulers are made more accountable to the ruled."

Yet, we might wonder how a public so politically inactive and poorly informed can possibly hold their elected representatives accountable. How can people control their representatives when they know so little about their legislative stands and, in many instances, do not even know their names? Such widespread ignorance would appear to give politicians virtually a free hand to make their own decisions, because they would assume most people do not know, or even care, what they are doing. As one member of Congress admitted, "In my district, they think I am a fighter. I can do anything I want down here and they will say, 'He is the greatest fighter we have ever had down there.' No one pays attention to the votes."[40]

The pluralist perspective discussed in the preceding chapter offers some comfort, however, by noting that we do not rely merely on something called "the public" to keep elected officials in check. The whole concept of the public is in some respects deceptive, because our population is really comprised of many "publics," or different opinion groups. We will find that some attentive citizens and opinion leaders will remain sufficiently interested in an issue to keep informed and politically active. They will write letters to their Representative and to the editor of the local newspaper, follow political events closely on television, and, most important, inform others of the issue. In the words of one Representative, "While the rank and file don't attach much importance to your committee assignment and your effectiveness, there are a handful of people in almost every community who will attach importance to them, and they are the ones who have considerable influence on public opinion."[41] In other words, politicians know they usually are being observed in their activities and must consider constituents' possible responses to their policy decisions if they are to avoid falling from favor.

Moreover, we are told, it may not be crucial whether most citizens are attentive and vigilant as long as politicians *believe* people remain aware of their activities. Even though members of Congress may suspect a general apathy among constituents, they may nevertheless prefer to overestimate rather than underestimate their own public visibility. In some measure, this caution reflects the difficulties Representatives encounter in learning what their constituents want or feel. Representatives know constituents mostly from dealing with organized groups and individuals who *do* write letters, who *will* contribute campaign money, and who *have* expressed an interest in their legislative activities. Moreover, they probably know they can win or lose an election by only a small fraction of the total electoral vote. If the number of informed voters is large enough, it can have considerable impact on their chances of survival. They know that some people back home will abandon them at the polls if their legislative efforts fail to conform to expectations. Of course, constituents who are the most visible to their Representative will probably reap the most benefits from the Representative's efforts in Congress—a fact that may not comfort either the apathetic majority or the poor and disorganized.

Finally, governmental leaders may be aware that there are limits to how far they can pursue a policy without suffering popular repudiation. Following a severe inflation, a scandal, or an unpopular war, public consciousness may increase and result in pressure for the removal of those considered responsible. Herbert Hoover's defeat in 1932, following the stock market crash and the onset of the Great Depression, and the decision by Lyndon Johnson not to run for reelection in 1968, following an unpopular and protracted war in Southeast Asia, suggest the potency of public opinion and sentiment.

The case of the Watergate scandal is particularly illuminating. As the story came together piecemeal in the most damaging ways—in newspaper headlines and televised committee hearings—the strain on the reputation of Richard Nixon and his party became more and more obvious. Shattering the initial assumption that most Americans were indifferent to the Watergate issue, the *Wall Street Journal* in April 1973 published the results of a poll showing that, even at that early stage of the scandal, 91 percent were aware of it—and that one in five Independent voters and two in eleven Republicans said it might turn them against the GOP. A few weeks later, a Harris poll showed that fully 63 percent of those surveyed did not believe the official White House version of Watergate while only 9 percent accepted its accounting of the case. As we know, the publicity stemming from Watergate and its aftermath compelled Richard Nixon to dump most of his closest associates in an effort to contain the damage already done. Among those purged were two successive Attorney Generals, his chief of staff, chief domestic advisor, private lawyer, and staff counsel. And, finally, facing the specter of his own impeachment and removal from office, he resigned in disgrace.

Positive and Negative Views

Some observers also believe that, because politicians must be sensitive to potential shifts in public opinion and because enough citizens do keep an eye on government, the large amount of non-participation in America is no real cause for concern. In fact, as we saw earlier, supporters of the pluralist theory feel that universal participation is neither possible nor especially desirable.[42] They point out that nothing would be gained by encouraging participation of people who are relatively uninformed and likely to have the least understanding of democratic principles. Because such people are less capable than most of making rational political choices and are more likely to be swayed by dangerous propaganda and the tirades of demagogues, encouraging them to participate may bring only disaster to the democratic process. Moreover, a highly demanding electorate, marked by extreme political differences, might result in a political system torn apart by internal bickering. Moderate levels of participation and interest provide maneuvering room for changes in public policy, a buffer zone between opposing extremes. "If everyone were highly active in politics," one scholar has argued, "or if everyone were passively obedient, it would be more difficult to maintain system balance between responsiveness and power to act."[43]

Other political observers, however, remain disturbed about the present levels of nonparticipation. They insist that those who do not become actively involved in politics are not adequately represented. It is typically the poor and the downcast who are left out of the decision-making process. The farther down the income and educational scale, the more likely are people to abstain from voting, to be politically uninformed, and to be neglected by the political system. As to the argument that heightened awareness could bring further conflict to the political process, they counter that, considering the urban riots in the 1960s, noninvolvement in the political process may be far more dangerous. Whenever large numbers of people feel excluded from the usual political channels and are estranged from government, the potential for disruption and violence can become explosive. Finally, a basic tenet of democracy (see Chapter Nine) is that people who are affected by a policy decision deserve to have a say as to what that decision will be. To assert that any increase in participation would threaten the political system is to reject the inherent democratic ideal of providing everyone who wants and needs it a role in the decision-making process.

The solution, therefore, may not be to moralize about the need for more citizen involvement or to force people to vote. Because nonparticipation is associated with certain social and psychological conditions, it may be more worthwhile to work for needed institutional and social reforms: raise the quality of education and economic well-being; simplify residence and registration requirements; make the choices among the major political candidates more meaningful; and open up the decision-making process to greater numbers of citizens.

Almond, Gabriel, and Verba, Sidney. *The Civic Culture.* Princeton: Princeton University Press, 1963.

Best, James J. *Public Opinion: Micro and Macro.* Homewood, Ill.: Dorsey Press, 1973.

Campbell, Angus; Converse, Phillip E.; Miller, Warren E.; and Stokes, Donald E. *The American Voter.* New York: Wiley, 1964.

Dawson, Richard E., and Prewitt, Kenneth. *Political Socialization.* Boston: Little, Brown, 1969.

Erikson, Robert, and Luttbeg, Norman. *American Public Opinion: Its Origins, Content, and Impact.* New York: Wiley, 1973.

Flanigan, William H. *Political Behavior of the American Electorate,* 2d ed. Boston: Allyn & Bacon, 1972.

Greenstein, Fred I. *The American Party System and the American People,* 2d ed. Englewood Cliffs, N.J.: Prentice-Hall, 1970.

Recommended Reading

Key, V. O., Jr. *Public Opinion and American Democracy*. New York: Alfred A. Knopf, 1961.

Hess, Robert D., and Torney, Judith V. *The Development of Political Attitudes in Children*. Chicago: Aldine, 1967.

Milbrath, Lester W. *Political Participation*. Chicago: Rand McNally, 1965.

Nimmo, Dan D., and Bonjean, Charles M. *Political Attitudes and Public Opinion*. New York: McKay, 1972.

Notes

1. Richard E. Dawson and Kenneth Prewitt, *Political Socialization* (Boston: Little, Brown, 1969), p. 19.

2. Colin M. Turnbull, *The Forest People* (New York: Simon & Schuster, 1961).

3. Alexis de Tocqueville, *Democracy in America*, vol. 1 (New York: Schocken Books, 1961), p. 12.

4. David Wallace, *First Tuesday: A Study of Rationality in Voting* (New York: Doubleday, 1964), p. 231.

5. Marian D. Irish and James W. Prothro, *The Politics of American Democracy*, 4th ed. (Englewood Cliffs, N.J.: Prentice-Hall, 1968), p. 183.

6. Fred I. Greenstein, *Children and Politics* (New Haven: Yale University Press, 1965), p. 23.

7. *Gallup Opinion Index*, March 1974.

8. Bernard Berelson and Gary A. Steiner, *Human Behavior: An Inventory of Scientific Findings* (New York: Harcourt Brace Jovanovich, 1967), p. 102.

9. M. Kent Jennings and Richard G. Niemi, "Transmission of Political Values from Parent to Child," *American Political Science Review*, June 1968, pp. 175–80.

10. Richard E. Dawson and Kenneth Prewitt, *Political Socialization* (Boston: Little, Brown, 1969), p. 192.

11. Fred I. Greenstein, *Children and Politics* (New Haven: Yale University Press, 1965), p. 34.

12. Ibid., p. 26.

13. Edgar Litt, "Civic Education, Community Norms, and Political Indoctrination," *American Sociological Review*, February 1963, pp. 69–75.

14. Fred I. Greenstein, *Children and Politics* (New Haven: Yale University Press, 1965), p. 39.

15. F. Christopher Arterton, "The Impact of Watergate on Children's Attitudes toward Political Authority," *Political Science Quarterly*, June 1974, p. 269–88.

16. From *The Learning of Political Behavior,* edited by Norman Adler and Charles Harrington, p. 190. Copyright © 1970 by Scott, Foresman and Co. Reprinted by permission of the publisher.

17. Herbert McClosky and Harold E. Dahlgren, "Primary Group Influence on Party Loyalty," *American Political Science Review,* 1959, pp. 757–76.

18. S. E. Asch, "Effects of Group Pressure upon the Modification and Distortion of Judgments," in Dorwin Cartwright and Alvin Zander, eds., *Group Dynamics: Research and Theory* (New York: Harper and Row, 1960), pp. 151–62.

19. V. O. Key, Jr., *Public Opinion and American Democracy* (New York: Alfred A. Knopf, 1961), p. 355.

20. David Riesman with Nathan Glazer and Reuel Denney, *The Lonely Crowd* (New Haven: Yale University Press, 1961).

21. For a more thorough examination of political socialization studies, see James J. Best, *Public Opinion: Micro and Macro* (Homewood, Ill.: Dorsey Press, 1973).

22. Lester W. Milbrath, *Political Participation* (Chicago: Rand McNally, 1965), p. 20.

23. Survey Research Center, University of Michigan.

24. *Gallup Opinion Index,* February 1972.

25. U.S. Senate, Committee on Government Operations, "Confidence and Concern: Citizens View American Government, A Survey of Public Attitudes," pt. 1 (Washington, D.C.: U.S. Government Printing Office, 1973).

26. Lloyd A. Free and Hadley Cantril, *Political Beliefs of Americans: A Study of Public Opinion* (New Brunswick, N.J.: Rutgers University Press, 1968), p. 39.

27. *Gallup Opinion Index,* August 1971.

28. *Gallup Opinion Index,* December 1972.

29. V. O. Key, Jr., *Public Opinion and American Democracy* (New York: Alfred A. Knopf, 1961), p. 386.

30. U.S. Senate, Committee on Government Operations, "Confidence and Concern: Citizens View American Government, A Survey of Public Attitudes," pt. 1 (Washington, D.C.: U.S. Government Printing Office, 1973).

31. Herbert McClosky, "Consensus and Ideology in American Politics," *American Political Science Review,* June 1964, p. 365.

32. Herb Caen, *San Francisco Chronicle,* 16 December 1969.

33. *Gallup Opinion Index,* December 1972.

34. *Gallup Opinion Index,* December 1972.

35. Morris Rosenberg, "Some Determinants of Political Apathy," *Public Opinion Quarterly,* Winter 1954, pp. 349–66.

36. Ibid.

37. Ibid.

38. Quoted in Robert Sherrill, *Why They Call It Politics,* 2d ed. (New York: Harcourt Brace Jovanovich, 1974), p. 316.

39. Margaret Mead, *And Keep Your Powder Dry: An Anthropologist Looks at America* (New York: William Morrow, 1942), pp. 165–66. © 1942 William Morrow & Company, Inc. Used with permission of William Morrow & Company, Inc.

40. Quoted in Charles L. Clapp, *The Congressman: His Work As He Sees It* (Washington, D.C.: Brookings Institution, 1963), p. 373. © 1963 by the Brookings Institution, Washington, D.C. Used with permission of the Brookings Institution.

41. Quoted in Charles L. Clapp, *The Congressman: His Work As He Sees It* (Washington, D.C.: Brookings Institution, 1963), p. 108. © 1963 by the Brookings Institution, Washington, D.C. Used with permission of the Brookings Institution.

42. See, for example, Bernard Berelson et al., *Voting: A Study of Opinion Formation in a Presidential Campaign* (Chicago: University of Chicago Press, 1954).

43. Lester W. Milbrath, *Political Participation* (Chicago: Rand McNally, 1965), p. 146.

4 Political Parties:
The Limits of Participation

*A**mong* the many kinds of American institutions offering
a route to power, political parties have in many ways reigned
supreme. Throughout our history, parties have given hope to
countless ambitious power-seekers that they would be selected
as candidates for such high public office as Congress or the Presidency and provided with the funds and organization needed to
achieve victory. As in many other countries, parties in the United
States have served as conspicuous links between citizens and government, and have figured prominently in the personal strategies
for political influence among many successful brokers of power.
Parties have represented an important source of access to the
political system—as well as a source of frustration—even to those
intending to engage only marginally in political activities.

Yet, one of the most interesting features of political parties in
this country is that they have no written constitutional base. Although the Constitution spells out many of the duties of Congress,
the President, and the Supreme Court, it makes no mention of
political parties. The Founding Fathers who framed the Constitution had little experience with parties and probably could not
have foreseen the important roles they would serve in the future.
In fact, they abhorred the whole idea of parties, on the grounds
that they would undermine a legislator's moral independence and

encourage undesirable divisions and factionalism. George Washington, in his famous farewell address in 1796, cautioned against "the baneful effects of the spirit of party." He feared that political parties, in their endless pursuit of selfish partisan goals, might destroy national unity at a time when the new country was struggling to survive. John Adams, his Vice-President, agreed with him, saying: "There is nothing I dread so much as the division of the Republic into two great parties. . . . This, in my humble opinion, is to be feared as the greatest political evil under our Constitution." Even Thomas Jefferson, who later became a key figure in the establishment of rival political parties, declared in 1789, "If I could not go to heaven but with a party, I would not go there at all."

Needless to say, parties developed anyway. Even though the Founding Fathers considered a party system to be, as Frank Sorauf puts it, "an extra-constitutional excrescence not to be dignified by mention in the constitutional document," parties began to take shape as different groups clashed over economic issues, foreign policy, and the proper role of the federal government. As the eighteenth century came to a close, there were two national parties: the Democratic-Republicans and the Federalists. The political campaign became the common route to public office, and candidates who previously had boasted of their independence now supported a party line.

But the antipathy toward parties in this country, surprisingly, has not disappeared. Many Americans today share the Founding Fathers' distrust of political parties. As Table 4-1 shows, among college students the performance of parties has received the lowest "favorable" rating of nine major American institutions—well below that of high schools, police, the courts, and business. More-

Table 4-1. How Students Rate American Institutions

	Excellent	+	*Good*	=	*Percent Favorable*
Universities	12		56		68
Family	23		35		58
Business	12		44		56
Congress	7		49		56
Courts	6		40		46
Police	6		34		40
High schools	4		33		37
Organized religion	7		26		33
Political parties	2		16		18

Source: *Newsweek* Poll by the Gallup Organization, *Newsweek*, 29 December 1969, p. 43.

Table 4-2. The Distribution of Sentiment on Items Pertaining to Support for the Party System

	Strongly Agree	Agree	Disagree	Strongly Disagree	Don't Know
The parties do more to confuse the issues than to provide a clear choice on them.	4%	50%	20%	1%	5%
Our system of government would work a lot more efficiently if we could get rid of conflicts between the parties altogether.	9	44	28	6	4
The political parties more often than not create conflicts where none really exist.	5	59	15	**	7
It would be better if, in all elections, we put no party labels on the ballot.	3	19	54	13	3

Source: Adapted from Jack Dennis, "Support for the Party System by the Mass Public," *American Political Science Review*, September 1966, p. 605.

over, according to another study, a majority of Americans believe that parties confuse more than clarify issues, that parties tend to encourage conflict, and that the government would perform more efficiently without party discord. (See Table 4-2.)

The reason parties rank low in popular esteem is not entirely clear. Perhaps a tradition of bad feelings toward them has simply been perpetuated since colonial times. Or perhaps parties have been sullied by their close association with politics, which, as indicated in the preceding chapters, many Americans perceive as a dirty business. In any event, one poll taken early in the Watergate scandal found that, although 31 percent of adult Americans regarded the affair as "a serious matter," 53 percent dismissed it as "just politics—the kind of thing both parties engage in."[1]

The Trademark of a "Party"

But what exactly is a "political party"? How do we distinguish between a party and, say, an interest group or political movement? As is true of many other concepts in political science, a party is difficult to define and catalog. "As there are many roads to Rome and many ways to skin a cat," Frank Sorauf has quipped, "there are also many ways to look at a political party."[2]

One traditional way of distinguishing a party from some other kind of political group is to examine its *purpose*. According to some political scientists, the unique goal of a party is to capture public office, to exercise the powers of government. An interest group, in contrast, strives merely to influence governmental policy on specific issues. It does not attempt to assume responsibility for running the government itself. The American Medical Association, for instance, may try to affect policies relating to medical practices, but it is not interested in deciding foreign policy as well.

A major problem with this definition, however, is that some organizations carrying the label of a party do not actively seek control of the government, either. Members of the Prohibition and Libertarian parties, for instance, often assert they have little realistic chance of gaining political control and are more interested in using elections to publicize their cause and sway public opinion. They reason that even though they have little hope of winning elections, they can attract more attention by fielding candidates for office than by working behind the scenes as an interest group. As John Hospers, the 1972 presidential candidate for the Libertarian party confessed, "We're not even going to watch the votes very closely. But as a mouthpiece for ideas, I happily consented to run."[3]*

Perhaps then a more useful way to differentiate between parties and other groups is not according to their purpose but rather according to their *method* of satisfying their objectives: only parties run candidates for public office under their own banners. Although other kinds of political organizations, such as interest groups, may try to mobilize public support for their views, they do not do so by nominating candidates for public office; no one runs for Congress, for example, under the specific banner of the National Rifle Association or the United Brotherhood of Carpenters.

Contributions and Broken Promises

Whatever the objectives or methods of political parties, we might wonder what the relevance of parties is to political action. In what ways can parties help, or perhaps hinder, those who desire to become actively involved in the ongoing political process?

Political scientists invariably point out that parties in this country serve a number of important functions for both the politi-

*Copyright Newsweek, Inc. 1972, reprinted by permission.

cal system and the individual citizen. Parties provide eager new recruits for government, offer information on current issues, help organize the creation of policy, serve as useful watchdogs on those in power, and even help regulate political conflict. Most of these functions, in fact, bear directly on the opportunities for participation at various levels of the political system—not only for ordinary citizens but for political elites as well. Although several prominent features of the American party system—which we will examine more closely later—work counter to the fulfillment of these functions, parties are still looked to by many as an important element in the struggle for political influence.

Channel for Action

Certainly one of the most important responsibilities of parties is to provide a channel for those trying to affect policy making in some direct way. Several important party activities, including the political campaign and the nomination of candidates for office, draw upon the resources of ordinary citizens. For example, those citizens who seek expanded opportunities for political action may serve as delegates to county and state party conventions, sit on local party platform and policy committees, or even help recruit candidates for local offices.[4]

Indeed, those willing to spend the time to find out how the party in their state chooses delegates to its quadrennial national convention may succeed in influencing the selection of the party nominee for President. In recent years, pressures have been increasing on both the Democratic and Republican parties to encourage greater grass roots participation in the presidential nomination process. In the Democratic party, especially, there have been sustained efforts to wrest control over the selection of delegates from local party bosses meeting in smoke-filled back rooms and to hand over that selection process to a broader segment of the voting population. Following the riots and turmoil at the 1968 Democratic National Convention in Chicago, a reform-minded commission, headed by Rep. Don Fraser and Sen. George McGovern, set new guidelines requiring more participation by women, minorities, and young people. State party conventions were told to increase representation of these groups "in reasonable relationship to their presence in the population of the state." As a result of these guidelines, more than 20 percent of the delegates to the 1972 Democratic National Convention in Miami were under the age of thirty, about 40 percent were women, and about

15 percent were black. Moreover, more than 85 percent of the delegates had never before attended a convention.

However, the question remains whether the opportunities for participation shared by the 1972 delegates signified a permanent transformation of party politics. Some observers have noted that, with McGovern's crushing defeat the following November, the drive toward increasing grass roots participation has apparently yielded to a resurgence of old-line party activists. Newer rules adopted in 1974, for example, resulted in some significant compromises in the quota system. Still, the lesson learned in 1972 will not easily be ignored. Reformers in the Democratic party, as well as in the Republican party, likely will continue to press for greater mass participation in the presidential nomination process.

Education for Action

For political action to carry any significance at all, it must be based on some understanding of relevant political issues and controversies. Even voting in an election would be largely meaningless if one knew virtually nothing about what was at stake, or what the policy proposals touted by the various candidates would mean for the country.

In this respect, parties are also looked to as an important source of political education. Citizens often rely on campaign speeches, debates between candidates, and press releases for information on the qualifications of candidates and their policy differences. Moreover, many Americans depend on the party out of power to point out the errors of the incumbent party and to acquaint them with alternative policy proposals. As the old party-hater Thomas Jefferson declared in 1824, "The parties are censors of the conduct of each other, and useful watchmen for the public."

The extent to which the major parties actually educate and inform voters remains debatable, however. Some critics charge that, although parties do occasionally focus public attention on issues during campaigns, candidates rely too extensively on emotional speech making and simplistic television commercials that exploit voters' insecurities and prejudices. "The claim that parties 'educate the public,' " scoffs one scholar, "is open to serious reservation if education means mobilizing facts . . . and impartially appraising problems and solutions. Hyperbole, exaggeration, the oversimple solution, and demagoguery too often characterize the educational efforts of party activists."[5] More will be said about the style of political campaigns in Chapter Five.

Support for Office Seekers

Going a step further, party support is often regarded as an essential asset for those who seek an expanded political role by running for public office. Although American parties have been too feeble to guarantee all-out assistance for individual candidates, they nevertheless have been looked to for help in mounting a winning campaign. Candidates will knock on the door of the local party headquarters seeking campaign workers to handle advertising and publicity, help raise funds, and draw up a salable campaign platform. They will also depend on a steady stream of party volunteers eager to ring doorbells, lick stamps, and encourage potential supporters to register and vote.

But, even when such direct assistance is not forthcoming, candidates still rely on the party label to gain the support of voters who habitually champion that party. By running on the Democratic party ticket, they may hope to capture many Democratic votes regardless of their own personal views and qualifications. Indeed, how many candidates have not had to rely on a party label to disguise their lack of qualifications for public office? It is clear that without the aid of such a label, candidates—good and bad— would have to depend totally on their own resources to reach and win the support of voters.

Bridge for Cooperation

In addition to aiding candidates, parties often assist those who presumably have made it to the summits of power. At the national, state, and local levels, parties are looked to for help in creating public policy. Members of Congress, for example, often rely on the party leadership to steer a program over the various legislative hurdles and to help staff committees, define responsibilities, and select the presiding officers (such as the Speaker of the House). The parties additionally are viewed as an essential bridge between Congress and the President. The President frequently will appeal to the loyalties of fellow party members in the House and Senate to muster support for his prized legislative proposals. He knows their common party allegiance and their mutual desire to establish an effective party program can provide potent incentives for cooperation between the two branches of government.

Still, the two major parties have not always proved effective in aiding the formation of public policy. Each party has fallen short in terms of organization and discipline, and has been undependable in coordinating the policy-making activities of government. As we will see, some critics contend that certain party reforms must be implemented before either party can effectively meet its organizing and coordinating responsibilities.

Context for Conflict

Finally, it has frequently been suggested that parties provide a controlled and legal context for political conflict. By introducing new candidates for public office, and by serving as legitimate sources of opposition, they provide a peaceful means for citizens and groups with opposing views to pursue (and take turns sharing) political power. They offer an alternative to violence and revolution in bringing about changes in the control of government.

Moreover, by supporting candidates and by espousing certain views, parties represent the interests of voters, translating their demands directly into public policies. In so doing, it is argued, they help promote stronger bonds of allegiance to the political order; they give individuals a feeling that their interests are being articulated, and thus maintain support and legitimacy for the system.

However, once again, American parties do not always adequately represent all groups or encourage complete support for the system. As ruling-elite theorists contend, the Democratic and Republican parties are too similar and moderate in their programs to represent all segments of opinion in our society. Many Americans—including large segments of the poor, the alienated youth, and members of ideological minorities (like socialists)—do not believe their interests and needs are being articulated by either major party. And, since third parties usually do not possess sufficient strength to influence policy making, many people have resorted to violence as a way of expressing their demands—in the process, creating tension and conflict neither party can resolve.

Democrats and Republicans: The Differences

Before turning to the more interesting features of American parties, we might consider a matter perhaps more laden with myths and shrouded in emotion than any other in American politics, namely, the differences between Democrats and Republicans. Since about two-thirds of all American adults still identify in some way with one of these two parties, many undoubtedly believe their party embodies the country's major virtues. Although they may be unable to define the essential differences between the two parties—if indeed such differences exist—they most likely subscribe to some popular notion of what distinguishes Democrats from Republicans. Clinton Rossiter, for example, irreverently

Blacks tend to vote democrat, city people tend to vote democrat, young people tend to vote democratic

Table 4-3. Vote by Groups in Presidential Elections since 1952 (based on Gallup poll survey data)

	1952 Stevenson	1952 Eisenhower	1956 Stevenson	1956 Eisenhower	1960 Kennedy	1960 Nixon	1964 Johnson	1964 Goldwater	1968 Humphrey	1968 Nixon	1968 Wallace	1972 McGovern	1972 Nixon
National	44.6%	55.4%	42.2%	57.8%	50.1%	49.9%	61.3%	38.7%	43.0%	43.4%	13.6%	38%	62%
Sex													
Men	47	53	45	55	52	48	60	40	41	43	16	37	63
Women	42	58	39	61	49	51	62	38	45	43	12	38	62
Race													
White	43	57	41	59	49	51	59	41	38	47	15	32	68
Nonwhite	79	21	61	39	68	32	94	6	85	12	3	87	13
Education													
College	34	66	31	69	39	61	52	48	37	54	9	37	63
High School	45	55	42	58	52	48	62	38	42	43	15	34	66
Grade School	52	48	50	50	55	45	66	34	52	33	15	49	51
Occupation													
Prof. & Business	36	64	32	68	42	58	54	46	34	56	10	31	69
White-collar	40	60	37	63	48	52	57	43	41	47	12	36	64
Manual	55	45	50	50	60	40	71	29	50	35	15	43	57
Age													
Under 30 years	51	49	43	57	54	46	64	36	47	38	15	48	52
30–49 years	47	53	45	55	54	46	63	37	44	41	15	33	67
50 years & older	39	61	39	61	46	54	59	41	41	47	12	36	64
Religion													
Protestants	37	63	37	63	38	62	55	45	35	49	16	30	70
Catholics	56	44	51	49	78	22	76	24	59	33	8	48	52
Politics													
Republicans	8	92	4	96	5	95	20	80	9	86	5	5	95
Democrats	77	23	85	15	84	16	87	13	74	12	14	67	33
Independents	35	65	30	70	43	57	56	44	31	44	25	31	69
Region													
East	45	55	40	60	53	47	68	32	50	43	7	42	58
Midwest	42	58	41	59	48	52	61	39	44	47	9	40	60
South	51	49	49	51	51	49	52	48	31	36	33	29	71
West	42	58	43	57	49	51	60	40	44	49	7	41	59
Members of Labor Union Families	61	39	57	43	65	35	73	27	56	29	15	46	54

Source: *Gallup Opinion Index*, July 1975.

summed up the differences this way: "A gathering of Democrats is more sweaty, disorderly, offhand, and rowdy than a gathering of Republicans; it is also more likely to be more cheerful, imaginative, tolerant of dissent, and skillful at the game of give-and-take. A gathering of Republicans is more respectable, sober, purposeful, and businesslike than a gathering of Democrats; it is also more likely to be more self-righteous, pompous, cut-and-dried, and just plain boring."[6]

Although, as we will see, the characteristics of the American party system make it impossible to pin down the differences between Democrats and Republicans in such definitive terms, political scientists do draw some distinctions between the two parties on the basis of their group support and ideological tendencies.

Group Support

In the first place, the two major parties differ historically in terms of the occupational, ethnic, racial, and other social groups each attracts for relatively long periods of time. As we can see in Table 4-3, Democratic presidential candidates have tended to draw greater support from nonwhites, younger voters, Catholics, union members, and manual workers, whereas Republican candidates have tended to attract the college-educated, professional and business groups, older voters, and Protestants.

Obviously, these are only tendencies. Neither party commands the exclusive support of any group. Plenty of Democrats are college-educated, attend a Protestant church, or own a business. Likewise, many Republicans are Catholic, young, or belong to a union. Nor does either party historically draw support always from the same groups. Prior to the 1930s, for instance, Jewish and black voters tended to be predominantly Republican.

The 1972 presidential election shattered many traditional voting patterns, largely because of the record defection (33 percent) among Democrats. Union members, youth, Catholics, and manual workers all switched in large numbers from their usual Democratic voting habits to support Richard Nixon. Although such defections were not as dramatic in local and state elections, party loyalties may be weakening among certain groups to the point that such loyalties may no longer be a reliable means of distinguishing between the parties. According to a March 1974 Gallup poll, more people now consider themselves Independents (34 percent), wedded to neither party, than identify themselves as Republicans (24 percent). Many observers attribute the growth of independent voters to increasing disenchantment with the political system, a long-term trend merely amplified by Watergate.

Ideology

However, many observers contend that in addition to group support, the two major parties differ in terms of their ideological tendencies. They argue that Democratic leaders and activists (such as governors, Senators, and campaign workers) tend to be more "liberal" or "progressive" than their Republican counterparts. Democrats are more inclined than Republicans to experiment with new governmental programs, to favor expanded regulation of the economy, and to support more extensive health and welfare programs. This greater inclination is due, at least in part, to the kind of group support the Democrats have maintained. "The fact that the Democratic party has built a national coalition of urban, lower socio-economic and minority groups," Frank Sorauf argues, "lies beneath its espousal of a wider social-welfare program than the Republicans have favored."[7]

One way to determine the ideological differences between Democratic and Republican leaders is to examine the voting records of Congress members. For some years now, the self-proclaimed "conservative" Americans for Constitutional Action (ACA) and the "liberal" Americans for Democratic Action (ADA) have been doing just that—rating the votes of Democratic and Republican members of Congress on key legislation. Generally speaking, the conservative ACA awards its highest ratings to members who favor a strong defense posture, a competitive market system, private ownership of production, and states' rights. The liberal ADA, on the other hand, awards its top marks to members who favor lower defense spending, welfare reform, civil rights, and environmental protection. Thus, for the 1973 congressional session, twenty-two Republicans and only five Democrats in the Senate received positive scores of 70 percent or better from the conservative ACA. At the same time, thirty Democrats and only five Republicans received positive scores of 70 percent or better from the liberal ADA.[8]

What then about the voters? Are there ideological differences also among the rank and file? There do appear to be such differences, although they are perhaps not as strong as among policy makers. A recent Gallup poll finds that only one-third as many Republicans as Democrats identify themselves as "liberal." Republican voters, in fact, identify their political views as "conserva-

Table 4-4. Party Identification and Ideology

	Conservative	Middle of Road	Liberal	No Opinion
Republican	57%	30%	11%	2%
Democrat	31	29	33	7
Independent	41	31	25	3

Source: *Gallup Opinion Index*, August 1972.

tive" almost five to one over "liberal," whereas Democratic voters divide almost evenly between the two extremes. (See Table 4-4.)

Moreover, a study published in June 1972 indicates that Democratic and Republican voters are tending to express increasingly different degrees of support for certain political and social issues. (See Table 4-5.) Voters with strong Democratic identifications now give about twice as much support as Republican voters to such issues as aid to education, medical care, governmental guarantees of full and fair employment, and school integration.

Table 4-5. Party Identification and Policy Position, 1956, 1960, 1964, and 1968 (in percentages supporting "liberal" position)

Party Identification	Aid to Education				Medical Care				Job Guarantee			
	1956	1960	1964	1968	1956	1960	1964	1968	1956	1960	1964	1968
Strong Democrat	80.0	66.8	51.0	53.6	74.2	74.5	78.2	81.3	75.6	71.2	52.6	53.1
Weak Democrat	78.1	59.0	44.1	38.3	67.3	60.2	65.2	72.1	64.0	62.4	38.4	39.7
Independent	71.0	53.2	39.3	32.9	55.8	56.7	57.2	55.3	55.0	56.6	31.0	27.0
Weak Republican	68.7	39.1	21.5	22.5	51.4	47.5	43.5	39.3	59.5	43.9	25.9	24.9
Strong Republican	67.7	44.5	15.5	12.0	45.9	54.2	23.6	42.7	51.5	52.7	16.1	25.4
Gamma	.15	.20	.34	.36	.24	.18	.45	.41	.19	.16	.31	.25

Party Identification	Fair Employment				School Integration				Foreign Aid			
	1956	1960	1964	1968	1956	1960	1964	1968	1956	1960	1964	1968
Strong Democrat	73.3	63.0	56.3	61.9	38.7	39.8	53.7	58.9	49.5	51.4	64.7	51.3
Weak Democrat	71.3	63.1	42.9	43.5	44.4	37.5	43.2	44.6	55.4	48.8	59.2	45.8
Independent	66.6	65.4	50.3	37.7	48.8	47.1	49.0	37.3	49.9	53.2	57.5	42.7
Weak Republican	70.8	62.7	36.3	37.8	49.3	43.0	50.5	37.4	48.2	54.0	56.6	47.0
Strong Republican	66.8	65.9	20.6	31.3	38.8	41.5	34.8	31.5	51.4	61.5	49.7	41.8
Gamma	.04	– .02	.22	.24	.04	– .01	.08	.43	.01	– .03	.08	.04

Source: Gerald M. Pomper, "From Confusion to Clarity," *American Political Science Review*, June 1972, p. 417.

Party Characteristics and Citizen Confusion

Since most Americans continue to identify in some way with a political party, we might expect considerable enthusiasm for party affairs. If people identify with a party, then it would seem likely that they would be eager to help push that party toward electoral victory. Yet only a relatively small proportion of the adult population (about 3 or 4 percent) make an effort to influence the selection of party candidates or help in a campaign. The actual direction of party affairs is left to small cadres of local party activists who devote considerable time and money to ensure party success at the polls.

Although many reasons may account for the low participation, some observers believe several prominent characteristics of the party system itself are partly to blame. They contend that the lack of discipline, the ideological potpourri, and the overlapping features of the two major parties prevent many people from seeing any clear connection between their own participation and eventual public policies. Indeed, most Americans tend to be confused about what the two major parties ultimately represent. They do not fully understand, for example, how the Democratic party at different times in its history could gain the support of both southern segregationists and the majority of black voters. Nor can they easily distinguish between the two major parties on policy issues—especially in foreign affairs, where members of both parties in Congress, and both Lyndon Johnson and Richard Nixon, supported the Vietnam War. The British writer, James Bryce, after visiting this country in the late nineteenth century, observed that a European is always asking Americans to explain the distinctive tenets of the two parties. "He is always asking," Bryce quipped, "because he never gets an answer."[9]

But, whether or not confusion about the parties discourages political participation, we might take a look at the prominent features of the American party system. At least, we may gain a better understanding of the basis for the confusion.

A Tradition of Disunity

Certainly one contributing factor to the confusion has been the fragmentation of party leadership. Although most of us may regard the Democratic and Republican parties as national bodies, they are little more than loose alliances of state and local parties

Table 4-6. National Party Organization

The National Convention   On paper, the supreme authority in both the Democratic and Republican parties is the national convention, which meets only a few days every four years to select a presidential candidate, settle disputes, and write a party platform. During the rest of the time, the direction of the party is turned over to the national committee and its chairman.

The National Committee   The national committee usually is composed of one man and one woman from each state and the territories, who are commonly selected by state delegations to the national convention. The committee meets only rarely, mainly to assist in the presidential campaign and to arrange for the next national convention.

The National Committee Chairperson   Most of the committee's responsibilities are assumed by the committee leader and staff. Usually chosen by the party's presidential candidate after the convention, the chairperson's main functions are public relations, research, and fund raising for the presidential campaign. Otherwise, his or her powers are marginal.

The Congressional Campaign Committees   Composed of members of the House and the Senate, these committees solicit speakers and money for candidates who face serious opposition. In both parties, friction prevails frequently between these committees and the presidentially oriented national committee.

that converge every four years at a national convention to select a candidate for President. For most of American history, each of the states—and not any national body—has directed party operations. This reflects the federal system of government in this country, a system in which power is constitutionally divided among national and state governments. Each state boasts its own unique constitution, and its own special rules concerning elections and the functions of parties. As a result, Democratic and Republican party groups differ enormously in form and membership from one state to another, with each local group responding to its own distinct rules, policy needs, and constituencies.

Naturally, this does not mean that the Democratic and Republican parties have operated totally without any national organization. (See Table 4-6.) But in each major party, the national organization has focused primarily on the election of the presidential candidate and has not intruded into state and local party campaigns. It has not, for example, chosen the party's candidates for Congress or for state political offices. "Despite all the appearances of hierarchy in the American party organization," Frank Sorauf has observed, "in no important way does any national party unit limit the autonomy of the state and local party organizations. With virtually no exceptions, the latter pick their own officers, nominate their own candidates, take their own stands on issues, raise and spend their own funds."[10]

This decentralization has been severely criticized, not only for confusing many voters but for making it difficult for either party to maintain party unity on issues. Because members of Congress, for example, have frequently gained their nominations and financial support from local and state party bosses and special-interest groups, they often have succeeded in building their own base of power independent of the national party leadership. They have realized that the national party leadership can do little to help or hurt their chances for reelection. As one member of Congress boasted, "They can't do a thing to me as long as they don't have any patronage to dish out. They don't give me any campaign money so they can't take that away."[11] Thus, a prevailing feature of Congress has been that members of each party ignore pleas for party unity when voting on important issues. In the Senate during 1974, for example, the average Democrat voted with his or her party only 63 percent of the time, while the average Republican voted with his or her party only 59 percent of the time.[12]

In fact, the undisciplined character of the two major parties has extended to voters as well. Although many voters still cast their ballots on the basis of party loyalty, evidence clearly shows that an increasing number are now splitting their votes between the two parties.[13] In the 1972 elections, as we have seen, many Democrats supported Richard Nixon for President while, at the same time, voting for Democratic candidates in state and local elections. In fact, out of the twelve states in 1972 in which voters chose candidates for President, Governor, and U.S. Senator, only in North Carolina did they support the same party (Republican) for all three offices.[14] Thus, while many political analysts debate the significance and wisdom of ticket-splitting, the fact remains that voters have been under no obligation to support the party with which they register. They have paid no dues nor signed any pledges that could prevent the kind of desertion that occurred among Democrats in the 1972 elections.

Concern about disunity, in fact, prompted more than two thousand Democratic party delegates (ranging from Alabama Governor George Wallace to the members of the Congressional Black Caucus) to hold their own "mini-convention" in Kansas City in December 1974. The convention marked the first time in American history that a major party has tried seriously to incorporate its disparate elements under a binding national constitution. In three days of seminars and debates, the delegates labored to reach conciliation and mend old party wounds. They fashioned the party's first formal charter and reached some important compromises on the volatile issues of minority representation and quotas. Most of the delegates hoped to stem the tide of independent voters by opening up the party to a broader cross section of the population. They felt that a strong, organized party could present a more unified stand on key issues and could force the local organizations to bring more minority voters, women, and young people into the party's embrace. Obviously, the delegates realized that any new-found unity would be at best only fragile. The years of divisiveness within the Democratic party would not likely be forgotten in just three days, or even in three years. Yet, most of the delegates still hoped that some remnant of unity would last at least through the 1976 presidential election, forestalling the corrosive bickering that had crippled the party in 1972.

The hopes of these delegates were bolstered to some extent by a number of dramatic events in January 1975. In that month, a caucus comprising all the Democrats in the House of Representatives assaulted one of Congress's most venerable traditions: the seniority rule, under which committee leaders have been selected on the basis of their length of service on a committee. For the first time in memory, three powerful committee chairmen—eighty-one-year-old Wright Patman of Banking and Currency, seventy-three-year-old F. Edward Hebert of Armed Services, and seventy-five-year-old W. R. Poage of Agriculture—were dumped from their posts. Their ouster followed the removal a few weeks earlier of Wilbur Mills from the chairmanship of the powerful Ways and Means Committee, after Mills had been caught red-handed in a series of drunken escapades with a local strip-tease artist, Fanne Foxe. In the opinion of many observers, the defrocking of the four committee chairmen signaled a dramatic shift in power from the small group of generally conservative, autocratic committee leaders to the more liberal caucus of all the Democrats in the House. It served as a warning to all members that seniority would no longer protect those who defied the party majority and its elected leadership on critical policies. (For more on the change, see Chapter Seven.)

Also in that month, the U.S. Supreme Court helped strengthen both the Democratic and Republican party leadership by ruling that the national party conventions could refuse to seat delegates chosen in state conventions. The ruling clarified who had authority over the delegate-selection process, giving the national leadership in each party the power to impose stricter criteria on each of the fifty states in their method of selecting delegates to the national party convention. The state party organizations could be compelled, for example, to include more minorities, women, and youth in their delegations to the national convention, thus further opening up the presidential nominating process to groups traditionally excluded from that process.

Not all party reformers, however, welcome the drive toward

unifying the parties—at least not from the standpoint of citizen action. Some contend that the present decentralization of the parties actually encourages citizen participation in party affairs. Since many important decisions, including the selection of candidates for local public office, are made at the district and state levels, citizens remain relatively close to the real power centers of their party. If all major party decisions were centralized at the national level, most citizens would find it more difficult to have some impact on party policy. We will return to this point at the end of the chapter.

A Potpourri of Ideology

In addition to sharing a tradition of disunity, the Democratic and Republican parties have tended to be ideologically mixed. Both parties have continued to elect members to Congress who span the spectrum of liberal and conservative philosophy. In fact, there are perhaps as many ideological differences *within* each party as there are between them. The Democratic party, for example, not only attracts "liberals" like Edward Kennedy of Massachusetts and George McGovern of South Dakota but "conservatives" such as Herman Talmadge of Georgia and Russell Long of Louisiana. Similarly, the Republican party—while not as diverse as the Democratic party—embraces not only "conservatives" like Strom Thurmond of South Carolina and Barry Goldwater of Arizona but moderate "liberals" such as Jacob Javits of New York and Charles Percy of Illinois. Obviously, the decentralized tradition of the two parties has a great deal to do with this ideological potpourri. As long as state and local organizations maintain some autonomy, politicians will tend to reflect the unique values and philosophy that characterize their own local power bases.

What then holds the Democratic and Republican parties together? Aside from the forces of tradition, most members of the same party do share some common views. Although Edward Kennedy and George Wallace, for example, have hardly seen eye to eye on civil rights and foreign policy, both have subscribed in principle to a number of other concepts—such as an active governmental role in welfare and the economy—that distinguish them from most Republicans. The sharing of views, combined with a mutual desire to see local party candidates win public office, are usually sufficient to surmount policy differences and hold members of the same party together.

Just the same, the tensions have sometimes reached the breaking point, as in 1968 when George Wallace bolted from the Democratic party to form his own American Independent party. Similar defections occurred in 1948 when Henry A. Wallace left the Democratic party to run for President on the Progressive party platform, and when in the same year southern Democrats stormed out of the Democratic national convention over the civil rights issue to support Strom Thurmond as their candidate for President. (Strom Thurmond later switched to the Republican party.) Even the generally less turbulent Republican party has suffered major defections, as in 1912 when the followers of former President Theodore Roosevelt bolted to support his Progressive party candidacy for another White House term.

"Not a Dime's Worth of Difference"

A third characteristic of the Democratic and Republican parties—and one subject to many criticisms—is that the programs of the two parties ultimately are not really different from each other. George Wallace used to complain in his 1968 presidential campaign that "there's not a dime's worth of difference" between Democrats and Republicans. Similarly, James Bryce once charged that "the two major parties are like two bottles, identical in size, shape, color, bearing different labels, but both empty."[15]

These are, of course, exaggerations; the two parties do express somewhat different ideological viewpoints. But, compared with the range of political parties in other countries—where the spectrum frequently runs from the extreme left to the extreme right—the Democratic and Republican parties are very similar and moderate. Although they may differ, for example, over the extent to which the government should regulate business, neither party advocates the total nationalization of industry. And, although they may disagree about policies of governmental economic assistance, few Democrats or Republicans advocate the abolition of social security or the elimination of the graduated income tax. In fact, both Democratic and Republican politicians seem to espouse many of the same values: free public education, a strong military defense, law and order, governmental subsidies for key industries, and so forth.

This similarity and moderation stems not only from their mutual support of certain traditions (like capitalism), but also from the pressures of two-party competition. With only the Democratic and Republican parties having a likely chance to gain control of government (for reasons we will discuss shortly), each party must attract many of the same groups to win an electoral majority. Each must offer programs and candidates having an appeal as broad-based as possible. As a result, the two parties tend to sound and look alike. "In some important respects," Clinton Rossiter concludes, "there is and can be no real difference between the Democrats and Republicans, because the unwritten laws of American politics demand that the parties overlap substantially in principle, policy, character, appeal, and purpose—or cease to be parties with any hope of winning a national election."[16]

Moreover, since both parties must draw support from a wide spectrum of the population, they cannot afford to be ideologically extreme. A party that daringly proposes a drastic modification of current policies or that caters exclusively to a small segment of society obviously risks alienating more voters than it attracts. The dramatic failures of both George McGovern in 1972 and Barry Goldwater in 1964 illustrate that strong ideological positions can be a handicap in presidential elections.

This then carries interesting implications for citizen action. If the two major parties refuse to offer clear and meaningful policy alternatives, then access to party decision making (when one can get it) may not be very meaningful. After all, if the pressures of two-party competition demand a bland policy approach, any effort to use the parties as channels for political action may accomplish little in the way of significant and lasting policy reform. As long as both parties try to attract as many different people as possible—without simultaneously alienating their own partisan loyalists—their campaigns and platforms will remain low-keyed and equivocal. Both parties will simply continue to indulge in what some cynically describe as "verbal exercises in calculated ambiguity."

One-Party Dominance

An additional feature of the American party system is the tendency toward one-party dominance. Although this feature may not necessarily contribute to citizen confusion, it contradicts the notion that the two major parties are closely competitive. In most congressional elections, for example, one of the two parties usually manages to maintain the upper hand for considerable periods of time. This means that in cities like Berkeley and Boston, Democratic candidates usually are elected to Congress without stiff opposition from Republican candidates. In fact, it has been estimated that about 75 percent of all congressional districts are

In a one party area your vote would do the most good in the primaries

Table 4-7. The Fifty States Classified According to Degree of
Interparty Competition, 1956–1970

One-Party Democratic	Modified One-Party Democratic	Two-Party		Modified One-Party Republican
Louisiana (.9877)	North Carolina (.8332)	Hawaii (.6870)	New Jersey (.5122)	North Dakota (.3305)
Alabama (.9685)	Virginia (.8235)	Rhode Island (.6590)	Pennsylvania (.4800)	Kansas (.3297)
Mississippi (.9407)	Florida (.8052)	Massachusetts (.6430)	Colorado (.4725)	New Hampshire (.3282)
South Carolina (.9292)	Tennessee (.7942)	Alaska (.6383)	Michigan (.4622)	South Dakota (.3142)
Texas (.9132)	Maryland (.7905)	California (.6150)	Utah (.4565)	Vermont (.2822)
Georgia (.9080)	Oklahoma (.7792)	Nebraska (.6065)	Indiana (.4450)	
Arkansas (.8850)	Missouri (.7415)	Washington (.0647)	Illinois (.4235)	
	Kentucky (.7170)	Minnesota (.5910)	Wisconsin (.4102)	
	West Virginia (.7152)	Nevada (.5742)	Idaho (.4077)	
	New Mexico (.7150)	Connecticut (.5732)	Iowa (.3965)	
		Delaware (.5687)	Ohio (.3837)	
		Arizona (.5663)	New York (.3835)	
		Montana (.5480)	Maine (.3820)	
		Oregon (.5387)	Wyoming (.3537)	

Scale: 1.0000 = completely Democratic; .0000 = completely Republican.

Source: Austin Ranney, "Parties in State Politics," in Herbert Jacob and Kenneth Vines, *Politics in the American States: A Comparative Analysis,* 2d ed., p. 87. Copyright © 1971 by Little, Brown and Co.

generally safe for one major party or the other; whatever changes in party strength that do occur in Congress result mainly from the defeat of incumbents in the other 25 percent of the districts where the two parties are closely competitive.[17] Thus, taking into account the usual built-in advantages of incumbency, when we look at the results of the 1974 elections (supposedly a year of assault against incumbents), we find that more than 85 percent of the Congress members who ran for reelection were victorious.

One-party dominance also emerges in statewide elections for Senator and Governor, especially in the South and parts of the Midwest. As Table 4-7 indicates, although in most states the Democrats and Republicans are closely competitive, in some states (like Louisiana, Alabama, Mississippi, South Carolina, Kansas, and Vermont) one of the two parties manages to win a majority of elections to state offices.

There is some evidence, however, of a trend away from one-party control over statewide and congressional elections. For example, during the past two decades Republicans have won a growing number of elections in the South. In the recent 93rd Congress (1973–1975), seven of the twenty-two southern Senators were Republicans, as were one-third of the southern Representatives in the House. Still, the Democratic party tradition in the South has been so strong historically that it is likely to prevent the two parties from becoming fully competitive there for some time to come.

Moreover, when we look back through history, we find few times when the Democrats and Republicans have been evenly matched at the national level with control of the federal government alternating frequently between them. Instead, the usual pattern has been for one of the two parties to dominate the White House and Congress for a considerable period of time. "Our political solar system," one writer reflects, "has been characterized not by two equally competing suns, but by a sun and a moon. It is within the majority party that the issues of any particular period are fought out; while the minority party shines in reflected radiance of the heat thus generated."[18] As we can see in Table 4-8, since 1800 there have been at least three distinct periods in American history when either the Democrats or the Republicans virtually dominated the White House.

The first period, from 1800 to 1860, was dominated by the Democrats. During this entire sixty-year period, the opposition Whig party (which had replaced the Federalists) managed to win only two contests for President, electing William Henry Harrison in 1840 and Zachary Taylor in 1848. All the other thirteen presidential contests were won by the Democrats.

The second period, from 1860 to 1932, was dominated by the Republicans. During this long period, only two Democrats were elected President, each for two terms: Grover Cleveland (1884 and 1892) and Woodrow Wilson (1912 and 1916). The Republicans won all the other fourteen presidential elections, and were able to dominate Congress most of the time as well. One reason given for the rise to prominence of the Republican party (formed in 1854 by Whigs, antislavery Democrats, and third parties) was that, by the end of the Civil War, the Democrats had to bear the burden of being the party of the defeated South; the Republicans, on the other hand, were lauded as the party of Lincoln, the party

Table 4-8. Party Domination of the White House

DEMOCRATIC PERIOD

	Federalist, Whig	Jeffersonian-Republican Democrat
1800		Jefferson
1804		Jefferson
1808		Madison
1812		Madison
1816		Monroe
1820		Monroe
1824		J.Q. Adams
1828		Jackson
1832		Jackson
1836		Van Buren
1840	Harrison-Tyler	
1844		Polk
1848	Taylor-Fillmore	
1852		Pierce
1856		Buchanan

REPUBLICAN PERIOD

	Republican	Democrat
1860	Lincoln	
1864	Lincoln-Johnson	
1868	Grant	
1872	Grant	
1876	Hayes	
1880	Garfield-Arthur	
1884		Cleveland
1888	Harrison	
1892		Cleveland
1896	McKinley	
1900	McKinley-T. Roosevelt	
1904	T. Roosevelt	
1908	Taft	
1912		Wilson
1916		Wilson
1920	Harding-Coolidge	
1924	Coolidge	
1928	Hoover	

DEMOCRATIC PERIOD

	Republican	Democrat
1932		F. Roosevelt
1936		F. Roosevelt
1940		F. Roosevelt
1944		F. Roosevelt-Truman
1948		Truman
1952	Eisenhower	
1956	Eisenhower	
1960		Kennedy-Johnson
1964		Johnson
1968	Nixon	
1972	Nixon-Ford	

that had "preserved the Union." This, together with other factors, permitted the Republicans to enjoy for many decades the same mass support previously given the Democrats.

But during the third great period, from 1932 to 1968, the Democrats returned to prominence. They gained control of the White House for twenty-eight years, yielding it for only the eight years that Dwight Eisenhower was President (from 1952 to 1960). And, except for 1947–1949 and 1953–1955, the Democrats also dominated Congress. Apparently, just as the Civil War had dealt a severe blow to the Democrats, the stock market crash in 1929 and the Great Depression similarly defeated the Republicans. By the mid-1930s, the Democratic party had shed much of its image as the party of the Confederate South and was able to attract widespread support as the party of reform under Franklin Roosevelt.

Since 1968, however, the picture has been more confusing. The Republicans reclaimed the White House that year by electing Richard Nixon as President, and subsequently saw him win a landslide victory over George McGovern in 1972—a victory that prompted many observers to herald the "bankruptcy" of the Democratic party. Then, in 1974, Nixon resigned the Presidency. Although Gerald Ford's ascendance to the office kept the White House in Republican hands, the Watergate burglary and its aftermath appeared to shatter Republican hopes of renewed glory.

The Democrats, meanwhile, continued to dominate both houses of Congress and the state capitals. Following the 1974 elections, they even managed to pick up an additional forty-three seats in the House, three more seats in the Senate, and four new governorships—giving them their largest holdings in the statehouses since 1936. On top of that, a March 1974 Gallup poll indicated the lowest public support for the Republican party in more than thirty-eight years of Gallup poll measurement. While 42 percent of those surveyed classified themselves as Democrats, only 24 percent said they were Republicans.

Yet, despite these gains, the Democratic party has not clearly benefited in terms of new party adherents. The number (42 percent) considering themselves Democrats in the March 1974 poll was virtually the same as during the 1972 election. The largest actual gain was registered among Independents, who climbed to an all-time high of 34 percent—an increase of 5 percent since 1972 (and 14 percent since 1940). This high percentage of Independents seemed to reveal a growing disenchantment among the electorate with both major parties—tossing the future of both into the air.

Third-Party Alternatives

Many Americans who have become fed up with the similar and moderate traits of the Democratic and Republican parties have put their faith in third parties. They have given their support to and worked within alternative parties that, in their estimation, favor policies that neither of the two major parties have been willing to implement. In doing so, however, they have had to accept the enormous difficulties third parties have encountered in carrying out their programs. For most of American history, only the Democrats and Republicans have had sufficient strength to compete for the control of national government with any likely chance of success. Although third parties have surfaced in almost every major election, only the Republicans in the 1860s managed to gain national political power; and they did so only by displacing the Whigs.

Variety of Third Parties

Third parties have, of course, played an active role throughout the nation's history. Since the Constitution permits any native-born American over thirty-five years of age to run for President, elections in this country have brought forth an abundance of eager competitors for the job. The Socialist-Labor party, for example, has run a candidate for President in almost every election during this century. In the 1972 elections, voters in all but ten states had an opportunity to vote for a score of presidential aspirants other than Richard Nixon and George McGovern. Among the most prominent of these candidates were John G. Schmitz (American party); Dr. Benjamin Spock (People's party); Linda Jenness and Evelyn Reed (Socialist Workers party); Louis Fisher (Socialist Labor party); Gus Hall (Communist party); John Hospers (Libertarian party); and Earle Harold Munn (Prohibition party). There was even a former State Department official who jokingly launched his own twenty-eight-state campaign to promote the ideas of the so-called National Association of Professional Bureaucrats party, with the motto: "When in charge, ponder; when in trouble, delegate; when in doubt, mumble." None of these third-party hopefuls, however, came close to the 13.5 percent captured by George Wallace in 1968. Combined, they received only 1.4 million votes of the more than 77 million cast in 1972—a total of only 1.7 percent.[19]

In the past, there have been many kinds of third parties, each with a different reason for existence. Some, like the American Communist and the American Nazi parties, have been highly doctrinaire, demanding the overhaul of the entire economic and political system. Others, like the Progressives in 1912 and the Dixiecrats in 1948, have been basically "splinter parties," that broke off in protest from the Democrats or the Republicans. Still others, like the Prohibitionists and the Libertarians, have been primarily "educational parties," using the electoral process to gain publicity for their ideas. Other third parties have included: the Anti-Masons in the 1830s, who contested only one presidential election and then disappeared; the "Know-Nothings" in the 1850s, an anti-Catholic, anti-Irish Native American party so secretive its members pretended to have heard nothing about it (hence the name); the Vegetarian and Prohibition parties, opposed to meat and to alcohol; and the Mugwumps, Republicans who bolted from

one strong issue is apt to bring 3rd party into existence

Table 4-9. Votes Captured by Third-Party Presidential Candidates

		Popular vote	
Year	Party	Total	Percentage
1832	Anti-Masonic	101,051	8.0
1840	Liberty	7,053	.3
1844	Liberty	62,197	2.3
1848	Free Soil	291,616	10.i
	Liberty	2,733	.1
1852	Free Soil	156,297	4.9
1856	Know-Nothing	849,872	21.1
1860	Constitutional-Union	591,688	12.6
1880	Greenback	308,649	3.4
1884	Greenback	175,066	1.7
	Prohibition	150,957	1.5
1888	Prohibition	250,122	2.2
1892	Populist	1,029,960	8.5
1904	Socialist	402,714	3.0
	Prohibition	259,163	1.9
1908	Socialist	420,858	2.8
	Prohibition	252,704	1.7
1912	Progressive	4,127,788	27.4
	Socialist	901,255	6.0
1916	Socialist	585,974	3.2
1920	Socialist	915,490	3.4
1924	Progressive	4,832,532	16.6
1948	States' Rights	1,176,125	2.4
	Progressive	1,157,326	2.4
1960	Unpledged Elector States	491,527	.7
1968	American Independent	9,906,141	13.5
1972	American	1,099,400	1.4

Source: Data from the *Congressional Quarterly Weekly Report*, 29 September 1967.

their party in 1884 in protest against the presidential nomination of James C. Blaine and who were once jokingly described: "I am a mugwump ... my mug is on one side of the fence and my wump is on the other."

Some third parties even have attained sufficient strength to affect the outcome of a presidential election or to elect members to Congress. One of the most successful, although short-lived, parties was the Populists, a coalition of the Farmers' Alliance and the Federation of Labor that gained prominence in the 1890s. Although it failed to attract a national following, it was able in 1894 to elect six Senators and seven Representatives to Congress. In this century, the most impressive third-party showing was by Teddy Roosevelt's "Bull Moose" Progressive party, a group of liberal Republicans who left the party in 1912. The Progressives captured 27 percent of the popular vote that year—more than the Republican incumbent William H. Taft—and thus brought victory to the Democratic candidate Woodrow Wilson.

Third parties have enjoyed successes also in state and local politics. The Socialist party, for example, has elected mayors in Bridgeport and Hartford, Connecticut, and in Milwaukee, Wisconsin. In Minnesota during the 1920s and 1930s, the Farmer-Labor party—not the Democratic party—provided the main opposition to the Republican party in most state and congressional elections; in the 1940s, the Farmer-Labor party even won the governorship. Similarly, in New York State, the Conservative party in 1970 sent James Buckley to the U.S. Senate, dumping the Republican incumbent Charles Goodell.

Reasons for Failure

The main pattern, however, has been for third parties in both state and national elections to suffer a common fate: few victories at the polls and a relatively short existence. No third party has ever captured the Presidency, and only a few have occupied more than a handful of seats in Congress. As Table 4-9 shows, only six third parties since 1832 have collected more than 10 percent of the popular vote in a national election: the Free Soil party in 1848; the "Know-Nothings" in 1856; the Constitutional-Union party in 1860; the Progressives under Theodore Roosevelt in 1912; the Progressives under Robert La Follette in 1924; and the American Independent party under George Wallace in 1968.

In a sense, the absence of powerful third parties seems rather surprising in view of the many regional, economic, and social differences in this country. We might expect many parties to flourish in Congress and in the state legislatures, each representing a different segment of our society. Yet, the United States is one of the few places in the world where powerful third parties have not been able to thrive. Norway, Italy, West Germany, Switzerland, and many countries in Africa and Latin America all have had several strong competitive parties. Although political scientists have been unable to agree on any overall explanation for the persistence of only two major parties in this country, several hypotheses have been offered.

Easily the most popular is that the sytem of electing candidates reinforces two-party competition.[20] In the United States, the "single-member district system" applies to all federal elections, meaning that only one Representative may be elected from a congressional district no matter how many candidates are running—it is simply a case of winner-take-all. (The same is true of the presidential election, where the candidate who receives the most popular votes in a state receives all its electoral votes.) This means that even if a third party wins 20 or 30 percent of the votes all over the country, it still is not rewarded with a single seat in Congress.

In such countries as West Germany, Norway, and Sweden, a different system of "proportional representation," with multi-member districts, is used. Under this system, a number of candidates are elected from each district and are assigned seats in the legislature in proportion to their percentages of the popular vote. This means that parties failing to win a majority of votes may still be represented in the legislature; their campaign efforts are not entirely wasted.

Consider, then, what might happen if the United States converted to a system of proportional representation. A party like the American Independent, winning 20 or 30 percent of the popular vote, might control 20 or 30 percent of the seats in Congress. In 1936, New York City actually approved such a system, deciding it would be more responsive to the true divisions of opinion among the electorate. As a result, the voters in 1945 elected to the City Council not only fourteen Democrats and three Republicans but also two American Labor party candidates, two Liberals, and two Communists. But the presence of the two Communists met such stiff opposition that in 1947 the city reinstated the tradition of one member per district. Thus, during the next election in 1949 only Democratic and Republican candidates won seats on the City Council.[21]

Nevertheless, the election of only one member per district does not provide a complete explanation for Democratic and Republican party supremacy. It does not explain why third parties have been unable to gain enough support to displace either of these two parties. Another popular hypothesis is that the United States has simply had a historical tradition of two-party competition, first inherited from the split between the Whigs and Tories in England and then reinforced by the division between the Federalists and Anti-Federalists over ratification of the Constitution. The pattern of two dominant competitive parties became entrenched at this early stage and has been perpetuated ever since.

Moreover, the traditional allegiances of voters to the two dominant parties have been difficult for third parties to break. After more than a century of Democratic and Republican party supremacy, most voters have become used to supporting one of these two parties. They have acquired their partisan loyalties from their parents at an early age and probably will support the same party throughout their adult lives. Because these loyalties tend to pass from generation to generation, the Democratic and Republican parties enjoy a tremendous historical and psychological advantage over smaller and more sporadic third parties.

It is also possible that many third parties are too ideologically extreme or specialized to gain widespread support. In contrast to France and Italy where both socialist and communist parties flourish, this country never has given much support to parties outside the mainstream of capitalist ideology. The fact, as we saw in the preceding chapter, that many Americans are unwilling to allow socialists and communists to express their views would seem to preclude much support for their platforms and candidates. Beyond that, the programs of many third parties probably are too narrow and specialized to appeal to a wide range of opinion. Not enough people feel strongly about a single issue, such as prohibition or vegetarianism, to cast their vote for a special-interest third party. And even if they do feel strongly about the issue, they may consider it impractical to lend their support given the tradition of electing only one member per district. By discouraging "wasted" votes for third-party candidates, the electoral system—and the psychology of voters—reinforces the two-party pattern.

Third parties also face tremendous legal and financial obstacles. In the first place, they are confronted by the statutory difficulties of getting on the ballot in many states. For a party to appear on the ballot in California, for instance, it must *either* register at least 1 percent of the total number of registered voters in the state *or* file a petition signed by a number of voters equal to 10 percent of the total vote cast for governor in the previous election. And to remain on the ballot in subsequent elections (without having to repeat this procedure), one of its candidates for statewide office must capture at least 2 percent of the total vote cast *and* the party must maintain at least 1/15 of 1 percent of the total registration. These requirements are tough for many small parties, although both the American and the Peace and Freedom parties qualified for the 1972 election in California.

The high costs of campaigning, accentuated by the increasing reliance on television (see Chapter Five), pose even more serious problems for third parties. Even though the American and the Peace and Freedom parties were able to get on the ballot, both had to scrounge for nickel-and-dime contributions. Neither party could compete with the national total of $90 million spent by the Democratic and Republican presidential candidates in 1972. Without funds, they could not gain publicity; and without publicity, neither party could hope to gain enough support to win public office.

Finally, the failure of third parties often results from the ability of the Democrats and Republicans to steal their thunder. A third party sometimes proposes a promising idea—such as the direct election of Senators, the progressive income tax, or the regulation of banks—only to have the two major parties appropriate the idea when it becomes popular. The unique appeal of the third party is thus undercut, and it loses whatever support it had started to gain. In 1968, for example, both Hubert Humphrey and Richard Nixon picked up, and ran on, the "law and order" issue sparked by George Wallace. By doing so, they capitalized on part of his appeal and probably undermined his third-party candidacy.

Value of Third Parties

So what contributions do third parties make to the political system? Despite their inability to gain mass public support or to play a major role in policy making, these parties do provide some important services.

In the first place, third parties often express the views and demands of those who are disgusted with the Democratic and Republican parties. Although third parties normally are unable to translate these views and demands into concrete policies, they at least provide a forum for alternative viewpoints. Without third parties, in other words, many more persons might abstain from voicing their political concerns.

In addition, third parties sometimes draw public attention to controversial issues ignored by the two major parties. In contrast to Democratic and Republican party candidates, who usually are afraid of alienating regular supporters and always are trying to attract new ones, third-party candidates are frequently more outspoken on specific issues. Whether it is because third-party candidates tend to be more ideological or because they see little hope of gaining control of the government, they have been able to publicize and endorse issues for their own sake. Third-party candidates in the past, for example, called for the primary election, old-age pensions, universal and compulsory education, women's suffrage, and the initiative and referendum well in advance of their acceptance by Democratic and Republican candidates.

But, besides drawing attention to controversial issues, third parties sometimes directly affect the programs of the two major parties. By threatening to steal the thunder of the Democrats and Republicans with a popular campaign issue—as Wallace attempted with the law-and-order issue in 1968—third parties sometimes compel the other two parties to alter their long-term policy orientations and to adopt ideas endorsed by third-party candidates. This occurred, for example, in the 1890s when the Democratic party absorbed the Populists and in 1924 when the Democratic party adopted many of the Progressive programs of Robert La Follette. "The evidence seems to suggest," one scholar has concluded, "that the rather large-scale, episodic, nonrecurring minor-party movements must be regarded . . . as integral elements of the so-called two-party system. They spring from the center of the political melee, and in turn they affect the nature of the major parties and the relationship between them as they cumbersomely make their way from election to election."[22]

Evaluation: "The Headless Horsemen"

As we noted earlier, most Americans continue to shun active participation in party affairs. Although many reasons may account for this, several of the party characteristics we have examined have been regarded as contributing factors. This has led to some specific proposals for reforming the American party system in order to clarify the policy differences between the parties and to encourage wider and more meaningful citizen participation. For voters to perceive a clear connection between their political acts and eventual public policies, they need to see more than just two unstructured parties in the guise of "headless horsemen," galloping from election to election bearing few substantive policy alternatives.

Two-Party Choice

A number of critics contend, first of all, that elections in this country have rarely done more than replace the "in" party with the "out" party, substituting "Tweedledee" for "Tweedledum." Because the Democratic and Republican parties have tended to seek broad-based support in order to win control of government, both have tried to pamper and please many of the same groups, thus assuring bland similarity. Their doing so not only has obscured the choices available to citizens but has failed to encompass various alternative points of view.

To remedy this shortcoming and encourage stronger third parties, some suggest we adopt a system of proportional representation and a more equitable way to finance campaigns (see Chapter Five). Advocates of such a multiparty system insist that it would expand the number of choices presently available. It would encourage representation of a wider range of opinion in Congress and would endow party membership with greater meaning.

Opponents of a multiparty system, however, fear that stronger third parties would only lead to chaos and instability. Under a two-party system, compromises are continually made *within* each of the two parties, and one party can usually carry the major responsibility for governing—especially if it dominates both the White House and Congress. However, under a multiparty system, it might be difficult for one party to capture even a sufficient majority to dominate Congress. Governments would have to be constructed out of alliances of several different parties (Socialists, Prohibitionists, Democrats, and so forth), creating unstable and fragmented situations similar to those found in pre–de Gaulle France and Italy.

However, such pro and con arguments remain at best tenuous, because it is unlikely that an objective appraisal of multiparty systems can be made. After all, we know that multiparty systems (as well as two-party systems) differ from country to country, reflecting diverse social and political traditions. For example, in Italy, multiparty governments have lasted an average of only ten months, while in Holland the average life of such governments has been about four years. Given the unique political traditions of this country, it is almost impossible to predict the long-term consequences of having stronger third parties vying with the Democrats and Republicans for control of government. Whether political instability, fairer representation, or even increased voter participation would result from having a multiparty system may depend less on the number of parties than on many other social and political factors.

Ideologically Mixed Parties

As an alternative to having a multiparty system, some critics believe the two major parties would offer voters more meaningful alternatives if they were reorganized along more consistent ideological lines. This reorganization would enable voters to choose more readily between the parties and to locate responsibility more easily for the policies they propose. Thus, we should metaphorically throw the two parties into a huge sack, shake the sack vigorously, and then pour out the contents into two new separate piles—one "liberal," the other "conservative." This realignment could be accomplished, for example, by shifting conservative southerners from the Democratic into the Republican party and by moving northern Republican liberals over to the Democratic side.[23]

However, any permanent ideological realignment may be difficult to maintain. In the first place, few politicians and voters can be labeled strictly "liberal" or "conservative." Although many southern Democratic Senators, for instance, may be regarded as "conservative" on civil rights and foreign policy, they may be quite "liberal" on many economic and welfare issues. Similarly, although many voters may take a "liberal" position on governmental regulation of business, they may be very "conservative" on busing and law enforcement.

In the second place, neither party is likely to define itself as strictly "liberal" or "conservative" if that means alienating large numbers of undecided and ideologically moderate voters. According to some analysts, this is precisely what occurred in 1972 when George McGovern's candidacy enabled the Republicans to preempt the center and win the votes of many moderate Democrats. For either party to solicit only "conservative" or "liberal" support would be to sacrifice flexibility and pragmatism—to throw out an essential part of its political strategy.

Some observers also fear that, even if the parties could sharpen the ideological distinction between them, this would only intensify conflict and polarization. If the moderating influences in each party were removed, elections would be fought between extremes; campaigns would become less restrained and opportunities for compromise would be reduced. Thus, even though voters might benefit to some extent by choosing between more ideologically distinct parties, the stability of the system itself would suffer. However, such fears are probably exaggerated, because the moderating tendencies of two-party competition in this country appear to be too pervasive to permit strongly ideological parties to flourish.

Party Discipline

A third, and final, criticism of the two major parties is that they have been too decentralized and undisciplined to translate their campaign promises into effective policies. The Democrats and Republicans have been unable to forge their multifarious state and local organizations into unified party machines capable of implementing policies demanded by voters. Voters have had no assurance that the party they support would in fact carry out even the vague policies that were promised. Hence, their incentive to vote has remained low.

Moreover, because of the lack of party discipline, politicians have tended to be swayed more by local interest groups than by national party goals. Since state and local party organizations have had control over nominations and have helped solicit campaign support, legislators have often succumbed to the wishes of local interests that could ensure their reelection.

Consequently, some critics have welcomed the efforts in recent years to make the two parties more centralized and disciplined— that is, to give the parties a greater capacity to lay down national programs that party members in Congress and elsewhere would have to support. Many years ago, in fact, the Committee on Political Parties of the American Political Science Association offered several recommendations for reform[24] that anticipated not only some of the reforms hammered out in the 1974 Democratic party "mini-convention" in Kansas City, but also the 1975 assault on the seniority tradition in Congress. One recommendation was to emulate the British party system by requiring all those elected under a party banner to support that party's national programs. To accomplish this, the committee advocated giving greater authority to the national leadership of each party so that it could implement official policies and discipline any congressional or other party member who refused to abide by the party line. This discipline could be enforced, for example, by having the congressional party caucus select committee chairmen on the basis of party loyalty and service rather than on the basis of seniority—thus undermining much of the control of congressional policy making by local interests.

However, a number of reservations also have been expressed about the committee's recommendations, such as that members of Congress should not be held more accountable to the demands of the national party leadership than they are to those of their district.[25] Even though local elites may exert a disproportionate influence on legislators, this may be preferable to giving national party leaders too much power, thus further removing representatives from the influence of citizens at the local level. What it may come down to, in other words, is a choice between improving the efficiency—and, as some argue, the representativeness—of the national party leadership or maintaining the existing ties between legislators and their districts.

Whatever may be the eventual outcome of the reform debate, the ultimate consideration should be the improvement of the parties' abilities to promote citizen participation. The parties should not only make the vote worthwhile by presenting meaningful policy alternatives, but they should also keep themselves open to both new party activists and rank-and-file voters. Otherwise, many of those with the motivation to try their hand at party politics—as convention delegates, candidates, or just campaign volunteers—will be disheartened by the vacuous party programs and the insensitivity to demands for policy reform.

Recommended Reading

Binkley, Wilfred E. *American Political Parties*. New York: Alfred A. Knopf, 1965.

Bone, Hugh A. *American Politics and the Party System*, 3rd ed. New York: McGraw-Hill, 1965.

Burns, James MacGregor. *The Deadlock of Democracy: Four-Party Politics in America*. Englewood Cliffs, N.J.: Prentice-Hall, 1963.

De Vries, Walter, and Torrance, Lance, Jr. *The Ticket-Splitter*. Grand Rapids, Mich.: William B. Eerdmans, 1972.

Duverger, Maurice. *Political Parties: Their Organization and Activity in the Modern State*. New York: Wiley, 1955.

Fenton, John H. *People and Parties in America*. Glenview, Ill: Scott, Foresman, 1966.

Keefe, William J. *Parties, Politics, and Public Policy in America.* New York: Holt, Rinehart and Winston, 1972.

Key, V. O., Jr. *Parties, Politics, and Pressure Groups,* 5th ed. New York: Crowell, 1964.

Rossiter, Clinton. *Parties and Politics in America.* Ithaca: Cornell University Press, 1960.

Saloma, John S., III, and Sontag, Frederick H. *Parties: The Real Opportunity for Effective Citizen Politics.* New York: Alfred A. Knopf, 1972.

Sindler, Allan P. *Political Parties in the United States.* New York: St. Martin's Press, 1966.

Sorauf, Frank J. *Party Politics in America.* Boston: Little, Brown, 1968.

————. *Political Parties in the American System.* Boston: Little, Brown, 1964.

1. *Gallup Opinion Index,* May 1973.

2. Frank J. Sorauf, *Political Parties in the American System* (Boston: Little, Brown, 1964), p. 1.

3. John Hospers, quoted in *Newsweek,* 23 October 1972, p. 47. Copyright *Newsweek,* Inc., 1972; reprinted by permission.

4. For some specific action strategies, see John S. Saloma III and Frederick H. Sontag, *Parties: The Real Opportunity for Effective Citizen Politics* (New York: Alfred A. Knopf, 1972).

5. Hugh A. Bone and Austin Ranney, *American Politics and the Party System,* 3rd ed. (New York: McGraw-Hill, 1965), p. 662.

6. Clinton Rossiter, *Parties and Politics in America* (Ithaca, N.Y.: Cornell University Press, 1960), p. 117.

7. Frank J. Sorauf, *Political Parties in the American System* (Boston: Little, Brown, 1964), p. 63.

8. See *Nation's Business,* September 1974.

9. James Bryce, *The American Commonwealth,* 1893.

10. Frank J. Sorauf, *Party Politics in America* (Boston: Little, Brown, 1968), p. 113.

11. Quoted in Charles L. Clapp, *The Congressman: His Work As He Sees It* (Washington, D.C.: Brookings Institution, 1963), p. 358.

12. *Congressional Quarterly Weekly Report,* 25 January 1975.

13. See, for example, Walter De Vries and Lance Torrance, Jr., *The Ticket-Splitter: A New Force in American Politics* (Grand Rapids, Mich.: William B. Eerdsmans, 1972).

14. See the *Congressional Quarterly Almanac,* 1972.

15. James Bryce, *The American Commonwealth,* 1893.

Notes

16. Clinton Rossiter, *Parties and Politics in America* (Ithaca, N.Y.: Cornell University Press, 1960), p. 108.

17. See, for example, William J. Keefe and Morris S. Ogul, *The American Legislative Process and the States* (Englewood Cliffs, N.J.: Prentice-Hall, 1968), pp. 109–14.

18. Samuel Lubell, *The Future of American Politics* (Garden City, N.Y.: Doubleday, 1956), p. 212.

19. For more information, see the *Congressional Quarterly Weekly Report*, 10 March 1973.

20. See, for example, Maurice Duverger, *Political Parties* (New York: Wiley, 1955).

21. Belle Zeller and Hugh A. Bone, "The Repeal of P.R. in New York City—Ten Years in Retrospect." *American Political Science Review*, December 1948, pp. 1127–48.

22. V. O. Key, Jr., *Parties, Politics, and Pressure Groups*, 5th ed. (New York: Thomas Y. Crowell, 1964), p. 279.

23. For an argument that such a realignment may already be occurring, see Kevin P. Phillips, *The Emerging Republican Majority* (New York: Doubleday, Anchor Books, 1969).

24. Committee on Political Parties of the American Political Science Association, *Toward a More Responsible Two-Party System* (New York: Holt, Rinehart and Winston, 1950).

25. See, for example, Austin Ranney and Willmoore Kendall, *Democracy and the American Party System* (New York: Harcourt, Brace, 1956); William J. Keefe, *Parties, Politics, and Public Policy in America* (New York: Holt, Rinehart and Winston, 1972).

5 Television and Other Media:
Information for Action?

M*ost* of us pass a great part of our lives watching television, reading newspapers and magazines, and listening to the radio. Watching television is especially popular, as shown by the fact that, besides sleeping and working, it is what most of us spend the greatest amount of time doing. It has been estimated that in most homes the television set is turned on an average of six hours a day and that by the time the average student graduates from high school, he or she has spent more hours in front of the television set (fifteen thousand hours) than in school (twelve thousand hours).

Because of their commanding presence, television and other communications media have great relevance to those of us concerned about our relationship to the political system. The media do, after all, supply much of the information on which we must base our political actions. Because most of us have few alternative sources of information, we are enormously dependent on the media for our awareness of current issues, political candidates, and changes in the ongoing struggles for power. We know that unless we can acquire such awareness, we are not likely to gain easy access to, or effective influence over, the policy-making process.

Moreover, as we will see in Chapter Nine, the media have great relevance as instruments and avenues for political action. Those of us who can employ the media to communicate our ideas—whether we happen to be ordinary citizens or members of the power elite—will enjoy a considerable advantage over others in reaching the public and creating new policy issues. As long as television and other media spread information on politics, they must be considered essential tools for political influence by those intent on contributing to the information process.

But whether or not we intend to use the media to expand our influence or obtain information for purposes of political activism, it is a safe bet the media have played a major role in our own education. Television especially has become so ubiquitous that it not only provides the bulk of family entertainment but has become the main source of information about world events. According to studies by the Roper Organization, 64 percent of those surveyed in 1972 said they received most of their news about what is happening in the world from television (see Table 5-1).

In fact, the Roper studies revealed that television not only has become the public's main source of news; it has been accepted, as Table 5-2 indicates, increasingly as the most reliable source—apparently supporting the popular maxim that "seeing is believing."

These findings lead some observers to fear that those who control television may be able to manipulate our views and opinions. If indeed we receive most of our information about world events from television—and are not very critical about what we re-

Table 5-1. Where People Get Their News

"First, I'd like to ask you where you usually get most of your news about what's going on in the world today—from the newspapers or radio or television or magazines or talking to people or where?"

Source of most news:	*12/59* %	*11/61* %	*11/63* %	*11/64* %	*1/67* %	*11/68* %	*1/71* %	*11/72* %
Television	51	52	55	58	64	59	60	64
Newspapers	57	57	53	56	55	49	48	50
Radio	34	34	29	26	28	25	23	21
Magazines	8	9	6	8	7	7	5	6
People	4	5	4	5	4	5	4	4
Don't Know or no answer	1	3	3	3	2	3	1	1
Total mentions	154	157	147	153	158	145	140	145

Source: The Roper Organization, "What People Think of Television and Other Mass Media 1959–1972," published by the Television Information Office, May 1973.

ceive—those who dominate the medium may have inordinate power to mold our perspectives on politics.

We need to consider, therefore, not only whether our opinions and perspectives are at the mercy of television and other media, but whether the media have supplied the information we need to undertake effective political action. We also need to consider the media's potential impact on our perceptions of government, as well as their effect—if any—on our interest in and awareness of current issues. These questions are obviously related, for if the media present only inadequate, one-sided, or distorted information, then probably we can expect our political awareness and behavior to be correspondingly affected.

Consider the vote. As we will discuss further in Chapter Nine, one of the most basic forms of political action is voting for candidates in an election. Because our choices are based not only on our party preferences but on information supplied by the media, such information ideally should be as useful and accurate as possible. But if it should turn out that the media, especially television, have been employed in political campaigns primarily to "sell" slogans and manufactured images of candidates, then one of our most fundamental acts of political expression will have been based on distorted and misleading information. Thus, in evaluating the relationship between the media and our political behavior, we can begin with the charge that our votes have been corrupted by the use of Madison Avenue selling techniques in political campaigns.

Table 5-2. What Sources They Most Believe

"If you got conflicting or different reports of the same news story from radio, television, the magazines and the newspapers, which of the four versions would you be most inclined to believe—the one on radio or television or magazines or newspapers?"

Most believable:	12/59 %	11/61 %	11/63 %	11/64 %	1/67 %	11/68 %	1/71 %	11/72 %
Television	29	39	36	41	41	44	49	48
Newspapers	32	24	24	23	24	21	20	21
Radio	12	12	12	8	7	8	10	8
Magazines	10	10	10	10	8	11	9	10
Don't know or no answer	17	17	18	18	20	16	12	13

Source: The Roper Organization, "What People Think of Television and Other Mass Media 1959–1972," published by the Television Information Office, May 1973.

Advertising in Campaigns: The Corruption of the Vote

As we are aware, it is virtually impossible to enjoy our favorite television shows without facing endless commercials imploring us to buy this or that hair spray, chewing gum, or deodorant. Commercials are as much a part of our viewing entertainment as the programs they interrupt. What we are not always aware of is that these commercials sell more than just nonessential products. They also sell inflated promises of beauty and youth, social acceptance, and heightened sexual prowess. Vance Packard, in his famous book *The Hidden Persuaders*,[1] accused advertisers of exploiting consumers' anxieties and insecurities in order to sell products that allegedly would alleviate them. Advertisers, Packard charged, try to convince potential consumers that unless they buy a certain brand of deodorant or mouthwash, they will suffer the rejection of family and friends alike. Consider, for example, the familiar slogan for Certs mints: "If he kissed you once, will he kiss you again?" Or, the tiresome formula for Dial soap: "Aren't you glad you use Dial? Don't you wish everybody did?" Both commercials promise that, by using these products, consumers can avoid social disapproval.

Advertisers do more, however, than exploit insecurities; they also exploit consumers' social values and sexual desires. They make exaggerated claims that by coloring one's hair with Super-Brunette, by driving a Triumph sports car, or by smoking a small Winchester cigar, one can magically transform his or her sexual image. A team of psychologists suggest that consumers are being sold the "Cinderella effect." "Cinderella," they write, "was a rejected girl until she acquired a beautiful gown and a coach. . . . The adjusted American hopes that the goods he acquires will transform him in similar fashion into an exciting, desirable person. When he gets a new convertible (or she gets a new dress or a mink coat) there is an exhilarating period in which he imagines that such a transformation has taken place."[2]

What about advertising in political campaigns? Can commercials similarly "sell" candidates for public office by compelling voters to buy exaggerated claims and promises? Can presidential and congressional hopefuls be packaged on television like racy automobiles and sweet-tasting mouthwashes—making them consumable by exploiting people's values and insecurities?

During every major election, television screens throughout the country become showcases for the modern wizards of American politics—the creators of political commercials. In many expensive campaigns, the same technical experts who peddle cat food, cosmetics, and hair sprays are employed to "sell" aspiring politicians to voters. Jack Tinker and Partners, for instance—the firm responsible for many of the popular Alka-Seltzer commercials—was hired in 1966 to create ads for Nelson Rockefeller's reelection campaign for Governor of New York, in large part because the Alka-Seltzer ads were so clever. And the firm accepted the challenge because, as Managing Partner Myron McDonald unabashedly put it, "We looked at the Governor almost as though he were a product like Alka-Seltzer."[3]

Indeed, when advertising specialists are employed to direct media campaigns for candidates, we can expect them to rely on the same marketing strategies used in commercial advertising. Just as they try to determine what will appeal to consumers before marketing a new product, advertising specialists survey voters to discover what qualities they are seeking in presidential and congressional candidates. They examine different regional and social groups to find out where certain slogans and messages will be effective—and where they will be wasted. In both commercial and political advertising, the same consideration applies: find out what people want, and then give it to them in the most glittering package possible.

Usually, such a package comes in the form of a "spot commercial"—a short one-minute political advertisement that typically projects a single dramatic theme. It is commonly employed to build a favorable image of a candidate or to present an unfavorable view of an opponent by exploiting public fears and anxieties. One of the most controversial one-minute spots was used briefly by the Democrats in 1964 against Senator Barry Goldwater. To discredit Goldwater's support for the testing of nuclear weapons, the film showed a little girl standing innocently in a meadow, picking petals from a daisy. As she finished counting the petals, the scene dissolved into a countdown of an atomic test, concluding with a billowing mushroom cloud. "The stakes," a voice warned, "are too high for you to stay home."

Similarly, a commercial used by the Republicans in 1968 tried to exploit voters' feelings toward the Vietnam War and the soaring domestic crime rate, by portraying the incumbent Democratic administration as responsible for both. Without dialogue, the commercial flashed successive pictures of Vice-President Hubert Humphrey, American soldiers in a Vietnam trench, and a small child peering out a window in a city slum. "This time," a message pleaded at the end, "vote like your whole world depended on it."

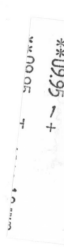

In the 1972 campaign, commercials presented by an organization calling itself Democrats for Nixon attacked George McGovern's welfare and defense proposals through the use of symbolic devices. In one such ad, a voice somberly announced: "The McGovern defense plan: He would cut the Marines by one-half. He would cut Air Force personnel by one-third and intercepter planes by one-fourth. . . ." With each statement, a hand swept away portions of toy soldiers, miniature warships and planes. The voice then concluded: "President Nixon doesn't believe we should play games with our national security."

For the most part in 1972, however, both Nixon and McGovern relied less on this kind of emotional advertising than on commercials resembling documentaries and news segments. Both candidates believed voters in 1972 would be swayed more by low-keyed documentary-style commercials than by negative, opponent-baiting advertising. The Nixon spots, for example, in an undisguised effort to plug his achievements in foreign affairs, featured footage of his 1972 trips to Peking and Moscow. Similarly, the McGovern commercials, in an apparent effort to temper his reputation as an "ultraliberal," showed his informal chats with groups of "hard hats" and factory workers.

Some observers believe this documentary approach—whether in the form of a newsreel or "man on the street" interview—probably will be used increasingly in future campaigns. It avoids the negativism of the older-style commercials and is particularly suited to portraying candidates in the most favorable light possible. Advertising specialists can shoot hours of film, taping together thirty-second and one-minute spots of candidates at their best and disposing of the remainder showing them as they normally are. In short, the documentary approach provides a means of exposing candidates under controlled conditions, while suggesting to voters that the presentations are natural and unrehearsed.

But whatever style of political commercials they employ in future campaigns, candidates probably will continue to take advantage of one-minute spots. The reasons are easy to understand. Apart from being less expensive than longer ads, short political commercials can be tucked conveniently into popular television shows like "The Waltons" and "All in the Family," to reach those voters who happen to be watching. Spot commercials can catch voters unaware, exposing them to the messages before they can turn them off. Indeed, as some campaign managers see it, the only effective way to reach many voters is to sneak up on them, surprising them with a political message while they sit before their sets complacently enjoying something else.

Moreover, one-minute spots can grab the attention of voters by projecting single dramatic themes using graphic visual effects similar to those found in commercial ads. Candidates have found that viewers are not as irritated by and bored with short commercials as they are with longer ones, especially if the commercials do not preempt their favorite shows. Adlai Stevenson once made the mistake in the 1950s of replacing an "I Love Lucy" show with a campaign address. As a result of this unforgivable act, Stevenson later received a letter from an irate viewer who wrote: "I Like Ike and I Love Lucy. Drop Dead."

It appears, therefore, that instead of using television to illuminate the issues and to acquaint voters with their qualifications, candidates have allowed themselves to be merchandized for public consumption like boxes of detergent. When Joe McGinniss, in his book *The Selling of the President 1968*,[4] revealed the premium that campaign managers place on good lighting, makeup, and a format tailored to the *expectations* of viewers, he demonstrated how carefully packaged campaigns have become. He showed that a campaign manager's task is not so much to reveal a candidate's stand on the issues as to display whatever personal qualities are likely to win votes.

Criticism of the spot commercial, and of political advertising generally, has been sufficiently severe to spark a number of proposals for reform. But before we look at some of these proposals, we must consider whether television commercials really do change people's minds. In view of the efforts of Madison Avenue advertising specialists to "sell" political candidates, are people actually persuaded by television campaigns?

Television and Political Opinion

Probably, as we will see, the media do have considerable impact on political perceptions over the long run, especially in affecting attitudes toward social crises, personalities, and political events—the Watergate scandal being a recent example. But, evidence indicates that for the short ten- to twenty-week duration of a typical political campaign, television and other media are relatively ineffective as a basic means of changing most people's minds. While the information spread during campaigns may be distorted, it tends to be interpreted in ways that reinforce the political opinions acquired from the family, school, and friends.

Several hypotheses have been offered to account for this.[5] One is that many people selectively *expose* themselves to television programs, magazines, and campaign speeches with which they already agree. They seek out information sources that reinforce their opinions rather than those that contradict them. Democrats, for example, are likely to listen more attentively to speeches of Democratic candidates than to those of Republican opponents. Apparently, it is often psychologically easier for people to absorb information that bolsters their present views than to confront new information that challenges them.

This does not mean that people can always avoid information that conflicts with their opinions. Television spot commercials, for instance, usually can attract viewers' attention before they can change the channel. And when debates between opposing candidates are aired, it is difficult for viewers to ignore one candidate entirely and pay attention only to the other.

Moreover, changes in opinion sometimes occur when there are strong cross-pressures, as indicated in Chapter Three, or when people confront potentially dissonant situations that require adjustments in their thinking. This may happen when they see a politician they respect courting the favor of one they dislike—thus forcing a change of opinion toward one or possibly even both. One can only speculate how some Republicans reacted to the televised coverage of Richard Nixon's amiable conversations with Mao Tse Tung on his 1972 visit to China.

The impact of the media during campaigns depends not only on the sort of messages sent, however, but on how messages are construed. People not only select the messages they wish to hear; they selectively *interpret* them as well. Instead of merely absorbing information from the media like human sponges, voters color and shape it according to their own predispositions. Thus, a Democrat may watch a Republican candidate in a political commercial without ever getting the message that was intended. The voter may interpret the commercial to mean what he wants it to mean, not what the candidate was trying to say.

This tendency to perceive information selectively has been noted even in people's reactions to physical phenomena. Psychologists have found in several intriguing experiments that people's perceptions of moving lights, shapes of objects, and even sizes of other people are determined in part by what they are used to seeing—or wish to see. If people suddenly are confronted with an unusual phenomenon, it often will be altered to fit their normal expectations.[6]

But even beyond selectively interpreting information, people also tend to *recall* selectively certain messages more than others. They remember only the information they agree with, conveniently forgetting that which they find disagreeable. Obviously, the demarcation line between selectively remembering something and selectively perceiving it in the first place is difficult to draw. It is difficult to determine, for instance, whether Democratic voters selectively tune out certain parts of a Republican commercial, or whether they correctly perceive the entire message but do not retain it.

Finally, as we discussed earlier, messages carried by the media frequently go through a "two-step flow." Rather than persuading people directly, the messages often are interpreted by a smaller number of "opinion leaders" who pass on their interpretations to others. Whether these opinion leaders happen to be union officials, teachers, or just friends and neighbors, their views on the information conveyed by the media may have greater impact than the original information itself. A televised campaign speech or congressional committee hearing may not affect viewers' opinions as greatly as what someone they respect says about the event later on. And in the process the opinion leader may alter the information to conform to his or her own views.

"With a Little Help from My Friends"

If these selective processes then reduce the likelihood that television campaigns will change political views, why do candidates continue to rely heavily on television in their efforts to become elected? Most of them certainly are aware that voters reinforce their existing opinions and are not totally susceptible to commercial messages. Consequently, candidates must derive advantages from using television in their campaigns that take account of and offset the limitations implied.

Reinforce Partisan Support

One reason for using television is to bolster weak support and persuade loyalists to trek to the polls rather than stay at home. Almost two-thirds of all American voters still identify with one of the two major parties, so it is important for Democratic and Republican candidates alike to broaden their party base and persuade as many potential supporters as possible to vote. Indeed, many elections can be won just by ensuring the turnout of partisans who are inclined to vote along party lines.

But this is often a difficult task. Many potential supporters are affiliated only weakly with a party and, for a variety of reasons, seldom vote. Consequently, the candidate must rely on television campaigns to reach these people and persuade them to lend their support. He must identify his views with theirs and convince them—as though peddling a popular brand of deodorant soap—that unless they support his candidacy they will suffer the consequences. Thus, although television campaigns may not change the minds of voters who cling loyally to the opposing party, they can reinforce the support of partisan voters whom the candidate minimally needs to win.

Attract Independents

A second reason for using television is to attract the support of the growing number of Independent and undecided voters (see Chapter Four). These people remain uncommitted to any party candidate and may be susceptible to the right kind of media campaign. Because their party bonds are weak, they may not be as subject to the same selective processes—exposure and perception especially—that insulate other voters from the emotional pitches of partisan politics. And, in a close election, the uncommitted voters can swing the election either way. "It seems clear," one scholar concludes, "that professional politicians drive themselves and their organizations to influence every remaining undecided voter in the hope and expectation that they are providing or maintaining a winning margin."[7]

An intriguing question thus arises. If the number of Independent voters continues to climb, does this mean that television commercials that stress personality will play an ever-growing role in political campaigns? It would seem that as more voters religiously split their tickets, candidates will find it less valuable to identify closely with a certain party. Instead, they will be tempted to lean even more heavily on commercials that display their independent qualifications and personal attractiveness.

However, although the presence of more Independent voters may lead to an even greater use of television commercials in campaigns, these voters likely will remain difficult to drag to the polls. While many Independent voters refuse to adhere to a party because of principle or a desire to consider the issues, others—especially after Watergate—are turned off to politics generally. Thus, rather than being easy targets for conversion, frequently they require a media effort even greater than is required for other voters.

Publicity for Unknown Candidates

Certainly a third, even more basic, reason to use television in a campaign is to gain added visibility. An unknown candidate running against a popular incumbent especially needs television to attract attention to himself and overcome the traditional support favoring the incumbent. "Because the newcomer is unknown" Dan Nimmo suggests, "his managers know that voters will not come to his public appearances, peruse his literature, note his displays, or read about him in newspapers. He must therefore wage his campaign in the voters' homes when residents settle down to be entertained."[8]

Indeed, in many statewide and national elections, television can be the crucial factor in assuring a victory at the polls. By using television, a candidate can display his charms to millions of potential voters with no more effort than that needed to reach hundreds in a speech before a town hall gathering. With an extensive television campaign of spot commercials and speeches, a relatively obscure candidate can become known quickly to millions of party loyalists, Independents, and opinion leaders whose support he needs for an electoral victory.

A Window on the Political World

In considering the relationship between the communications media and our political opinions and behavior, we should keep in mind that the media can have significant long-range effects other than just influencing our votes during campaigns. Because our relationship to the media is a lifetime experience, the media undoubtedly present images of government and the world that indirectly affect our social and political views over the long run. For example, our attitudes toward violence, sex, and authority are very likely influenced by the television programs, films, comic books, and magazines to which we are exposed during our lifetimes.

One problem, however, is that if we review studies on the long-term influences of television and other media, we will encounter an abundance of contradictory findings. We will learn that social scientists have experienced considerable difficulty in agreeing on the precise long-term impact of the media, in part because they must take into account millions of messages—from the media and other sources—to which we are exposed.

For the purposes of this chapter, however, we might consider ways in which the media may have affected our perceptions of government and politics—keeping in mind that several interpretations are possible. Since the media play such important roles in providing us with information, we might want to know whether such information has been reliable, how it has influenced our views of government, whether it has increased our awareness of and interest in political issues, and how it has affected our views of candidates.

Information on Politics

To begin with, much of the information we receive—information on which we must base our actions—has been slanted by those who exercise economic controls over the media. In this country, many television stations, publishing houses, and newspapers are multimillion-dollar enterprises owned and controlled by large corporations like Westinghouse, ITT, and RCA. These enterprises rely heavily for their profits on advertising by other large corporations, and often share the same values as other economic elites.

As we noted earlier, advocates of the ruling-elite theory regard television and other media ultimately as instruments of powerful elite interests. They see the economic and political control over the content of the media as a means by which the elite can perpetuate their own values and self-interests. By controlling the media, the elite not only determine the flow of information to the public but give the public few opportunities to obtain radically different or critical viewpoints.

Although the charges of ruling-elite theorists are somewhat exaggerated (certainly neither the chairman of General Motors nor the joint chiefs of staff regard magazines like *Playboy, Ramparts,* and *Ms.* as the best vehicles for their interests), the media over the long run do not give "equal time" to all current points of view. Most television stations and newspapers in the United States are fundamentally commercial enterprises that cater to a mass audience and are not prone to emphasize political perspectives that have not yet become fashionable or "newsworthy." Thus, radically new political ideas are rarely presented with much enthusiasm by most of the media, and tend to be limited to a few magazines and newspapers with relatively small distribution. (Of course, this situation may reflect the public's own narrow selective orientations as well as the economic and political realities of media ownership.)

Moreover, the media's interpretations of political occurrences are rarely unbiased. Newspapers, magazines, and television stations—whether considered "liberal" or "conservative"—interpret events in terms of their own political perceptions, rarely offering totally dispassionate or nonideological coverage. Even when political reports aim toward objectivity, selective perception and interpretation remain as inescapable for those in the media as for anyone else. Although most people may realize that the evening news consists largely of a selective view of the "important" events of the day, they may still mistake the news as a total portrait of reality. They may still confuse the compelling and highly selective fragments pieced together by reporters and media executives, with the whole of politics for that day. An interview with a U.S. Senator standing outside a committee room may give viewers an idea of what occurred behind closed doors, yet it is only a fragment of information seen momentarily through the eyes of one participant. Thus, any information the public relies on for effective political action cannot be considered over the long run to be complete or objective, and must necessarily be supplemented by alternative experiences and viewpoints.

However, despite these limitations, television and other media have not totally neglected to provide essential political information. Even though much of the information over the long run has been biased and narrow (and has hardly reflected any radical ideology), the media, contrary to the ruling-elite view, have furnished citizens with information on the activities of public officials and have helped expose deception in government. In fact, the news media frequently have collided with governmental officials who have tried to bring reporters around to an uncritical view of governmental policies—often without success.

This conflict flared frequently during the Nixon administration, which suffered repeated embarrassment from a number of sensational revelations in the press and on television: the ITT settlement, the Watergate break-in, the illegal campaign contributions, the White House tapes and transcripts, and evidence of Nixon's

★WANTED★

NAME: WALTER CRONKITE, CBS NEWS.
ALIAS: JOHN CHANCELLOR, DAVID BRINKLEY, TOM BROKAW, NBC;
ERIC SEVAREID, DAN RATHER, DANIEL SCHORR, CBS;
HARRY REASONER, ABC.
CHARGED WITH REPORTING: WATERGATE BREAK-IN AND COVER-UP;
OBSTRUCTION OF JUSTICE; COMPILING ENEMY LIST; FAKING OF
STATE DEPT CABLES; PERJURY (NUMBER OF COUNTS UNDER
INVESTIGATION); WIRETAPPING; SECRET CAMPAIGN FUNDS;
THE ITT SETTLEMENT; GOVERNMENT FUNDING TO IMPROVE
HOMES AT SAN CLEMENTE AND KEY BISCAYNE; NUMEROUS
RESIGNATIONS OF WHITE HOUSE STAFF; FINANCIAL DEALS
AND RESIGNATION OF SPIRO AGNEW; JUSTICE DEPT RESIGNATIONS.
ARMED AND DANGEROUS WITH MICROPHONES AND CAMERAS.
· NOTIFY ·
PROSECUTOR RICHARD M. NIXON
OR
LOCAL COMMITTEE TO REELECT THE PRESIDENT

Paul Conrad
© The Los Angeles Times, 1973

own culpability in the Watergate cover-up. In fact, the Nixon administration had been hostile to the news media from its inception—unleashing biting criticisms of the media through Spiro Agnew's alliterative speeches, refusing to divulge details to the press about administration policies, threatening local radio and television stations with withdrawal of their licenses, and employing the Justice Department to intimidate news reporters into handing over confidential information to grand juries. As NBC correspondent John Chancellor remarked, "Other Administrations have had a love-hate relationship with the press. The Nixon Administration has had a hate-hate relationship."

The role of the press in uncovering the Watergate scandal particularly illuminated the bitter conflict that can erupt between the news media and government. At the initial outbreak of the story in the summer of 1972, administration officials complained sarcastically about the willingness of the press to play fast and loose with information derived from "hearsay" and "unofficial sources." Shortly after the break-in at the Watergate office and apartment complex, White House Press Secretary Ronald Zeigler chastised the *Washington Post* for blowing a "third-rate burglary" out of proportion. He chided reporters for printing "stories based on hearsay, character assassination, innuendo or guilt by association." The press, however, justified its stories on the principle of the public's "right to know." In fact, as the Watergate story unfolded, the press contended that the multitude of leaks on Watergate were warranted by the growing evidence that members of the administration were engaged in a wide-ranging cover-up of criminal activities. When official statements turned out to be false, the press felt it could not be blamed for turning to unofficial sources to get at the truth.

There were, obviously, dangers in this approach, as there would be in any effort to separate fact from rumor. As reporters Bob Woodward and Carl Bernstein acknowledged, there were times when they resorted to unorthodox methods to get the low-down on the Watergate story.[9] But it is certain that without persistent investigation and reporting by the press, the vast scenario of the scandal would have remained hidden. Despite the powers of the Presidency used to try to cover up the scandal, the press—together with the courts and independent prosecutors—succeeded in unraveling many of the threads. As New York Times columnist James Reston wondered, "Would this scandal have reached the present point of disclosure if the press had not reported the secret testimony of witnesses in this case? Is a government which had knowledge of this kind of political espionage and sabotage, and then tried to conceal the facts, entitled to bar reporters from getting beyond the screen of secrecy?"[10] Even the administration and the Pulitzer Prize Committee eventually acknowledged the press's responsibilities in the case. By the end of May 1973, the Washington Post received not only a public apology from Ronald Zeigler for his earlier comments but the coveted Pulitzer Prize for its coverage of the Watergate story.

Political Interest and Awareness

In addition to considering whether the media have provided useful information, we might consider whether television programs in particular have had much impact on political awareness, interest, and participation. When television first burst upon the political scene in the 1950 and 1952 elections, many observers believed it to be the greatest innovation in politics since radio. They marveled at television's ability to bring the outside political world into American homes, at its capacity to make millions of viewers direct witnesses to the pageantry of politics. Indeed, for the first time in history, most Americans could observe, in the quiet leisure of their living rooms, the sweaty hoopla of a party convention, the tensions of a presidential address, even the machinations of a committee hearing in Congress.

Yet, has the advent of television raised the level of public involvement and interest in politics? Has it broadened public understanding of major issues and events? According to several prominent and controversial studies, television does not appear to have stimulated greater interest and participation in politics.[11] In fact, as we will see shortly, there is even a possibility that television has discouraged such interest and participation.

One popular signpost of public attention to politics is the turnout in elections. Supposedly, if television has heightened political interest, one would find a larger percentage of Americans today marching to the polls. Yet, voter turnout has increased only barely during the past thirty or so years. As we may recall from Chapter Three, voter turnout in presidential elections since 1948 has stabilized at just over 60 percent—only slightly higher than the percentages recorded during the preceding twenty years. In fact, in the 1972 elections, the number of voters dipped below 55 percent, a percentage lower than in either 1936 or 1940—well before the advent of television. And, in the 1974 congressional elections, voter turnout plunged to only 38 percent. Although a number of social factors—such as increased mobility, a breakdown in party loyalties, and a deepening cynicism toward politics—also may be depressing voting levels, the expanding role of television in political affairs has not been accompanied by a surge in voter turnout.

Nor does there appear to be any dramatic rise in the public's knowledge of government and political issues. As we also saw in Chapter Three, only about 46 percent of those surveyed in 1973 could correctly identify their Representative in Congress—a proportion only slightly higher than in the late 1940s. In 1971, at the time the Supreme Court ruled that the *New York Times* and *Washington Post* could publish the "Pentagon Papers," 45 percent of those polled said they knew nothing about the issue.[12] In other words, despite television, there is little evidence of the kind of accelerated public interest in, and understanding of, politics that many originally anticipated.

Several explanations for this exist, including the charge that television has failed to educate the public. As stated earlier, American television has catered to mediocrity by saturating the airwaves with commercial entertainment that "disturbs no gray cells." Although most Americans report television as their main source of news, the amount of television time devoted to provocative political questions has been miniscule. Except for coverage of unusual political happenings, such as Watergate, there have been few sophisticated and provocative presentations of current social and political events.

Indeed, some critics charge persuasively that the very presence of television has dulled sensibilities. Despite its capacity for exciting visual drama, most television fare has been low-keyed, commercial, and dull. It has encouraged passivity, demanding—unlike books and radio—almost no imagination or involvement by the viewer.*Anthropologist Margaret Mead made an observation more than a decade ago that remains applicable today. Television, she warned, "threatens to be a negative social influence, a way of accustoming people to dreary half-attention, just satisfying enough to dampen anyone's desire to read a book, or go out, or start a conversation; a way of keeping husbands home with their shoes off, of entertaining in-laws without effort. . . . Without a very large admixture of real events, real plays, real political excitement, real music, TV threatens the country with apathy at a time when we grievously need a stimulant."[13]

But the total responsibility does not rest with television alone. The same selective processes discussed earlier keep many people from watching even the few educational programs about politics that do surface on television. Those who remain disinterested in politics simply will not sit through programs of a political nature, regardless of their content or frequency. When the Senate Watergate hearings were televised during the summer of 1973, the networks were flooded by thousands of letters from irate viewers who complained angrily about the hearings' preemption of their favorite afternoon soap operas and game shows. Even though television can bring dramatic historical events into American homes, it cannot ensure that people will pay attention; it cannot guarantee that the ideas and images it projects will stimulate people to reflect on their significance.

Views of Politics and Government

There may be an added consequence of television, however, that affects people's perceptions of politics and desire to participate. As we have seen, most Americans today regard politics as a "dirty business," and cast a cynical eye on the activities of government. Perhaps, as Kurt and Gladys Lang suggest, this cynicism has been nurtured by the tendency of television news programs to highlight the unusual and negative aspects of politics—the battles, scandals, and crises—and thus to present a somewhat distorted view of the political process. "Television's style in chronicling political events," they argue, "can affect the fundamental orientation of the voter toward his government. It can undermine or bolster public confidence in the viability of political institutions and in the ability of political leaders to discharge their responsibilities."[14] During 1973 and 1974, for example, the highlights of television coverage of Washington politics included the Watergate hearings, the White House tapes controversy, the indictment and conviction of high governmental officials, the impeachment deliberations, and the abdications of President Nixon and Vice-President Agnew. Although these events did not mark all the accomplishments of national government during that period, the extensive coverage of these events on television undoubtedly reinforced many people's distrust of politicians. Whereas before, people may have suspected that politics was riddled with corruption and dishonesty, now they had proof.

Obviously, television does not create such events; crises and scandals in government were inflicted on citizens long before the introduction of television. But the ability of the medium to dramatize these events and bring them visually into the living room may reinforce defensive reactions to politics and serve to justify lack of interest and participation.

Also, television coverage may create an added sense of remoteness in that political events often gain a distant and unreal aura. The disgust with politics, Kurt and Gladys Lang reflect, may be "nothing but a defensive reaction against . . . reality that is overbearing, against the unfamiliar and the frightening, where 'remote' events and invisible powers seem to determine the destiny of the individual who can do nothing about it."[15] Indeed, we cannot expect information to motivate people to participate if they feel

DOONESBURY   **by Garry Trudeau**

they do not have access to power. If television is indeed a window on the political world, it is also a partition. It keeps viewers at arm's length, showing them crises and suffering thousands of miles away that they feel they cannot prevent. In this society, a wide chasm separates the enormous flow of information and the opportunities to act. Television exposes people to problems of society, yet does not offer them a corresponding channel for effective action. Thus, it can be argued that television and other media tend to breed frustration. In the absence of a meaningful relationship between information and the ability to act, viewers receive no alleviation of the tensions produced by knowing that a problem exists and yet feeling too impotent to solve it. (For more on this point, see Chapter Nine.)

Television and Candidates' Personalities

A final, and somewhat different, question about television is what long-term effect it may have on our perceptions of candidates. Because of television, do candidates with the best "images"—the most careful packaging—indeed stand the best chance of winning public office?

According to some observers, the introduction of the "television personality" into political campaigns has been the most significant development in the age of television. Although campaigns revolved around personalities long before television arrived, the medium, they charge, has placed a greater premium on superficial characteristics—the attractive face, the broad smile, the commanding presence—than on intelligence and ability. It has given tremendous impetus to candidates who conform to the expectations of a commercial entertainment medium, in which a physically attractive appearance is a definite plus. According to Bob Price, who served as campaign director for former New York Mayor John Lindsay, "You don't have to look as good as Lindsay, but if you look bad, it's a minus. An ugly, able man is less likely to be nominated than fifty years ago."[16] Thus it has been argued that even some former Presidents, if they were alive today, might have a difficult time winning national office. Although Abraham Lincoln, for example, was a striking man in several respects, his high-pitched voice, angular features, and trimmed beard might not endear him to a contemporary television audience.

Marshall McLuhan even suggests that television favors not only attractive candidates but those with certain kinds of personal-

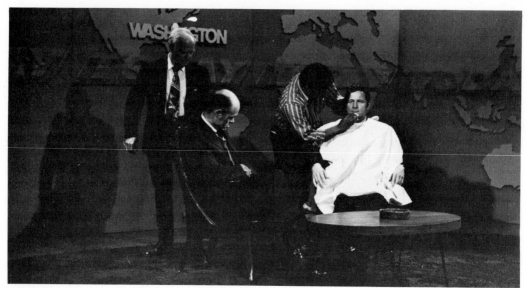

Senator Birch Bayh

ities.[17] For candidates to be embraced by viewers today, he contends, their projected images must be attractive and soft—an image he defines, in part, as "cool." They must not appear too loud or abrasive, invading the intimacy of the living room with an overbearing presence—a tendency of Hubert Humphrey that some observers believed ensured his presidential defeats. Thus, according to McLuhan, during the Great Debates in the 1960 presidential campaigns, the "blurry, shaggy texture" of John Kennedy triumphed over the "sharp, intense image" of Richard Nixon. To many voters who watched the debates, Nixon did not appear as appealing as Kennedy regardless of what the two men were actually saying. As Theodore White recounted, "Probably no picture in American politics tells a better story . . . than that famous shot of the camera on the Vice-President as he half slouched, his 'Lazy Shave' powder faintly streaked with sweat, his eyes exaggerated hollows of blackness, his jaw, jowls, and face drooping with strain."[18] Even Nixon himself admitted, "I spent too much time . . . on substance and too little time on appearance. I paid too much attention to what I was going to say and too little to how I would look."[19]

We must not, of course, carry this point too far; certain appearances do not always ensure victory or defeat. Many candidates are elected to public office who do not fit the stereotypes established by McLuhan or anyone else. Nevertheless, media specialists and campaign managers do take account of appearance and personality in the broadest sense, deliberately placing candidates in staged settings that offer selected views of their most pleasing qualities. As we have seen, in both 1968 and 1972 Nixon's campaign managers were careful to avoid the mistakes of the 1960 campaign. Although Nixon for many people still exhibited the "sharp, intense image" described by McLuhan, most of his appearances were carefully controlled. A great deal of attention in 1968 was devoted to projecting the "right" image—"The New Nixon," as his campaign managers dubbed it—in the belief that a "correct" projection would bring success, whereas a "wrong" projection would lead to defeat.[20]

This then raises the question we began with: Does television give advertising agencies and campaign managers a chance to fool the American public—to corrupt their vote—with staged presentations and false images? Does television, in other words, permit a candidate's qualifications (or lack of them) to become more perceptible to the public, or does it allow them to remain hidden and disguised?

Some believe that because of the pervasiveness of media campaigns, candidates are not required to stand exposed before the voters. They do not have to reveal their true personalities. Instead, most of their appearances are controlled and staged, and their commercials offer only one-sided, artificial images fabricated by their campaign managers. Sometimes, candidates may depend too much on their campaign managers. As those who saw the film "The Candidate" may recall, when it finally dawns on actor Robert Redford in the last scene that he has been elected U.S. Senator, he turns to his manager and asks, "What do we do now?"

Others believe, however, that television tends to reveal rather than disguise the qualities of candidates. In a typical national campaign, candidates are in the spotlight so many times, and seen in so many different circumstances, that most voters *can* get a good idea of what sorts of persons they really are. During the 1972 presidential primaries, for example, Senator Edmund Muskie was mercilessly unmasked by television. In the most dramatic instance, network television caught him sobbing in front of the *Manchester Union Leader* offices as he tried to respond to charges contained in a phony letter published by that New Hampshire newspaper. "It changed people's minds about me, of what kind of guy I was," Muskie later admitted. "They were looking for a strong, steady man, and here I was weak."[21] Thus, in the opinion of some observers, despite the efforts of image-makers to present only the most favorable aspects of their candidates, television will reveal many of the true qualities of those hoping to gain public office.

It should be pointed out, of course, that it is difficult for most people ever to know from television alone whether the images of candidates are accurate. Only those who know the candidates firsthand can gauge the degree of distortion, if any, by television. In fact, television can both reveal and mask the qualities of political hopefuls, depending on the style of their campaigns. Nevertheless, given the reliance on advertising and staged presentations, most campaigns tend to project the images of candidates campaign managers want voters to see. As one scholar has concluded, "Possibly a more reasonable approach would be to state that television *can* unmask a charlatan, if those responsible for use of camera and microphone want to do so. But given control over the television situation—makeup, lighting, camera angles, speechwriting, teleprompting, and the like—there is no reason in the world that the basic appearance of a candidate cannot be acceptable. (It may not be a crashing success, but there are specialists in the field of personal public relations and deportment who could get a man past either Emily Post or the casual voter.)"[22]

Evaluation: The Buying and Selling of Votes

In view of the controversy surrounding the role of the media during campaigns, it is not surprising that a number of media-related reforms have come under consideration. It has been proposed, for example, that in order to base our most common form of political expression, the vote, on more reliable information, we need to eliminate political advertising and find more rational ways to present the views and qualifications of candidates. Also, it has been suggested that, to further "democratize" campaigns, we need to regulate campaign expenditures. Although the latter proposal involves more than just the media and already has resulted in specific legislation, its importance for future campaigns compels examination.

Campaign Advertising

As we would expect, the use of paid political advertising during campaigns has been severely criticized. Many justifiably insist that such advertising demeans the electoral process by transforming candidates into "products" suitable for packaging and by treating voters as consumers. As Adlai Stevenson once remarked, "This idea that you can merchandise candidates for high office like breakfast cereal—that you can gather votes like box tops—is, I think, the ultimate indignity of the democratic process."

But beyond the "indignity" of political advertising, there is a concern that voters are exposed only to the most superficial sides of candidates. By relying on interviews and surveys to probe the emotions of the public, and by using spot commercials to bring home the messages the public "wants to hear," candidates and campaign managers ensure that voters never receive the full information they need to make rational and intelligent choices at the polls. In this respect, political advertising remains even more odious than commercial advertising. "If a television commercial," Robert MacNeil contends, "makes you like the image of one kind of toothpaste enough to buy a tube, it is no great matter if you find you don't like the stuff after all. You can quickly revert to the brand you like. If a television commercial makes you like the image of a politician, it may be six years before you can change him and he is next to impossible to throw away."[23]

Consequently, there has been an increasing demand for campaigns in the latter half of the 1970s to rely less on trying to "sell" candidates and to become more issue- and problem-oriented. Instead of using traditional advertising techniques, campaigns should be structured around press conferences and debates, in which candidates must demonstrate an understanding of political problems and an ability to handle them. Television debates especially have been advocated as a proper forum for presenting candidates to the voters. They have the advantage of bringing together the major adversaries and thus overcoming the tendency to expose voters to only one side. And they give voters a more rational way to assess the candidates' qualifications.

However, since the televised debates between Richard Nixon and John Kennedy in 1960, there have been few similar confrontations between major candidates. (Probably the only subsequent notable debate was between Robert Kennedy and Eugene McCarthy prior to the 1968 Democratic primary in California.) Lyndon Johnson, for example, backed away from confronting Barry Goldwater in 1964, and Richard Nixon refused to face his major opponents in 1968 and 1972. Part of the reason for this unwillingness is that it is to the challenger's advantage, not the incumbent's, to stage a televised debate. A debate gives the lesser-known challenger needed exposure, provides him with a stature equal to the incumbent's in the eyes of voters, and puts the incumbent in a position of having to defend his policies. As John Kennedy reportedly remarked following his successful 1960 presidential campaign, "We wouldn't have had a prayer without that gadget."[24] Indeed, the outcome of the 1960 debates apparently has led most incumbents, as well as those candidates with greater name recognition generally, to refuse to engage in such confrontations.

There is some doubt, anyway, whether televised debates truly provide a significantly more rational approach to campaigning—especially considering that what candidates say may not be as important as how they look. As stated earlier, many who witnessed the 1960 debates on television responded more favorably to Kennedy's overall style than to Nixon's, allowing details of appearance to overshadow what the two men were actually saying. "Some scanty evidence from the Kennedy-Nixon debates," Kurt and Gladys Lang point out, "suggests that the dramatic improvement of Kennedy's personal image that followed the first debate did not extend to radio listeners. The relatively few who listened (mainly to car radios) were apt to call the debate a 'draw,' while viewers, who were witnesses to Kennedy's drive and energy and Nixon's apparent discomfort, credited Kennedy with a clear 'win.'"[25]

But whatever the reactions to debates or other unrehearsed forms of television campaigning, many people clearly would welcome an alternative to paid political advertising. As it stands now, instead of using the media to illuminate the issues and present their qualifications, candidates allow themselves to be "packaged" with all the razzle-dazzle of commercial advertising. As television correspondent Eric Sevaried has aptly concluded, "This is the age of appearances, when the wrapping seems more important than the contents."[26]

Campaign Financing

Another, even broader, target of reform relating to both political advertising and campaigns generally has been campaign financing. From the start of the Watergate scandal, hope was expressed that it finally might encourage reform of campaign financing abuses. Because so many of the "Watergate horrors" were made possible by an excess of campaign donations—many secretly and illegally obtained—advocates of campaign financing reform insisted it was an idea whose time had come.

In fact, in 1974 Congress responded to the growing pressures for campaign finance reform by enacting landmark legislation radically overhauling the traditional ways of funding federal election campaigns. Generally speaking, the legislation covered three major areas: (1) curbs on the amount of money candidates can

*"I bet if I had a million dollars I could hire
an image-maker and make you vote for me."*

Joseph Farris, Time Magazine © Time Inc.

collect and spend in their campaigns; (2) limits on the contributions by individuals and special interests; and (3) public financing of national campaigns. All provisions except those related to spending limits survived Supreme Court scrutiny in early 1976, and thus the new law bolstered the hope of some that campaign financing would no longer be an area of blatant abuse. However, before we look at the specifics of this legislation, we should consider some of the problems of campaign financing that prompted the drive toward reform.

For one thing, campaigns for national political office have become extraordinarily expensive. In most states, candidates may spend $150,000 or more to run for the U.S. House of Representatives. To run for the U.S. Senate, candidates may dole out close to $2 million, especially in populous states like New York and California. In fact, an estimated $400 million was spent by all political hopefuls in 1972—a jump of one-third over the amount spent in 1968.

In addition to inflation, the toilsome length of campaigns, and the growing number of eligible voters, television and other media expenses have contributed greatly to the escalation in campaign costs. This escalation can be seen both in the soaring costs of television and radio time (a half-hour of prime time on network television may cost upwards of $200,000) and in the practice of employing professional advertising firms. Many candidates believe that office seekers who cannot afford such media expenses (and this applies particularly to most third-party hopefuls) remain at a considerable disadvantage.

Although laws have been enacted over the years that place a ceiling on campaign expenditures, they have been either ignored or repealed. The Corrupt Practices Act of 1925, for example, was intended to limit spending by congressional candidates to 3¢ per eligible voter, with a maximum expenditure of $5,000 by candidates for the House and $25,000 by candidates for the Senate. But this legal limit was never enforced. Because the limit applied only to expenditures made with the "knowledge and consent" of the candidate, funds simply could be channelled through campaign committees that were not required to file reports.

A major concern of reformers has been that the large sums of money required to meet the exorbitant costs of campaigns have increased the influence of a relatively few wealthy contributors or "fat cats," to the detriment of average citizens. In 1972, for example, Richard Nixon's reelection campaign reaped more than $7 million from just twenty-seven individuals—nine of whom each contributed $250,000 or more. In fact, W. Clement Stone, a Chicago insurance baron, alone shelled out $2 million to the 1972 Nixon campaign—about $1 million more than had been first reported. The Hatch Act of 1940 was supposed to prohibit any person from contributing more than $5,000 to a candidate for federal office. But the loopholes in the law rendered it largely ineffective. A person who wished to part with more than $5,000 could simply contribute to a variety of separate party committees or candidates. Or, if a person wished to make a large contribution to a particular candidate, he or she only had to give in the names of other members of the family—such as the spouse, children, or in-laws. And in the absence of any serious intention to enforce the law, even blatant violations went unpunished. As a result, when compared with $250,000 donations, $5 or $10 contributions from ordinary citizens have tended to be virtually meaningless—these citizens simply have been priced out of the political system. As each election has ended, "fat cat" contributors have enjoyed an access to legislators that other citizens simply could not match.

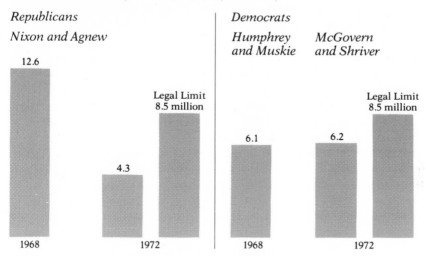

Figure 5–1. Presidential Radio and TV Spending
in General Elections — In Millions of Dollars

Source: Congressional Quarterly, Weekly Report, 12 May 1973. Data from
Federal Communications Commission. © 1973 Congressional Quarterly.

Furthermore, the pumping of large sums of money into campaigns has raised fears of corruption. In 1972, a number of giant corporations, including American Airlines and Gulf Oil, admitted to making illegal contributions running into hundreds of thousands of dollars to Nixon's reelection campaign, often in response to pressures from the White House itself. Many of these contributions were "laundered" through foreign subsidiaries and Swiss banks and turned up in the cash accounts of Watergate burglars and conspirators. As former New York Mayor John Lindsay remarked, "The contributions of Vesco, ITT, milk producers, airlines and others financed this kind of thing, whether they knew it or not. And most of them did know that, in return, they were buying some kind of political protection—an air-route franchise, immunity from SEC or antitrust prosecution, or license to engage in political pot-boiling in some Latin American country. Watergate was made possible by the use of political money raised under the umbrella of an election campaign—just as the bugging, housebreaking and other crimes occurred under the umbrella of national security."[27]*

*Copyright Newsweek, Inc. 1974, reprinted by permission.

Moreover, many reformers have realized that without a way to open the books on all contributions to candidates, voters cannot know how much candidates are indebted to special interests. Voters have no way of finding out how money is being spent, or how much money candidates have received from particular groups.

Consequently, legislation passed by Congress in recent years has been extremely significant. In 1971, for instance, Congress enacted the Federal Election Campaign Act—the first noteworthy campaign reform bill since the Corrupt Practices Act of 1925. Among its provisions, the new law required candidates for federal office to file detailed reports on all donations and expenditures exceeding $100. It also set limits on the amounts candidates could spend on media advertising (although these limits were later removed by new legislation and Supreme Court rulings).

One immediate result of the new act was to limit the amount that Richard Nixon and George McGovern could spend on radio and television time in 1972. According to a document published by the Federal Communications Commission, these two candidates actually spent only half as much on political broadcasts as was spent in 1968. As Figure 5-1 shows, Richard Nixon spent $4.3 million on broadcasting during the general election—approximately one-third as much as in 1968. Of course, the lower expenditure in 1972 was not attributable solely to the new campaign law. Richard Nixon's exposure as an incumbent President also made it less imperative for him to rely on as extensive a media campaign as in 1968. In addition, many Nixon television commercials were paid for by "Democrats for Nixon," a group headed by John Connally.

By ironic coincidence, in the same year the new Federal Election Campaign Act became law, the Watergate scandal became public. In fact, the revelations of the scandal may have been aided by the law's disclosure provisions. For example, the General Accounting Office issued a series of reports citing apparent violations of the 1971 Act by the Committee for the Reelection of the President (CREEP). These reports led to the indictment of the committee by the Justice Department on at least eight separate counts of campaign spending violation. Federal investigators charged that before and after the Federal Election Campaign Act took effect on April 7, 1972, the Nixon Reelection Committee had raised $10 million more than it reported. Investigators also found evidence that top Nixon hands had skimmed campaign money for personal use, and that campaign funds had been converted into Watergate "hush money."

Table 5-3. Provisions Included in the 1974 Campaign Reform Law (Following the 1976 Supreme Court Ruling)

1. No individual can give more than $1,000 to any candidate for President or Congress, and not more than $25,000 to all candidates for federal office during one campaign season.
2. No political organization—including labor union committees and other special-interest groups—can give more than $5,000 to any congressional or presidential candidate for any one election.
3. Candidates in presidential primaries raising $100,000 in amounts of $5,000 in each of at least 20 states (through gifts not exceeding $250) will receive matching public funds up to $4.5 million.
4. In the general election, each major-party candidate for President who accepts the prescribed spending limits will be assured of $20 million from the U.S. Treasury, which will be raised from the $1-checkoff on federal income tax returns.
5. Third-party candidates will be eligible for federal funding if their party obtained at least 5 percent of the total vote cast in the preceding election.
6. Criminal violations of the law will be handled by the Justice Department, with maximum fines for violating the law set at $50,000.

Thus, spawned by Watergate and a desire to limit the influence of big-money contributors, pressures increased on Congress to pass even more comprehensive reform legislation. Finally, in October 1974—two and one-half years after passing the Federal Election Campaign Act—Congress enacted the most far-reaching campaign financing law in American history (see Table 5-3). The new law, making its initial impact on the 1976 presidential election, set new limits on the amount of money that could be contributed by individuals or groups, or spent by candidates themselves, in congressional and presidential races. It also provided for public financing of presidential campaigns (although not for Senate or House races) and established an independent Elections Commission to enforce the law's provisions. According to the Center for Public Financing of Elections, which had lobbied actively for the measure, the new law represented "the only decent legacy of Watergate."

In January 1976, however, the law came under the scrutiny of the Supreme Court, which used its judicial review power to strike down some of its provisions. Although reformists were relieved to see most of the law upheld by the Court, the tight squeeze on campaign spending was loosened. The Court ruled that candidates could spend any amount they wished in seeking public office (although those accepting federal matching funds had to remain within the bounds originally set by the 1974 law). Moreover, a freer reign was given to individual citizens and "fat cats."

They still could not dump unlimited funds directly into a candidate's campaign till, but they were now free to spend extravagantly *on behalf* of a candidate—such as by paying for television spots and billboards. The Supreme Court also undercut the Federal Elections Commission which had been set up to enforce the new legislation. The Justices ruled that the commission could not wield the power of an executive enforcement agency because most of its members were appointed by congressional leaders instead of by the President.

The Court's partial assault on the 1974 law came in response to legal challenges by Senator James Buckley, Eugene McCarthy, and others who felt that limits on spending violated the constitutional right of free expression. They insisted that ceilings on campaign spending would give an unfair advantage to incumbents, who usually enjoy greater public recognition than challengers. The use of large sums of money, they argued, frequently has been the only way for relatively unknown challengers, particularly third-party candidates, to compete with incumbents.

But, the constitutional issues aside, the new ruling kept alive the old worries about the link between money and politics. With spending ceilings removed, those candidates who could raise substantial sums of money would continue to enjoy a significant political advantage over their less well-financed opponents. Money would still talk in politics—particularly in the struggle to achieve recognition through political commercials and other media blitzes.

Recommended Reading

Cirino, Robert. *Don't Blame the People.* New York: Random House, 1971.

Lang, Kurt, and Lang, Gladys E. *Politics and Television.* New York: Quadrangle/The New York Times Co., 1968.

McGinniss, Joe. *The Selling of the President 1968.* New York: Trident Press, 1969.

McLuhan, Marshall. *Understanding Media.* New York: McGraw-Hill, 1964.

MacNeil, Robert. *The People Machine: The Influence of Television on American Politics.* New York: Harper & Row, 1968.

Mickelson, Sig. *The Electric Mirror.* New York: Dodd, Mead, 1972.

Rubin, Bernard. *Political Television.* Belmont, Cal.: Wadsworth, 1967.

Whale, John. *The Half-Shut Eye: Television and Politics in Britain and America.* London: Macmillan; New York: St. Martin's Press, 1969.

Wykoff, Gene. *The Image Candidates: American Politics in the Age of Television.* New York: Macmillan, 1968.

1. Vance Packard, *The Hidden Persuaders* (New York: David McKay, 1957).

2. Snell Putney and Gail J. Putney, *The Adjusted American* (New York: Harper & Row, 1966), p. 188. Used with permission of Harper & Row, Publishers, Inc.

3. Quoted in Robert MacNeil, *The People Machine: The Influence of Television on American Politics* (New York: Harper & Row, 1968), p. 210. Used with permission of Harper & Row, Publishers, Inc.

4. Joe McGinniss, *The Selling of the President 1968* (New York: Trident Press, 1969).

5. See, for example, Joseph T. Klapper, *The Effects of Mass Communication* (New York: Free Press, 1960); David O. Sears and Jonathan Freedman, "Selective Exposure to Information: A Critical Review," *Public Opinion Quarterly*, Summer 1967, pp. 194–213.

6. See, for example, W. H. Ittelson and F. P. Kilpatrick, "Experiments in Perception," *Scientific American*, August 1951, pp. 50–55.

7. William H. Flanigan, *Political Behavior of the American Electorate*, 2d ed. (Boston: Allyn and Bacon, 1972), p. 108.

8. Dan Nimmo, *The Political Persuaders: The Techniques of Modern Election Campaigns* (Englewood Cliffs, N.J.: Prentice-Hall, 1970), p. 138.

9. Bob Woodward and Carl Bernstein, *All the President's Men* (New York: Simon & Schuster, 1974).

10. James Reston, *New York Times*, 9 May 1973. © 1973 by The New York Times Company. Reprinted by permission.

11. See, for example, Angus Campbell, "Has Television Reshaped Politics?" in Edward C. Dreyer and Walter A. Rosenbaum, eds., *Political Opinion and Electoral Behavior* (Belmont, Cal.: Wadsworth, 1966), pp. 318–23.

12. *Gallup Opinion Index*, August 1971.

13. Margaret Mead, "A Force That Can Change the Nature of Society," *TV Guide*, 10 March 1962, pp. 9–11.

14. Kurt Lang and Gladys E. Lang, *Politics and Television* (New York: Quadrangle/The New York Times Co., 1968), p. 306.

15. Ibid., p. 307.

16. Quoted in Robert MacNeil, *The People Machine: The Influence of Television on American Politics* (New York: Harper & Row, 1968), p. 138. Used with permission of Harper & Row, Publishers, Inc.

17. See, for example, Marshall McLuhan, *Understanding Media* (New York: McGraw-Hill, 1964).

18. Theodore H. White, *The Making of the President 1960* (New York: Atheneum), p. 289. Copyright © 1961 by Atheneum House, Inc.

19. Richard M. Nixon, *Six Crises* (Garden City, N.Y.: Doubleday, 1962), p. 341. © 1962 Doubleday & Company, Inc. Used with permission of Doubleday & Company, Inc.

21. Quoted in Theodore H. White, *The Making of the President 1972* (New York: Atheneum), p. 82. Copyright © 1973 by Theodore H. White.

22. Charles A. H. Thomson, *Television and Presidential Politics* (Washington, D.C.: Brookings Institution, 1956), p. 139.

23. Robert MacNeil, *The People Machine: The Influence of Television on American Politics* (New York: Harper & Row, 1968), pp. 193–94. Used with permission of Harper & Row, Publishers, Inc.

24. Pierre Salinger, *With Kennedy* (Garden City, N.Y.: Doubleday, 1966), p. 299. © 1966 Doubleday & Company, Inc. Used with permission of Doubleday & Company, Inc.

25. Kurt Lang and Gladys E. Lang, *Politics and Television* (New York: Quadrangle/The New York Times Co., 1968), p. 296.

26. Quoted in Bernard Rubin, *Political Television* (Belmont, Cal.: Wadsworth, 1967), p. 33.

27. John V. Lindsay, "Let's Get the Money Out of Politics," *Newsweek*, 20 May 1974, p. 18. Copyright Newsweek, Inc., 1974; reprinted by permission.

Participation at the Higher Levels

6 The President:
High Rolling in Politics

Those of us who have ever dreamed of wielding great political power probably have tried to envision what it would be like to be President of the United States. For many of us, the Presidency evokes images of fabulous pomp and ceremony, of subordinates jumping to obey authoritative commands, and of economic and social crises being whisked away by the force of executive decision. The President appears to be an individual who has made it to the summit of power, who has achieved the ultimate success in gaining access to and influence over the machinery of government.

Similar visions of success undoubtedly propel those candidates who campaign for the Presidency. Seduced by the glamor and power of the office, they will sacrifice almost anything to gain command of the White House. They will endure the hardships and humiliations of a national campaign, expose themselves and their families to endless probings and personal criticisms, and pump friends and enemies alike for the funds needed to "sell" their candidacy to the voters. Rather than accept the admonition of James Bryce, who once said that "great men are not elected President," they will view their campaign for the office as a testament to their own call to political eminence.

Part of the great lure of the Presidency is, of course, that it is an extremely adaptive office, responsive to the personality of each individual who sits in the White House. In contrast to the duties of Congress, which are quite specifically outlined in Article I of the Constitution, the vague duties of the President stated in the opening line of Article II—"The executive power shall be vested in a President of the United States of America"—ultimately allow for a great deal of flexibility. Each President has room to interpret his responsibilities to suit not only the needs of the times but his own personal philosophy. Although some Presidents have been reluctant to exercise great authority (Calvin Coolidge, for example, believed there already were too many laws and pledged not to recommend many new ones), other, more forceful Chief Executives (like Lincoln, Wilson, and the two Roosevelts) have interpreted the vague constitutional language to mean an absence of specific prohibitions and have acted accordingly to broaden their powers—setting precedents for future White House occupants. The nature of the office, John Kennedy reflected, demands that "the President place himself in the very thick of the fight" and that he "be prepared to exercise the fullest powers of his office—all that are specified and some that are not."[1]

Yet, the Presidency is not without its hazards. Those who eventually attain the office may experience frustration and defeat on a par with the glory and fame. As is true of any gamble involving high stakes, the pursuit of presidential power may either elevate an individual to greatness or plunge him into an abyss of failure and public disrepute. As shown by recent experiences with Vietnam and Watergate, errors of judgment and misconduct at such a height of political power as the Presidency can result in blunders of tragic proportions—tragic not only for the person occupying the office but for those affected by his decisions. Instead of winning a reputation for good will, a President may become a historic anomaly, a public mistake shared by all who supported him.

Consider the case of Richard Nixon. With his resignation in August 1974, he left behind a legacy of public distrust and cynicism that damaged more than his own reputation. By abusing the powers of his office, he helped further intensify public suspicion of politicians and political institutions alike, threatening to leave in wreckage the very office for which he had campaigned. His admitted complicity in the Watergate cover-up, compounded by his and Lyndon Johnson's calamitous Vietnam policies, took the Presidency through a period of growing public distrust that may be unrivaled in U.S. history. A 1973 Harris survey found that the Presidency ranked among the lowest in public trust of most American institutions, with only 19 percent of those questioned expressing confidence in the office.[2] And, as for Richard Nixon

THE WHITE HOUSE

WASHINGTON

August 9, 1974

Dear Mr. Secretary:

I hereby resign the Office of President of the
United States.

Sincerely,

[signature: Richard Nixon]

11.35 AM

The Honorable Henry A. Kissinger
The Secretary of State
Washington, D.C. 20520

HK

himself, columnist George Will summarized it this way: "The disgrace is permanent. There are not going to be any Richard M.
Nixon high schools, parks, highways, stadiums."[3]

Character and Presidential Performance

The possibility of failing or succeeding in the Presidency should
remind us that the personality and style each President brings
to the office affects both his performance as well as his responsiveness to the citizenry. His sensitivity to citizen concerns and
his capacity and willingness to confront social problems is inexorably bound up, not only with his possible ties to certain elite
interests (see Chapter Two), but with his character, motivations,
and view of the office. Indeed, those hoping to sway executive
decision making—through letters, pressure group activity, or demonstrations—must confront the question of presidential personal-

ity. Some observers insist, for instance, that the reluctance of both Lyndon Johnson and Richard Nixon to face up to the mounting protests against the Vietnam War revealed not only a stubborn commitment to military policy but also an almost paranoiac reaction to criticism and alternative views.

The realization, in fact, that personality ties in with conduct has led to some highly controversial psychological studies of presidential behavior. Political scientist James David Barber, for example, has drawn biographical sketches of eleven recent Chief Executives in an effort to understand more clearly the influence of character on the exercise of presidential power.[4] Since a President's character—his style, self-image, and world-view—may have a profound impact on national affairs, Barber suggests we analyze each future Chief Executive to predict his likely performance under stress, insisting that we can make such a prediction if we study his "psychological makeup." By examining his earliest childhood and adult experiences, we can anticipate what he will do while in the White House. Show us a child with an overbearing, cantankerous father and a domineering mother, and we may find a President beset by hostility and unpredictable impulses.

Taking this thesis even further, Barber contends that early experiences usually result in one of four different presidential types: "active-positives," "active-negatives," "passive-positives," and "passive-negatives." Barber uses the dichotomy "active" vs. "passive" to describe the amount of energy a President invests in the office, and the dichotomy "positive" vs. "negative" to indicate how a President feels about what he does. Thus, "active-positive" Presidents want most to achieve results and enjoy exercising political power. They tend to possess relatively high self-esteem as well as an ability to adapt to changing circumstances (Franklin Roosevelt, Truman, and Kennedy). "Active-negatives" also seek results, but they seldom get as much pleasure from the task. Their actions seem compulsive, and they tend to view life as a hard struggle to gain and maintain political power (Wilson, Harding, Johnson, and Nixon). "Passive-positive" Presidents are those who search for affection as a reward for being agreeable. They do not accomplish much, but they enjoy the adulation that comes with the office (Taft and Harding). The "passive-negatives" not only accomplish little but retreat from the demands and conflicts of the job by stressing vague civic virtues. For them, the burdens of politics tend to outweigh the enjoyments (Coolidge and Eisenhower).

Barber issues a special warning about the second type of presidential character: the "active-negative." This type of individual,

Barber believes, tends to be motivated by anxieties and guilts, and has difficulty controlling his aggressions. Because such a person sometimes confuses national policy with his own ambitions and becomes rigidly fixated on a policy regardless of the consequences—as Johnson did with Vietnam and as Nixon did with the Watergate cover-up—the "active-negative" President can be an especially dangerous individual who may bring on disaster.

There are, of course, weaknesses in such psychological interpretations from a distance. Although it might be possible to augment our understanding of presidential behavior by examining childhood and adult experiences, there are dangers in merely picking out certain incidents in the past to account for later actions. Such incidents may only seem to tie in with later actions and may not necessarily be typical of the individual's past, or future, behavior. When it comes to predicting presidential behavior, it may be difficult to know which experiences are truly the most significant.

The Burdens and the Glories

We should not become so involved, in any case, in examining the personality differences between individuals who occupy the White House that we ignore the special requirements of the office. The relationship between character and performance works both ways, in that the office influences the incumbent's behavior just as his behavior affects the office. Persons seeking the Presidency and those struggling to influence it must take into account the scope and complexity of the President's many competing responsibilities. As adaptive as the Presidency may be, the job still carries with it certain expectations.

A number of duties have been assigned to the office by the Constitution and by tradition that every President is expected to perform. He is supposed to direct the federal bureaucracy, propose new federal programs, serve as ceremonial head of state, lead his party, and assume major responsibility for foreign and military affairs. Although the discretionary nature of the office permits him to choose which of these duties to emphasize, the President cannot entirely ignore any of them. At various times during his reign he will find himself immersed in a problem that, as party leader or Commander in Chief, he is expected to solve. And he will find himself judged not only by the policies he personally initiates as President, but by how well he handles the other responsibilities thrust upon him.

The Weight of Bureaucracy

When a President takes office, he assumes command of one of the largest government bureaucracies in the world—an administrative enterprise employing more than three million people, with a payroll exceeding $70 billion a year. This is because the framers of the Constitution expected the President to take charge of the federal agencies that administer the nation's social and legal services. They stipulated in Article II that "The executive power shall be vested in a President of the United States" who shall "take care that the laws be faithfully executed."

Indeed, it is a safe bet that no other executive in government or industry has as many administrative responsibilities as the President. No other executive has as many buttons to push, as much money to spend, as many employees to supervise. As a result of the provisions in Article II and congressional statutes, the President is expected to oversee the entire federal bureaucracy and to appoint (or discharge) more than three thousand top officials outside the civil service system—including department and agency heads and U.S. ambassadors. On top of that, Congress since 1921 has expected the President each year to submit a budget covering the operating expenses of all federal agencies and programs—a budget that now exceeds $350 billion.

Of course, the President is not expected to administer the bureaucracy single-handedly. Most of the day-to-day responsibilities are delegated to subordinates who in turn place most of the burden on their underlings. Over the years, Congress has created a number of agencies to help the President make administrative decisions and enforce federal policies. In addition to his Cabinet and personal White House staff (which we will discuss later), the President is served by a number of agencies in the Executive Office (see Table 6-1). One of the most important of these agencies is the Office of Management and Budget, which helps the President review the financial requests of other federal agencies and serves as a watchdog to keep their spending within bounds after the money has been appropriated by Congress. Another is the Council of Economic Advisers, whose three economists (hired by the President) help him forecast, interpret, and manage national economic developments—although at times, as we know, with questionable competence. Still other important White House agencies include the National Security Council (to advise the President on foreign affairs) and the Domestic Council (to help formulate solutions to domestic problems).

However, despite the President's numerous assistants, his control over the federal bureaucracy is not absolute. It would be

Table 6-1. Organization of the U.S. Government

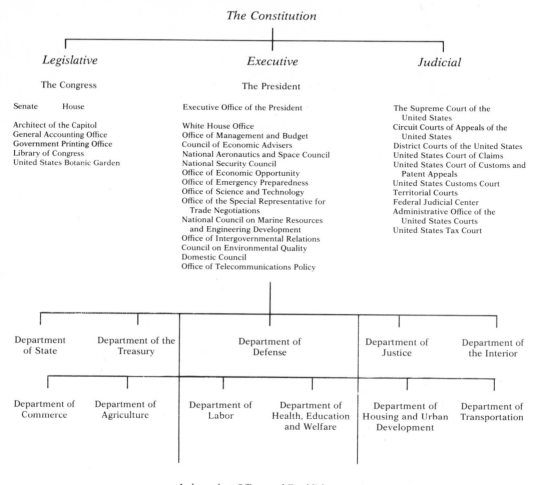

The Constitution

Legislative   *Executive*   *Judicial*

The Congress   The President

Legislative	Executive	Judicial
Senate House	Executive Office of the President	The Supreme Court of the United States
Architect of the Capitol	White House Office	Circuit Courts of Appeals of the United States
General Accounting Office	Office of Management and Budget	District Courts of the United States
Government Printing Office	Council of Economic Advisers	United States Court of Claims
Library of Congress	National Aeronautics and Space Council	United States Court of Customs and Patent Appeals
United States Botanic Garden	National Security Council	United States Customs Court
	Office of Economic Opportunity	Territorial Courts
	Office of Emergency Preparedness	Federal Judicial Center
	Office of Science and Technology	Administrative Office of the United States Courts
	Office of the Special Representative for Trade Negotiations	United States Tax Court
	National Council on Marine Resources and Engineering Development	
	Office of Intergovernmental Relations	
	Council on Environmental Quality	
	Domestic Council	
	Office of Telecommunications Policy	

Department of State	Department of the Treasury	Department of Defense	Department of Justice	Department of the Interior

Department of Commerce	Department of Agriculture	Department of Labor	Department of Health, Education and Welfare	Department of Housing and Urban Development	Department of Transportation

Independent Offices and Establishments

Administrative Conference of the U.S.	Federal Power Commission	National Science Foundation
Atomic Energy Commission	Federal Reserve System, Board of Governors of the	Railroad Retirement Board
Civil Aeronautics Board		Securities and Exchange Commission
District of Columbia	Federal Trade Commission	Selective Service System
Export-Import Bank of the U.S.	General Services Administration	Small Business Administration
Farm Credit Administration	Interstate Commerce Commission	Smithsonian Institution
Federal Communications Commission	National Aeronautics and Space Administration	Tennessee Valley Authority
Federal Deposit Insurance Corporation	National Foundation on the Arts and the Humanities	U.S. Civil Service Commission
Federal Home Loan Bank Board		U.S. Information Agency
Federal Maritime Commission	National Labor Relations Board	U.S. Postal Service
Federal Mediation and Conciliation Service	National Mediation Board	U.S. Tariff Commission
		Veterans Administration

Source: *U.S. Government Organization Manual*, 1970–71.

a mistake to assume that the President simply takes command and issues orders that subordinates instantly obey. As stated in Chapter Two, some observers view the federal bureaucracy as a powerful, independent "fourth branch" accountable to no one and swelling under its own irrepressible momentum. This view has considerable merits, for certain features of the federal bureaucracy encourage its independence from presidential authority. For one thing, while the agencies of the Executive Office just described operate in close contact with the President, a number of other important agencies operate relatively free from presidential direction. For example, most of the regulatory agencies—such as the Federal Communications Commission (FCC), the Civil Aeronautics Board (CAB), and the Securities and Exchange Commission (SEC)—are exempt from presidential domination because of their largely judicial functions. Because these commissions are charged with regulating private industry by granting licenses, setting fares, investigating deceptive advertising, and so forth, they are supposed to remain relatively independent of outside political pressures. (They have been justifiably criticized, however, for yielding to pressures from the industries they are supposed to oversee.) Thus, even though members are appointed by the President, they are not subject to removal by him. Most serve long, overlapping terms so that no one President can make all the appointments.

Furthermore, the enormous size of the federal bureaucracy, combined with the President's many competing responsibilities, does not allow him to keep in touch with thousands of administrative workers. Even though the President establishes guidelines for the programs he wishes to implement, the bureaucracy is so vast he can never be sure whether his programs will be carried out as he intends. The sheer size of the federal bureaucracy, one scholar notes, "makes it impossible for a President to know or see or influence personally more than a handful of those men whose day-to-day activities will determine whether some cherished policy is to succeed or fail."[5]

Adding to the President's problems is the federal bureaucracy's sluggishness and evasiveness. Although the President is in principle the "chief executive," he may experience frustration similar to that of ordinary citizens who have become entangled in bureaucratic red tape. As a top official of the Kennedy administration once concluded, "Getting the bureaucracy to accept new ideas is like carrying a double mattress up a very narrow and winding stairway. It is a terrible job, and you exhaust yourself when you try it. But once you get the mattress up it is awfully hard for anyone else to get it down."[6] In fact, the President may encounter even greater difficulties in forcing the bureaucracy to implement his programs than in persuading Congress to enact them in the first place. "Were the Presidents of the last fifty years to be polled on this question," Clinton Rossiter insists, "all but one or two, I am sure, would agree that the 'natural obstinacy' of the average bureau chief or commissioner or colonel was second only to the 'ingrained suspicions' of the average Congressman as a check on the President's ability to do either good or evil."[7]

In many respects, the federal bureaucracy has a will of its own separate from that of the White House or any other branch of government. Civil servants (who are not elected by the people) frequently make independent decisions that drastically affect other people's lives—where roads will be built, who will be eligible for welfare assistance, how safe drugs and automobiles must be. Many of these civil servants have toiled at their jobs for years, serving Presidents of both major parties. As Richard Nixon once remarked, "Presidents come and go, but the bureaucracy goes on forever." Often these civil servants are allied with influential members of Congress or special-interest groups who may not approve of a President's policies. In such instances, they may take policy matters into their own hands, purposely stalling the implementation of a President's program or even failing to carry it out at all. In Harry Truman's view, many of these "career men in government look upon the occupant of the White House as only a temporary nuisance who will soon be succeeded by another temporary occupant who won't find out what it's all about for a long time and then it will be too late to do anything about it."[8] Sometimes, a President may even be reluctant to pursue the matter with great vigor, especially if it might sour his relations with key members of Congress or special-interest groups whose support he desperately needs. As long as he has satisfied certain people by getting a program through Congress, he may not wish to risk further antagonizing those who opposed the program by forcing the bureaucracy to carry it out as intended.

An Architect of Policy

The President is deeply involved also in policy making and is, in fact, judged by the kinds of programs he proposes to Congress. Although the Constitution does not specifically refer to him as an architect of policy, it does outline a number of major legislative responsibilities—responsibilities that many Presidents regard as their principal reasons for assuming the office in the first place.

One of these responsibilities is expressed in the annual "State of the Union" message to Congress, in which the President spells out what needs to be done to settle the nation's woes. The constitutional basis for this message is found in the statement that he "shall from time to time give to the Congress information of the State of the Union, and recommend to their consideration such measures as he shall judge necessary and expedient."

Usually, the President addresses both houses of Congress after the opening of each session in January, taking full advantage of television coverage. Because he cannot personally introduce a bill into the House or Senate, he can use this annual address—as well as other forms of persuasion—to convince members of his party to enact certain policies. Most members of Congress, in fact, look to the President for policy leadership, even though they may ultimately reject his specific proposals. Because the President heads the federal bureaucracy and enjoys a national constituency, he is regarded by them as a focal point of legislation.

Even though a President is expected to provide legislative leadership, he cannot always count on success. It is easier for members of Congress to thwart White House plans than to initiate constructive programs of their own. Indeed, ruling-elite theorists and pluralists alike contend that the powers of the Presidency over legislation vary with the personalities of those who occupy the office, and that a President's real power depends ultimately on his ability to persuade. To win support for his programs, he must be able to deal aggressively, employ publicity, or do whatever else is required to convince skeptical legislators that, as one scholar noted, "what the White House wants of them is what they ought to do for their sake and on their authority."[9] In former President Harry Truman's words, "About the biggest power the President has, and I've said this before, is the power to persuade people to do what they ought to do without having to be persuaded. There are a lot of other powers written in the Constitution and given to the President, but it's that power to persuade people to do what they ought to do anyway that's the biggest. And if the man who is President doesn't understand that, if he thinks he's too big to do the necessary persuading, then he's in for big trouble, and so is the country."[10]

Proposing legislation is, of course, only the beginning. Another important legislative responsibility is to provide an occasional check on Congress by wielding the potent constitutional weapon of the veto—a weapon, incidentally, that plays no minor role in his ability to persuade. Because all new bills must be signed by the President, he has a virtual life-or-death power over policy. The mere threat of a veto can force a bill's sponsors in Congress to scurry to shape it to the President's desires.

One reason the veto is such a potent weapon is that a two-thirds majority of both the House and Senate is required to override. In fact, any bill the President receives within ten days before Congress adjourns that he does not sign (called a "pocket veto") automatically dies and cannot be overridden. As we can see in Table 6-2, Congress between 1933 and the early part of 1975 was able to override less than 3 percent of all presidential vetoes.

Table 6-2. Presidential Vetoes, 1933 to 1975

President	Regular	Pocket	Total	Vetoes Overridden
Roosevelt (1933–45)	372	263	635	9
Truman (1945–53)	180	70	250	12
Eisenhower (1953–61)	73	108	181	2
Kennedy (1961–63)	12	9	21	0
Johnson (1963–69)	16	14	30	0
Nixon (1969–1974)	25	15	40	5
Ford (1974–June 1975)	18	11	29	4

One major limitation of the veto is that the President must turn thumbs down on an entire bill, even though his objections to it might be only partial. Most state governors—including those of New York, Illinois, California, and Texas—command even greater power over some kinds of legislation than does the President, for they can employ an "item veto." This device allows them to strike out or "bluepencil" any part of an appropriations bill they disapprove of, while leaving the remainder intact. Because the President does not possess this item veto (although, as we will see in the next chapter, Richard Nixon attempted to use one), members of Congress sometimes can push through favored policies by attaching amendments ("riders") to bills the President is known to want. They know the President must either accept or reject the entire package—he cannot veto just the amendment. This was the very strategy that enabled Congress in July 1973 to end the bombing in Cambodia and Laos. By attaching the measure as a rider to an emergency $3.4 billion supplementary appropriations bill, a veto of the antiwar amendment by President Nixon was averted.

Erich Hartmann, Magnum Photos

The Ceremonial Side

In addition to his usual political chores as head of government, the President can find his calendar clogged with endless ceremonial functions as the nation's symbolic head of state. In countries like Britain and Norway, the two jobs are performed by different persons: the figurehead queen or king discharges most of the ceremonial duties as titular head of state—such as knighting prominent public figures or welcoming new foreign ambassadors—while the prime minister wields the real political power as head of government. But because the President holds both jobs at once, he may spend his time not only proposing and vetoing legislation but decorating astronauts, banqueting the Shah of Iran, rolling out the first egg for the Easter Bunny, or hosting delegations of Campfire Girls and World War II veterans. When he enters a hall on state occasions, he is usually welcomed with the Presidential anthem, "Hail to the Chief," and he is inaugurated—or buried—with all the ceremony and pomp reserved in other countries for royalty.

Although these ceremonial duties and trappings may seem unimportant, they are not. Often a President's personal magnetism and appeal can be augmented by his activities as the symbolic representative of the American people. Indeed, a good performance as chief of state can greatly enhance a President's public prestige, and hence become a potent weapon in his political arsenal. "A President's prestige," notes one scholar, "is a factor in his influence of roughly the same sort as his personal reputation:

a factor that may not decide the outcome in a given case but can affect the likelihood in every case and therefore is strategically important to his power."[11]

Naturally, the President's featured role in the spotlight can also attract attention to his character and style in ways not entirely flattering. Certainly, most Presidents have been subject to type-casting: Nixon as the used-car salesman; Johnson as the southern wheeler-dealer; and Kennedy as the youthful sophisticate. Ford suffered an image of being less than brilliant—an image fostered largely by Lyndon Johnson's famous wisecracks that Ford "could not walk and chew gum at the same time" and that he "played football too long without his helmet." Satirist Mort Sahl remarked dryly that Ford reminded him of the clerk who OK's a customer's check at Safeway.

But whatever relationship exists between a President's popular image and his role as ceremonial leader, his image can have a decided effect both on his popularity and on public confidence in the Presidency. Even though Ford, for example, was belittled for his lack of intelligence, he seemed to offer to many Americans a welcome contrast in style to that of his predecessor. Where Nixon's Presidency had been widely viewed as insular and devious, Ford's was immediately regarded as open and relaxed. Indeed, many people looked to Ford as a messiah to lead the nation out of the morass of Watergate. Apparently, the public mood had been so depressed by Watergate as to be at least temporarily bolstered by seeing the Presidency pass from the used-car sales-man to the Safeway clerk.

The President and Party

An interesting paradox each President must face is that he not only must serve as the ceremonial representative of the entire nation but must provide partisan leadership for his party as well. Many of the Founding Fathers would not have relished this latter role, since they conceived of the Chief Executive as a neutral figure removed from most factional squabbles. But because of his powerful position, he is expected to lead his party from the time he is nominated at the national convention—to select the party national chairman, campaign for local and state party can-didates, and use his prestige to attract needed campaign contribu-tions. "He is at once," Clinton Rossiter observed, "the least politi-cal and the most political of all heads of government."[12]

However, his leadership of the party can never extend too far.

Because of the decentralized nature of the Democratic and Republican parties, the President has little direct control over state and local party organizations; for instance, he can impose only marginal discipline over most congressional members of his party. Although some Presidents have exercised more party leadership than others, a President's relations with other members of his party tend to rest on mutual benefits; he requires their support for his legislative proposals, and the party depends on his prestige, direction, and such special favors as appointments.

There are also times when a President, due to loss of credibility or public support, is unable to provide his party with any effective leadership. This has happened to a number of Presidents, including Andrew Johnson, Warren Harding, and Harry Truman. Perhaps the most extreme example of a recent President who fell from party favor was Richard Nixon: his rapid decline in popularity during the Watergate investigations prompted a majority of Republicans to disavow ties to his policies. During the special off-year elections in the spring of 1974, Republican candidates, instead of seeking his appearance in their districts, pleaded for his absence. Even so, the party lost four normally strong GOP congressional districts that spring—including the one in Michigan previously represented by Gerald Ford. Given such a record of defeats—and the placement of the blame directly on Nixon's ties with Watergate—it came as no surprise that many Republicans, up for reelection in November, welcomed with relief the news of Nixon's resignation from office.

Architect of Diplomacy

Most Presidents probably have regarded their role as chief diplomat to be the inspiration for their most ambitious and important policies. Certainly many have had grandiose expectations of influencing world affairs, as we are reminded by Woodrow Wilson's determination to "make the world safe for democracy" and Franklin Roosevelt's "Four Freedoms." Richard Nixon declared on numerous occasions that the overriding goal of his tenure in office was to create a "lasting structure of peace in the world"—a goal that prompted his trips to Peking and Moscow in 1972 and his efforts to help settle the Arab-Israeli conflict in 1974.

In fact, the President's control over foreign affairs generally exceeds his control over domestic legislation and the federal bureaucracy. Although the President must share his diplomatic responsibilities with the Senate—which can either approve or reject his treaties and appointments of ambassadors—his position remains paramount. For example, only the President or his executive agent (like Henry Kissinger) can legally represent the United States in its relations with foreign governments. In 1936, the Supreme Court ruled that the President has "exclusive power ... as the sole organ of the Federal Government in the field of international relations."[13] Neither members of Congress nor private citizens may communicate officially with other governments on behalf of the United States. It is argued that diplomatic negotiations with other countries require a "single voice" and occasionally an element of secrecy that Congress, with its 535 diverse and conflicting personalities, cannot provide.

As a result, the President has the sole constitutional authority to decide if and when the United States shall officially recognize or break off relations with foreign governments. It was Dwight Eisenhower, for example, not Congress, who decided to sever diplomatic relations with Cuba in the late 1950s. It was Richard Nixon, not Congress, who finally established a diplomatic liaison with China in 1972.

The President also has the exclusive constitutional authority to negotiate formal treaties with other countries. Although the Senate must approve all treaties by a two-thirds vote, it seldom has failed to do so: historically it has approved more than 90 percent of the treaties submitted. One of the few dramatic instances in which Congress refused to ratify a major presidential treaty occurred in 1919 when it turned down the Treaty of Versailles and its provision for United States membership in the new League of Nations.

Actually, the President does not even have to depend on Senate concurrence for most negotiations with other countries. He may bypass it entirely through the use of "executive agreements," which, unlike treaties, do not require formal Senate approval (although they may be thwarted by Congress if appropriations are required to carry them out). Although most executive agreements have been used for such routine matters as postal or patent arrangements, a substantial number have been quite important. These agreements include the establishment of U.S. military installations in countries like Spain and Turkey, the annexation of Texas in 1845, the "Open Door" policy in China in 1889, and the exchange of U.S. destroyers for long-term leases on British naval bases in 1940.

Although the Constitution does not specifically authorize executive agreements, the Supreme Court in 1937—following many decades of such agreements—declared that the President may independently negotiate with foreign governments as part of his treaty-making responsibilities. Thus, ever since Woodrow Wilson failed to win Senate ratification of the Versailles Treaty, Presidents increasingly have relied on this device. Each year a President may sign close to 100 executive agreements, while resorting to treaties only in matters of great international significance or when Senate approval is assured. From 1946 until the end of 1974, for example, the United States concluded 6,317 executive agreements and only 411 treaties, according to State Department figures.

Naturally, the frequent use of this device has sparked considerable criticism. Some critics fear that the President's resort to executive agreements (which often are negotiated in secret since they do not require Senate approval) places too great a responsibility in one person's hands. In 1953, Senator John Bricker proposed a constitutional amendment to prohibit the practice entirely; but it failed to win Senate approval by one vote. Later, in the summer of 1972 after it had been revealed that some of President Nixon's agreements with foreign governments had been kept secret from Congress, the House and Senate passed a new law requiring the President to submit to both houses within sixty days the text of any international agreement. Under the law, if the President should decide an agreement is too sensitive for public disclosure, he may send it only to the Foreign Relations Committee for review. But, in the opinion of some critics, the new law, while it limits the President's power to some degree, does not sufficiently curtail the President's authority to conduct such secret agreements in the first place.

Control over the Military

The President can also back up his diplomatic responsibilities with his command over the military. The Constitution empowers the President to "be Commander in Chief of the Army and Navy ... and of the militia of the several states, when called into the actual service of the United States." This means that the President can draw his sword and personally lead the troops into battle—an action, however, to which only George Washington resorted during the Whisky Rebellion of 1794. It is generally forgotten that almost one-fourth of our Presidents have been army generals, including: George Washington, Andrew Jackson, Zachary Taylor, Franklin Pierce, Ulysses S. Grant, Rutherford B. Hayes, James Garfield, Benjamin Harrison, and Dwight Eisenhower.

Although the Constitution grants Congress the sole authority to "declare" war and appropriate military funds, Presidents have had virtually a free hand to conduct military operations. Over the years, the United States has been engaged in more foreign military adventures under presidential direction than in wars formally declared by Congress. One estimate is that Presidents have ordered troops into battle without a congressional declaration of war at least 150 different times. In fact, even the five legislatively sanctioned wars—the War of 1812, the War with Mexico, the Spanish-American War, and the two World Wars—were declared only at the insistence of the President. Since the close of World War II alone, Presidents have taken a number of dramatic military steps without formal congressional approval: the dropping of two atomic bombs on Japan in 1945; the "intervention" in Korea in 1950; the invasion of Cuba at the Bay of Pigs in 1961; the landing of more than twenty thousand troops in the Dominican Republic in 1965; and the invasion of Cambodia in 1970.

The explanations for such military actions sometimes result in peculiar interpretations of the Constitution. "There is nothing in the Constitution," Saul K. Padover has written, for example, "that says the President may not wage war at his discretion. The Constitution merely states that only Congress can 'declare war.' But it does not say that a war has to be 'declared' before it can be waged."[14]

Frequently, Presidents have even combined their domestic responsibility "to take care that the laws be faithfully executed" with their role as Commander in Chief. During the Civil War, Abraham Lincoln called out the militia to seize railroads and telegraph lines and to blockade Southern ports, and suspended the writ of habeas corpus. Similarly, during World War I and World War II, Woodrow Wilson and Franklin Roosevelt wielded extraordinary powers over the economy and civil rights. In fact, the President's potential powers as Commander in Chief at home are almost boundless. During the past forty years Congress has passed hundreds of statutes permitting a President to take decisive actions in many domestic areas without waiting for congressional approval. Under these statutes, the President could legally refuse to allow any one of us to enter or leave the United States, seize control of all radio and television stations, institute martial law, and take control of our private capital and personal property. And he could take these extraordinary measures simply by declaring the existence of a "national emergency."

Many scholars contend that the framers of the Constitution never intended the President to command such sweeping military power. Abraham Lincoln, long before assuming office, wrote that it was the power of kings to involve their citizens in war that the Founding Fathers "understood to be the most oppressive of all kingly oppressions; and they resolved to so frame the Constitution that no one man should hold the power of bringing this oppression upon us."[15] The major reasons the framers gave the President command of the military were to ensure civilian control over the armed forces and to allow quick response to a sudden attack on the United States. Any protracted or offensive conflict, however, would be conducted only after a congressional declaration of war. But, because the framers did not define the difference between "war" and any action short of it, Presidents have felt relatively free to initiate military actions.

As a result, many citizens have been frustrated in their attempts to influence the President in military matters. Despite the framers' avowed intentions to ensure civilian control over the armed forces, many Americans have complained that the White House has too frequently assumed a fortress stance—a "Pentagon mentality"—in the face of citizen pressures. Clamorous protesters against the Vietnam War, for example, continually met firm resistance from Presidents Johnson and Nixon on the issue of American withdrawal from Southeast Asia. In fact, ruling-elite theorists make a persuasive argument that the ties between the White House and the Pentagon have resulted in a rigidity of thought, an unwillingness on the part of most Presidents and their advisors to accept criticism of military policies.

Numerous justifications have been offered, of course, for expanded presidential control over military policy. One argument holds (somewhat feebly) that only the President has full access to the information and expertise needed to act decisively. Only he is supplied with daily intelligence reports compiled by experts in the Central Intelligence Agency, the National Security Agency, and the State and Defense Departments. Also, with annihilation of the country a terrifying possibility in the nuclear age, only the President can respond to foreign attack with quick life-or-death decisions. It is partly for these reasons (as well as an unwillingness to accept responsibility) that most members of Congress have been reluctant to curb the President—such as by withholding money for military operations—especially when they have been told that funds are required for the support of troops. During the Vietnam War, many of the same Senators and Representatives who complained bitterly about the war's unconstitutionality continued to appropriate the money to keep it going.

With rare exceptions, not even Supreme Court Justices have mustered a serious challenge to a President's military authority.

With the country's security possibly at stake, the Justices have repeatedly let the Chief Executive's decisions slip by, exempt from judicial review. They refused during World War II, for example, to interfere with Franklin Roosevelt's executive order placing thousands of Japanese-Americans in makeshift detention camps. They also refused during the Vietnam War to question the constitutional authority of Lyndon Johnson and Richard Nixon to carry out a prolonged war in Southeast Asia, or to decide whether the draft was legal without a congressional declaration of war.

This is not to say, however, that members of Congress in recent years have not tried to regain control over military policy. In November 1973, they imposed new limitations on the President's capacity to wage a protracted undeclared war. In a vote overturning President Nixon's veto, the House and Senate passed a War Powers Act, forbidding any President to send combat troops abroad for more than sixty days without a congressional declaration of war. Under the new Act, a President would still be free to take "emergency" military actions, but he would be required to report the reasons for his actions to Congress within forty-eight hours. Congress could then reverse his decision by passing a concurrent resolution of both houses, which would not be subject to his veto. Furthermore, unless Congress gave specific authorization to continue the military action, the President would be required to halt the operation after sixty days. In other words, the operation would have to cease if Congress simply did nothing. The President, under the Act, could extend this sixty-day period for an additional thirty days, but only to permit safe withdrawal of troops.

President Nixon, in his veto message, insisted the War Powers Act was unconstitutional because it "would purport to take away, by a mere legislative act, authorities which the President has properly exercised under the Constitution for almost 200 years." He, as well as other critics of the new Act, feared the President no longer would be able to respond effectively to a foreign "crisis" that called for strong military action. However, supporters of the Act replied that many previous crises—such as the Cuban missile threat in 1962—ended well under ninety days. And, in an age of possible nuclear attack, all too much decisiveness by a President can occur within ninety minutes, let alone ninety days. For these reasons, ironically, several members of Congress, including Rep. Ronald Dellums and Senator Thomas Eagleton, also opposed the Act, fearing it would only give the President virtually a free hand to undertake military adventures for ninety days without congressional approval—a fear borne out when Cambodian gunboats seized the freighter *Mayaguez* in 1975. Not until Ford had already ordered marines to rescue the ship's crew did he notify congressional leaders of his action; and for this he encountered little criticism from the leaders. More will be said about the President's military powers toward the end of the chapter.

The Judicial Side

Finally, although the Constitution assigns "the judicial power of the United States" to the courts, the President (as a check on the judicial branch) also undertakes certain judicial tasks. For one thing, he may overturn a court ruling by pardoning a person convicted of a federal (but not a state) crime. He may also reduce a sentence by granting a commutation, or temporarily delay punishment by granting a reprieve. In rare instances, he may even pardon an entire group (in the form of an amnesty) as Nixon and Ford were pressured to do for Vietnam War resisters and as Andrew Johnson did for Confederate soldiers after the Civil War. In no event can either Congress or the courts overturn his decision.

A pardon may, of course, stir considerable public controversy, as when President Ford stunned the nation in September 1974 by granting a "full, free and absolute" pardon to Richard Nixon. In an unprecedented display of presidential judicial prerogative, Ford pardoned his White House predecessor before any formal charges could be levied. The pardon covered not only Watergate-related activities but all other federal crimes Nixon might have committed as President. Although Ford regarded the pardon as an act of mercy in view of Nixon's deteriorated health, others felt it was premature and violated the principle of equal justice.

In addition to the pardoning power, a President has the judicial authority to fill all vacancies on the federal courts, including the Supreme Court. The power to appoint Supreme Court Justices—which, as we will see in Chapter Eight, is largely based on partisan considerations—remains one of the President's most sweeping powers. Since Supreme Court Justices are appointed for life, their selection can influence the course of national policy long after a President has left office. William O. Douglas, for example, one of the most powerful forces on the Court in the 1970s, was appointed by Franklin Roosevelt in 1939.

This important power is restricted by the fact that only a few vacancies on the Court may occur during a President's term. On the average, each President has been able to select only two Supreme Court Justices, although Nixon during his five-and-a-half-year term appointed four. Moreover, the President's power to appoint Supreme Court Justices is limited constitutionally by the fact that a majority of the Senate must confirm his choices. Although the Senate has ratified most appointments to the Court, it nevertheless has turned down 28 of the 130 Supreme Court nominations made in history. In recent years, for example, the Senate not only failed to act on Lyndon Johnson's nominations of Abe Fortas as Chief Justice and Homer Thornberry as Associate Justice in 1968; it also tossed out Richard Nixon's nominations of Clement Haynesworth in 1969 and G. Harold Carswell in 1970—a spectacular four rebuffs in a three-year period.

In Payment for Services

Confirming the special place of the Presidency in American politics, a variety of special compensations and benefits have been bestowed on the incumbent. In addition to being served by a large personal staff, the President enjoys a salary of $200,000 a year (taxable), plus an annual expense allowance of $50,000. For his personal comfort and convenience he has at his disposal a ninety-two-foot yacht, a fleet of Boeing 707 jets ("Air Force One"), helicopters, a staff of gourmet cooks and chefs, a butler, and even a White House projection room for private showings of first-run films. It has been estimated that an ordinary citizen would require an annual income of more than $50 million to live in the style of an American President.

When a President leaves office, he receives a lifetime annual pension of $60,000, free office space, up to $96,000 a year for staff assistance, and continued protection by the Secret Service. He receives these compensations, incidentally, even if he resigns. Even though Richard Nixon abdicated following accusations of illegal activities, he was still granted a pension and allowances for his years of White House service. He would not have received these benefits, however, if he had been forcibly removed from office through impeachment.

Some wonder whether all the perquisites of the office—especially the doting assistants and "yes men" who inevitably come with the job—do not eventually take their toll, sheltering a President from "the real universe of living." As George Reedy, former Special Assistant to President Lyndon Johnson, observed during his tenure at the White House, "A President moves through his days surrounded by literally hundreds of people whose relationship

Cornell Capa, Magnum Photos

to him is that of a doting mother to a spoiled child. Whatever he wants is brought to him immediately—food, drink, helicopters, airplanes, people, everything but relief from the political problems." In fact, Reedy hypothesized, perhaps "the burdens would be lighter, the urban poor would be better served . . . if Presidents had to face the same minor social penalties that the rest of us do. An occasional 'go soak your head' or 'that's stupid' would clear the murky, turgid atmosphere of the White House and let in some health-giving fresh air."[16]*Naturally, the degree to which a President remains insulated in the office and allows the pomp and ceremony to go to his head depends a great deal on the individual. As we have noted, each President responds differently to the office, depending on his motivations and style. Some find comfort in the fact that Harry Truman, on leaving the White House, paid for his own train ticket back to Independence. And when he arrived, people back home found him, as Bernard Berenson put it, "as natural, as unspoiled by high office as if he had risen no further than alderman of Independence, Missouri."[17]

Recruitment to the Presidency

Most Americans, it is true, will never discover what sort of President they would become. Most do not have enough money for an extensive campaign, cannot claim the required past service in a high political office like U.S. Senator, and cannot muster the ambition or make the personal sacrifices to be a full-time, back-slapping politician.

The legal qualifications for the job are actually not very restrictive. One only has to be at least thirty-five years old, native-born, and a resident of the United States for at least fourteen years. However, as a result of tradition and social prejudices, the Presidency has been occupied primarily by white, well-to-do men. So far, out of the thirty-eight Presidents in our history, none has been a woman or a member of a racial minority. In fact, prior to the election of John Kennedy in 1960, many even assumed only Protestants could be seriously considered for the job.

There are at least some signs this situation may change. As Table 6-3 shows, the number of Americans saying they would vote for

Table 6-3. Vote for a Woman for President? (34-year trend)

	Yes	No	No Opinion
Latest	66%	29%	5%
1969	54	39	7
1967	57	39	4
1955	52	44	4
1949	48	48	4
1937	31	65	4

Source: *Gallup Opinion Index*, August 1971.

a woman for President has climbed noticeably during the past several decades—a period that has witnessed intensified efforts by women to gain increased rights. In a 1971 poll, persons of each sex held comparable views, with an average of 66 percent saying they would vote for a woman for President.

Public support for a nonwhite candidate for President also appears to be increasing. For example, as Table 6-4 indicates, a majority of Americans in 1971 said they would vote for a black candidate for President.

It should be noted, however, that about one of every four persons surveyed still refused to support qualified candidates solely on the basis of their sex or race. Moreover, even the positive

Table 6-4. Vote for a Black Candidate for President?

	Yes	No	No Opinion
1971	69%	23%	8%
1969	67	23	10
1967	54	40	6
1965	59	34	7
1963	47	45	8
1958	38	53	9

Source: *Gallup Opinion Index*, November 1971.

responses among the majority in the surveys may have reflected largely what the respondents considered socially acceptable views. Still, if we take the responses at face value, the fact that support for female and for black candidates has increased at all may signal an eventual change in presidential politics. We may expect at the very least that someday the pronoun "he" will not be the exclusive referent to the President.

"All the President's Men"

In any examination of presidential powers and responsibilities, it is hardly sufficient to consider only the activities of the President. Each President is surrounded by counselors and assistants who either help or hinder him in the performance of his duties. Although the variety of posts held by these men and women is practically endless, two basic groups stand out in recognition and importance: the Cabinet and the "inner circle" of the White House staff. Let us consider each in turn.

The Cabinet

Many people may not realize that the presidential Cabinet stems, not from the Constitution, but from a politically expedient tradition honored by successive Presidents. Although the Constitution calls for the appointment of a "principal officer in each of the Executive Departments," each President so far has decided to form a Cabinet to help him administer the executive branch. The Cabinet usually consists of the heads (or Secretaries) of the eleven Executive Departments (see Table 6-5), who are appointed by the President with the consent of the Senate. Their ostensible duties are to supervise the work of their departments and to serve as advisors to the President.

Table 6-5. The President's Cabinet

Department	Date Established	Major Responsibilities
State	1789	Advises President on foreign policy; negotiates treaties; oversees foreign aid programs
Treasury	1789	Enforces federal revenue laws, coins money, and collects taxes
Interior	1849	Oversees nation's park services, natural resources, and Indian reservations
Agriculture	1862	Supports farm productivity research; administers crop surplus subsidies
Justice	1870	Enforces federal laws; represents federal government in legal matters
Commerce	1903	Promotes U.S. exports; administers Census Bureau and Patent Office
Labor	1913	Enforces minimum wage laws and labor safety regulations; oversees pension program services; decides wage disputes
Defense (Replaced the War Department)	1947	Maintains and directs U.S. military forces; awards defense contracts
Health, Education, and Welfare	1953	Administers pure food and drug laws, federal aid to education, and Social Security program
Housing and Urban Development	1965	Coordinates urban renewal; provides public housing assistance
Transportation	1966	Oversees federal highway and mass transit programs; enforces automotive and air safety standards

However, unlike the British Cabinet, in which elected members of Parliament share responsibility with the Prime Minister for policy direction, members of the American Cabinet often remain on the fringes of presidential decision making. The Cabinet in this country rarely has had the influence commanded by its counterparts in Britain and most other parliamentary systems. Although Cabinet members do enjoy considerable public prestige and a high salary ($60,000 a year), their powers and duties ultimately bear the personal imprint of the President they serve. Indeed, most Presidents tend to use their Cabinets and individual Secretaries as they see fit. Whereas Dwight Eisenhower, for example, met frequently with his Cabinet members for their collective advice, Richard Nixon made little use of his Cabinet as a consultative body, preferring instead to see one Secretary at a time or to ignore their advice almost completely. In fact, Nixon frequently was chided for being too isolated from his Cabinet officers—a criticism voiced publicly in 1970 by his Interior Secretary, Walter Hickel, who was subsequently dismissed.

For the most part, each President selects Cabinet members who share his political philosophy or who may help accommodate some interest group or faction of the party. As ruling-elite theorists point out, Cabinet officers frequently are brought in from private industry and finance, resulting in some overlapping of interests between the White House and economic elites. A President, for varying political reasons, may even snatch someone from the opposition party, as when Richard Nixon picked southern Democrat (and later Republican) John Connally in 1971 to head the Treasury Department. And, although most Cabinet members are chosen for their expertise, some are selected who have little or no experience in the subject area of the department they head. Such was the case when President Kennedy selected Robert McNamara (former head of the Ford Motor Company) as Secretary of Defense, and when President Nixon appointed Connally (former Governor of Texas) as Secretary of the Treasury.

It should be understood that even though Cabinet Secretaries are ultimately dependent on the President, they must also be responsive to Congress. Because their departments are funded by Congress, they may find themselves caught in the middle between congressional and presidential demands—an often tight and uncomfortable position.[18]

The White House Staff

While most Presidents do not rely heavily on their Cabinet for daily advice and policy orientation, they do lean on a cadre of special assistants in the White House Office. This "inner circle" of aides are not subject to Senate confirmation and are selected primarily for their expertise and/or personal loyalties. Drawn from industry, universities, the news media, or law firms, these top aides populate offices in the West Wing of the White House close to the President.

Each President molds this White House staff according to his own style, assigning titles and duties to suit his needs. Some assistants may serve as his links with Congress or the executive agencies. Others may smooth his relationships with the press or handle his appointments. Still others may advise him on foreign policy, provide legal counsel, or help draft his speeches. A President may assign the same individual a variety of tasks, switching him from assignment to assignment, and then dumping him when he no longer proves useful.

Because of their proximity to the President, White House aides can command considerable power. Ordinary citizens and governmental officials alike who have tried to gain access to a President have at times found themselves unable to vault over a wall of White House aides insensitive to their desires. This was especially true during the Nixon reign when chief of staff H. R. Haldeman and presidential counsel John Ehrlichman virtually dominated the executive branch. "By Nixon's time," Arthur Schlesinger reflected, "White House aides were no longer channels of communication. They were powerful figures in themselves, making decisions and issuing instructions in their own right, more powerful than members of the Cabinet—Kissinger more powerful than the Secretary of State or Defense, Haldeman and Ehrlichman more power-ful than the forgotten men who headed the domestic departments. But they were not, like members of the Cabinet, subject to confir-mation by the Senate or (pre-Watergate) to interrogation by com-mittees of Congress."[19] Until the Watergate scandal removed him from office, White House chief of staff H. R. Haldeman was espe-cially influential, deciding who would have access to President Nixon and who would not. Some observers described him as Nixon's personal "gatekeeper," as the man even the Washington power elite had to court and favor. Whenever a Senator or member of the Cabinet tried to telephone the President for a consultation, his call usually went first to Haldeman. Or, whenever an official wished to see the President personally, it was Haldeman who decided whether he would be admitted. "Rather than the President telling someone to do something," Haldeman said, "I'll tell the guy. If he wants to find out something from somebody, I'll do it."[20]

At least two clear dangers may arise from presidential use of staff. One is that a President may become too insulated in the White House, shielded by overzealous aides from outside citizen influ-ence and alternative information sources. Obviously, the way a President makes policy decisions is of great importance to us all. Generally, the first thing a President must do is demand up-to-date information. This information then has to be collected, analyzed, and boiled down by White House aides, in order to present mean-ingful options for the Chief Executive to consider. After the alter-natives are discussed in meetings with Cabinet members and staff, he may go into seclusion (as Nixon usually did) to make his deci-sions. Only later may a President discover that he received one-sided information or was shielded from the advice of people he should have seen. Of course, most Presidents, by selecting assis-tants who share their philosophy and prejudices, encourage this one-sidedness. They set the tone of the White House by choosing aides who are most like themselves.

Moreover, the personal ambitions of the aides themselves con-tribute to this one-sidedness of information. As assistants to a President, they exercise a degree of political influence few other Americans can experience, and are under great pressure to remain in the Chief Executive's good graces. As Philippa Strum has ob-served, "The Presidency is the supreme prize offered in American political life, but very few men can become President. For those to whom the White House is the symbol of the ultimate goal, the next best thing to the Presidency itself is the role of presiden-tial adviser. Those playing the role must suffer from the omnipresent, albeit subconscious knowledge that the fall from grace will be a very long and humiliating one. Under the circumstances, one can hardly expect the majority of advisers to escape the trap of yes-men."[21]

The other danger is that a President may delegate too much responsibility to his aides. Assistants anxious to please their boss may take on his behalf, independent actions that go well beyond the confines of the law. Although Nixon promised in 1968 to select "men who will command the public's respect," and who "will not have to check their conscience at the door," the actions of the staff he picked heaped further disaster on his Presidency. The Senate Watergate hearings in the summer of 1973 revealed that top Nixon aides had employed the White House Office—apparently with Nixon's encouragement—as a private instrument to intimidate political opponents and carry out assorted forms of espionage. While presidential counsel John Ehrlichman promoted the investigation of opponents' drinking and sexual habits, counsel Charles Colson helped draft an "enemies list" of White House adversaries, ranging from Senator Edward Kennedy and Rep. Bella Abzug to football star Joe Namath and actor Paul Newman.

Revelation of such acts prompted at least one former Kennedy aide to contrast White House styles and to insist that many who have served as presidential assistants have regarded the White House Office as a source of great pride and stimulation. "An appointment to the White House of Roosevelt or Truman or Eisenhower or Kennedy or Johnson," noted historian Arthur Schlesinger, Jr., with perhaps considerable exaggeration, "seemed the highest responsibility one could expect and called for the highest standards of behavior. And most of us looked back at our White House experience, not with shame and incredulity, as the Nixon young men did, not as the 'White House horrors,' but as the most splendid time in one's life."[22]

If any figure in the Nixon administration did shine in the public eye—albeit with controversy—it was Henry Kissinger. A political scientist drawn from Harvard University in 1969, he served first as the top White House advisor on foreign affairs and later as Secretary of State for both Nixon and Ford. Throughout the history of political thought, philosophers such as Plato and Machiavelli have regretted the separation of the political thinker from the world of political action. They often felt frustrated having to examine and construct political theories without being able to translate their ideas into concrete policies. Yet, like many presidential aides before him, Kissinger was able by virtue of his proximity to the President to transcend the ivory tower of academe and help shape the structure of international relations. Perhaps only President Woodrow Wilson, also a former political scientist, was in a better position to leap from the realm of study and contemplation into the arena of political action.[23]

The Vice-Presidency: "The Hollow Shell"

While the Presidency has evolved into one of the most powerful offices in the world, the Vice-Presidency has remained merely a "hollow shell of an office." Some of the Founding Fathers even doubted the need for a Vice-President. In fact, several Vice-Presidents have felt that the office has been only a failure and humiliation. John Adams, the first person to hold the job, lamented that "my country has in its wisdom contrived for me the most insignificant office that ever the invention of man contrived or his imagination conceived." John Nance Garner, Vice-President under Franklin Roosevelt, went even further, contending that "the Vice-Presidency isn't worth a pitcher of warm spit." Indeed, although most of us probably can name or recognize all previous Presidents, how many are familiar with former Vice-Presidents? Consider some of the Vice-Presidents who have been lost to history:

George Clinton (1805–1812)	Henry Wilson (1873–1875)
Elbridge Gerry (1813–1814)	William A. Wheeler (1877–1881)
Daniel D. Tompkins (1817–1825)	Thomas A. Hendricks (1885)
Richard M. Johnson (1837–1841)	Levi P. Morton (1889–1893)
George M. Dallas (1845–1849)	Garret A. Hobart (1897–1899)
William R. King (1853)	Charles W. Fairbanks (1905–1909)
John C. Breckinridge (1857–1861)	James S. Sherman (1909–1912)
Hannibal Hamlin (1861–1865)	Thomas R. Marshall (1913–1921)
Schuyler Colfax (1869–1873)	Charles G. Dawes (1925–1929)

The Vice-President actually draws only three clear duties from the Constitution: (1) to serve as the constitutional heir to the President; (2) to preside over the Senate; and (3) to exercise a Senate vote in case of a tie. As a measure of the insignificance of the last two tasks, former Vice-President Spiro Agnew, during the first half of the 1973 session in the Senate, presided for only 2½ hours out of the 667 hours the Senate had been sitting.[24] During the rest of the time, either the Senate Pro Tempore or a junior Senator wielded the Senate gavel. And, during his entire term as Vice-President, Spiro Agnew cast a deciding vote in the Senate only once: to break a tie in favor of the Alaskan pipeline amendment in July 1973.

Most contemporary Vice-Presidents are, of course, also assigned other duties by the President. They serve on the National Security Council, attend Cabinet meetings, travel abroad as the President's personal ambassador, and make public speeches that, for varying reasons, the President does not wish to make. But because these duties are at the President's request, they do not provide an independent power base for a Vice-President. In other words, a Vice-President's powers generally are what the President chooses to make them.

If the Vice-Presidency seems to be such an insignificant office, why then would any prominent politician want the job? One reason perhaps, apart from the $62,500 salary and fringe benefits, is that it may offer a convenient springboard to the Presidency. Although few Vice-Presidents have advanced to the White House by their own efforts, a number have eventually succeeded to the office in this manner—including John Adams, Thomas Jefferson, Martin Van Buren, and Richard Nixon. Moreover, eight Vice-Presidents have been thrust into the Presidency as a result of the death of the incumbent, and one (Gerald Ford) succeeded as a result of his predecessor's resignation. In all, thirteen out of the forty-one Vice-Presidents in our history—almost one third—eventually became President.

In view of these statistics, we might expect the selection of a Vice-President to be a careful process, aimed at choosing a person with great leadership capabilities. Yet the choice of Vice-President, Theodore White observes, "is the most perfunctory and generally the most thoughtless in the entire American political system."[25] Traditionally, the Vice-President is chosen by the presidential nominee in the closing hours of the national convention, with an eye to "balancing the ticket," adding regional and ideological symmetry to the campaign. John Kennedy, for example, chose Lyndon Johnson as his running mate in 1960 not solely for Johnson's loyalties and abilities but to get him out of the Senate and to strengthen the ticket's appeal in southern states. Similarly, Richard Nixon picked Spiro Agnew in 1968 not because of his character alone but to augment his appeal among conservative voters.

To many critics, this method of hurriedly picking a Vice-President, and for political expediency, is a mistake—a mistake

Table 6-6. Vacancies in the Vice-Presidency

Vice-President	Term Elected	Date of Vacancy	Reason	President
George Clinton (R)	1809–1813	4/20/1812	Death	James Madison
Elbridge Gerry (R)	1813–1817	11/23/1814	Death	James Madison
John C. Calhoun (D)	1829–1833	12/28/1832	Resignation	Andrew Jackson
John Tyler (Whig)	1841–1845	4/ 6/1841	Succeeded to presidency on death of President Harrison	William Henry Harrison
Millard Fillmore (Whig)	1849–1853	7/10/1850	Succeeded to presidency on death of President Taylor	Zachary Taylor
William King (D)	1853–1857	4/18/1853	Death	Franklin Pierce
Andrew Johnson (R)	1865–1869	4/15/1865	Succeeded to presidency following assassination of President Lincoln	Abraham Lincoln
Henry Wilson (R)	1873–1877	11/22/1875	Death	Ulysses S. Grant
Chester A. Arthur (R)	1881–1885	9/20/1881	Succeeded to presidency following assassination of President Garfield	James A. Garfield
Thomas Hendricks (D)	1885–1889	11/25/1885	Death	Grover Cleveland
Garrett A. Hobart (R)	1897–1901	11/21/1899	Death	William McKinley
Theodore Roosevelt (R)	1901–1905	9/14/1901	Succeeded to presidency following assassination of President McKinley	William McKinley
James S. Sherman (R)	1909–1913	10/30/1912	Death	William Howard Taft
Calvin Coolidge (R)	1921–1925	8/ 3/1923	Succeeded to presidency on death of President Harding	Warren G. Harding
Harry S. Truman (D)	1945–1949	4/12/1945	Succeeded to presidency on death of President Roosevelt	Franklin D. Roosevelt
Lyndon B. Johnson (D)	1961–1965	11/22/1963	Succeeded to presidency following assassination of President Kennedy	John F. Kennedy

Source: *Congressional Quarterly Weekly Report,* 22 September 1973.

made clear by the disastrous impact of Thomas Eagleton's selection on George McGovern's candidacy in 1972 and by Spiro Agnew's indictment and resignation in 1973. Indeed, Spiro Agnew will probably be saved from the obscurity of most Vice-Presidents. In October 1973, he became the second Vice-President in the history of the United States to resign, and the only one to do so after pleading "no contest" to a charge of federal income tax evasion. (John C. Calhoun also resigned the office, in 1832, to become a U.S. Senator.) Although Agnew denied other charges of wrongdoing, many suspected that he stepped down after the Justice Department agreed to drop charges of bribery, extortion, and conspiracy detailed in a forty-page document released through the federal court in Baltimore. Interestingly enough, a 1973 Gallup poll found that 42 percent of the American public thought the punishment handed Agnew (a $10,000 fine and three year's probation) was "too lenient," as compared with 38 percent who thought it was "fair," 12 percent who felt he should have gone to prison, and only 6 percent who thought the punishment was harsh.

Although no way exists to prevent any vice-presidential choice from turning into a disaster, pressure has been mounting for a change in the selection process. Politicians and voters alike have become increasingly insistent that each party offer greater assurance that it is presenting the person most qualified for the job. Consequently, in addition to the suggestion that the Vice-Presidency simply be abolished,[26] at least two major reform proposals have been discussed. One is to force individual presidential and vice-presidential candidates to pair up for the primary races. The other is to have a separate primary for all those campaigning solely for the Vice-Presidency. In each case, vice-presidential candidates would be exposed to the voters during the long ordeal of the primaries, offering the voters a chance to decide for themselves who would be best suited for the job.

One significant aftereffect of Agnew's resignation, of course, was to permit Richard Nixon to become the first American President to select a new Vice-President (Gerald Ford) during his administration. Before the ratification of the Twenty-fifth Amendment in 1967, there was no provision for filling the Vice-Presidency between elections if the office became vacant. Even though few people may have noticed, the United States prior to Agnew's resignation had been without a Vice-President sixteen times, for a total of more than forty years. (See Table 6-6.)

The Twenty-fifth Amendment stipulates that whenever a vacancy occurs in the Vice-Presidency, the President is to nominate a new Vice-President "who shall take office upon confirmation by a majority vote of both houses of Congress." It was through this amendment that Ford ascended to the office in late 1973 and was followed a year later by Nelson Rockefeller after Ford succeeded to the White House. This rapid succession of incumbents resulted in the country's having for the first time in history both a President and Vice-President who had not been elected at the polls. The new amendment also provides that the Vice-President shall become "Active President" either if the President informs Congress he is unable to perform his duties or if the Vice-President and a majority of the Cabinet declare the Chief Executive incapacitated—a provision that obviously carries some interesting implications. However, if the President should disagree with the prognosis of the Vice-President and Cabinet, then Congress must decide the matter within twenty-one days. If Congress should declare, by a two-thirds vote of both houses, that the President is indeed incapacitated, then the Vice-President continues to serve as acting

President; otherwise, the President resumes the powers and duties of the office.

Evaluation: The Imperial Presidency?

Having begun this chapter with a discussion of presidential character and the possibility of failing or succeeding in the White House, it seems fitting to conclude with a brief analysis of presidential power. Clearly, the desire of a President to get the most out of his opportunity to command power at the "highest political level" must be sufficiently restrained to protect the freedom and well-being of other citizens. The Watergate scandal and Vietnam War have forced many Americans to worry seriously about the misuse of presidential power, and to wonder how to resolve the conflict between the need for a strong Chief Executive and the potential for abuse of the executive office. Although each President brings his own personality and ambitions to bear on the White House, there is concern that the office has been entrusted with so much power that, in the hands of the wrong individual, the power will be misused.

This concern is, of course, hardly new. The framers of the Constitution in the late eighteenth century not only expressed similarly divided feelings about executive power but were deeply worried about its potential misuse. In fact, part of the reason the Constitution is so vague about the duties of the President is that the framers disagreed over how much responsibility to assign the office. On the one hand, they were convinced of the shortcomings of purely "legislative government" and believed the United States required a reasonably strong, independent executive. As Thomas Jefferson warned, "The tyranny of the legislature is really the danger most to be feared, and will continue to be so for many years to come." As a result, they provided for a President who was chosen separately from Congress, who originally could be elected for any number of terms, and who could veto all bills passed by Congress.

Yet, at the same time, the framers were afraid of the potential danger posed by too strong an executive. Following their pre-Revolutionary experience with the British King George III, they were careful to restrict the President's powers through a complex system of checks and balances: his appointments and treaties had to be approved by the Senate, his vetoes could be overridden by a two-thirds vote in Congress, and he could be impeached by the House and removed by the Senate.

But even though the framers expressed divided feelings about executive power—and wrote them into the Constitution—the historical tendency has been for the powers of the Presidency to expand. Despite the framers' expectation, for example, that Congress would be responsible for initiating new laws, all modern Presidents have introduced major legislative proposals. Moreover, despite the framers' intention to give only Congress the constitutional authority to declare war, more military actions—such as in Korea and Vietnam—have been initiated by presidential decree than by congressional declaration of war.

This expansion of presidential power has stemmed largely from the actions of forceful and ambitious Presidents, such as Lincoln, Wilson, and Franklin Roosevelt, who refused to accept limited roles for their Presidencies. Faced with new crises and challenging social demands, they extended the duties of their office and used its resources to accomplish goals they believed in. And they succeeded in getting away with it because a change in the times—a civil war, an industrial revolution, a world war, or a depression—called for strong actions.

Other factors also have been important. For example, members of Congress have contributed to an increase in presidential power by abdicating many of their responsibilities. As a result of a decentralized party system and Congress's own cumbersome procedures, Senators and Representatives alike have been either unwilling or unable to respond to new social and economic crises. Instead of setting their own agenda, they have been satisfied to let more of the major decisions pass to the White House.

In fact, the evolution of American society itself has augmented presidential responsibility in decision making. In foreign policy, for example, many Americans have come to support the idea that the President, and not Congress, should dominate military and foreign policy. With the coming of the nuclear age, many feel that only the President can respond to emergencies with appropriate speed and decisiveness, as John Kennedy did during the 1962 Cuban missile crisis. Similarly, in domestic policy many have come to expect the President, not Congress, to meet the problems of poor housing, crime, poverty, and discrimination. As the United States has grown in population (from 3 million people to more than 210 million) and has become plagued with all the social ills of an urban and industrial society, the President's responsibilities as Chief Executive have increased. Although Congress has continued to pass the laws and control the budget, the President has been expected to carry the major responsibility for implementing large-scale social programs.

Even the advent of radio and television probably has helped magnify the Presidency's importance. In contrast to the 535 members of Congress, the President is a single individual whose activities are constantly under the watch of the news media and the subject of public gossip. And, although most Presidents have criticized the media, each has used the media to his own advantage, relying on free air time—such as that provided for press conferences and television addresses—to reach the public over the heads of critics.

But, whatever may have contributed to the expansion of presidential power during the past two centuries, the debate concerning its consequences is unlikely to subside. Indeed, no issue in American politics is less likely to fade away than whether presidential power is too extensive and dangerous. On the one hand, some political observers—notably the pluralists discussed in Chapter Two—insist that the powers of the Presidency are not too extensive and that recent congressional actions, such as the impeachment hearings and the passage of the 1972 War Powers Act, show the resilient strength of the legislative branch.

In fact, they argue, presidential "power" is difficult to measure; how one views it depends on the policy area with which a President deals. Although recent Presidents have been more than a match for Congress in foreign affairs, they have been greatly constrained by Congress, the federal bureaucracy, and other forces in domestic affairs. Although President Kennedy, for example, achieved some notable successes with his major foreign policies (such as the Peace Corps and the Nuclear Test Ban Treaty), he was unable to persuade Congress to enact most of his "New Frontier" domestic policies (such as health insurance and civil rights legislation).

Anyway, pluralists argue, if presidential power should be limited, who could then take the initiative? Could Congress, with its 535 diverse personalities and cumbersome structure of committees and rules, possibly fill the vacuum? Certainly, any decision to alter the present balance of power between the White House and Congress would require major changes in Congress to make it more responsive to the times, to make it capable of exerting policy leadership. Until that time, they insist, only the President, with all the advice and assistance of the executive branch at his command, can provide adequate leadership.

Such a view of presidential power, however, does not soothe

those who fear that strong presidential leadership can serve evil as well as good ends. Many critics—notably the advocates of the ruling-elite theory—point out that presidential power in recent years has exceeded constitutional limits and has often been exercised to the detriment of the nation as a whole. This criticism has been echoed by scholars and members of Congress who insist that both Lyndon Johnson and Richard Nixon pushed the nation too close to a one-branch government. The House Judiciary Committee's impeachment inquiry, for example, pointed out that Nixon not only illegally impounded funds appropriated by Congress; he also withheld important information from the courts pertaining to criminal activities, directed the surreptitious surveillance of private citizens, and ordered an invasion of Cambodia without consulting Congress. (See Chapter Seven.) "The first concern," Arthur Schlesinger, Jr., wrote recently, "is that the pivotal institution of American government, the Presidency, has got out of control and badly needs new definition and restraint. . . . Unless the American democracy figures out how to control the Presidency in war and peace without enfeebling the Presidency across the board, then our system of government will face grave troubles." [27]

It may be remembered that only a few years ago many of these same critics of presidential power, focusing primarily on domestic affairs, fostered an almost uncritical cult of a strong Chief Executive. Such well-known scholars as Arthur Schlesinger, Jr., George Kennan, and Richard Neustadt championed strong-willed Presidents like John Kennedy and Lyndon Johnson (in his early years) who tried to use their office to solve such domestic problems as racial discrimination and poverty. They were critical of the fact that both Presidents were hampered in their efforts by a coalition of conservative Congress members loyal to the status quo.

Yet, following Vietnam and Watergate, many of these same scholars have joined the chorus denouncing the burgeoning of executive power—the "runaway Presidency," as Arthur Schlesinger has dubbed it. While still believing in the need for strong executive leadership in domestic policy, they lament the ever-expanding powers of the Presidency in foreign and military policy. Despite the long tradition of presidential control over military affairs, they insist that Lyndon Johnson and Richard Nixon went far beyond the limits of their predecessors in exercising military authority. "Only Presidents Johnson and Nixon," Schlesinger contends, "have made the claim that inherent Presidential authority, unaccompanied by emergencies threatening the life of the nation, unaccompanied by the authorization of Congress or of an international organization, permits a President to order troops into combat at his unilateral pleasure."[28]

Nor has the recent War Powers Act removed all the fears. In the first test of the Act—the 1975 *Mayaguez* incident—President Ford reestablished presidential authority to order military forces into play with hardly any consultation with Congress. In fact, many still regard the President's military authority as too dangerous, especially given the present technology of nuclear weapons. Indeed, the structure of power in the United States has become a true paradox in the twentieth century. "We have given power to the President," historian James MacGregor Burns has commented, "precisely in the area where his rash action might be uncheckable and irreversible—that is, in foreign and military policy—and we carefully fence him in, in those areas where Presidential errors could be limited and reversed—notably in domestic fiscal policy."[29]

Thus, a number of alternatives have been explored to shield the nation from future abuses of presidential power while simultaneously maintaining the President's leadership in foreign affairs. For example, since the President's assistants and Cabinet officers may be far too biased or under a President's spell to weigh properly alternative foreign and military options, it has been suggested that key members of Congress be brought into all deliberations. In the opinion of historian Henry Steele Commager, this could be accomplished by formally establishing a congressional committee composed of members of both parties, with whom the President must consult on all major military and foreign policy decisions. Such a committee would grant citizens an added voice in these vital areas and might even prevent a hasty decision by an overzealous President or aide. While such a committee might be useless in true emergencies—such as threat of invasion—such emergencies have been rare anyway. As Commager concluded, "With the exception of the Civil War . . . there are no instances in our history where the use of war-making powers by the Executive without authority of Congress was clearly and incontrovertibly required by the nature of the emergency that the nation faced. On the contrary, in almost every instance the long-run interests of the nation would have been better promoted by consultation and delay."[30]

This assumes, of course, that Congress has the will and capacity to play a more significant role in policy making—an assumption, as we will see in the next chapter, not all observers share.

Recommended Reading

Barber, James David. *The Presidential Character: Predicting Performance in the White House.* Englewood Cliffs, N.J.: Prentice-Hall, 1972.

Cronin, Thomas E., and Greenberg, Sanford D., eds. *The Presidential Advisory System.* New York: Harper & Row, 1969.

Egger, Rowland. *The President of the United States,* 2d ed. New York: McGraw-Hill, 1972.

Johnson, Lyndon B. *The Vantage Point: Perspectives of the Presidency.* New York: Holt, Rinehart and Winston, 1971.

Koenig, Louis W. *The Chief Executive,* rev. ed. New York: Harcourt Brace Jovanovich, 1968.

Miller, Merle. *Plain Speaking: An Oral Biography of Harry S. Truman.* New York: Berkley Publishing Co., 1974.

Neustadt, Richard E. *Presidential Power.* New York: Wiley, 1960.

Reedy, George E. *The Twilight of the Presidency.* New York: New American Library, 1970.

Rossiter, Clinton. *The American Presidency,* rev. ed. New York: Harcourt Brace Jovanovich, 1960.

Schlesinger, Arthur M., Jr. *The Imperial Presidency.* Boston: Houghton Mifflin, 1973.

Staff of *The Washington Post. The Fall of a President.* New York: Dell, 1973.

Strum, Philippa. *Presidential Power and American Democracy.* Pacific Palisades, Cal.: Goodyear, 1972.

Young, Donald. *American Roulette: The History and Dilemma of the Vice-Presidency.* New York: Holt, Rinehart and Winston, 1965.

Notes

1. Quoted in *A Thousand Days* by Arthur M. Schlesinger, Jr., p. 120. Copyright © 1965 by Arthur M. Schlesinger, Jr. Reprinted by permission of Houghton Mifflin Company.

2. U.S. Senate, Committee on Government Operations, "Confidence and Concern: Citizens View American Government, A Survey of Public Attitudes," pt. 1 (Washington, D.C.: U.S. Government Printing Office, 1973).

3. George Will, *Washington Post*, December 1974.

4. James David Barber, *The Presidential Character: Predicting Performance in the White House* (Englewood Cliffs, N.J.: Prentice-Hall, 1972).

5. Clinton Rossiter, *The American Presidency*, rev. ed. (New York: Harcourt Brace Jovanovich, 1960), p. 57.

6. Chester Bowles, quoted in *A Thousand Days* by Arthur M. Schlesinger, Jr., p. 683. Copyright © 1965 by Arthur M. Schlesinger, Jr. Reprinted by permission of Houghton Mifflin Company.

7. Clinton Rossiter, *The American Presidency*, rev. ed. (New York: Harcourt Brace Jovanovich, 1960), p. 55.

8. Quoted in James David Barber, *The Presidential Character: Predicting Performance in the White House* (Englewood Cliffs, N.J.: Prentice-Hall, 1972), p. 276.

9. Richard E. Neustadt, *Presidential Power* (New York: Wiley, 1960), p. 34.

10. Quoted in Merle Miller, *Plain Speaking: An Oral Biography of Harry S. Truman* (New York: Berkley Publishing Co., 1974), p. 10. Used with permission of Berkley Publishing Corporation.

11. Richard E. Neustadt, *Presidential Power* (New York: Wiley, 1960), pp. 92–93.

12. Clinton Rossiter, *The American Presidency*, rev. ed. (New York: Harcourt Brace Jovanovich, 1960), p. 28.

13. *United States* v. *Curtiss-Wright Export Corp.* (1936).

14. Saul K. Padover, "The Powers of the President," *Commonweal*, 9 August 1968, p. 524.

15. Abraham Lincoln to W. H. Herndon, 15 February 1848.

16. From *The Twilight of the Presidency* by George E. Reedy, pp. 33–34. Copyright © 1970 by George E. Reedy. Reprinted by arrangement with The New American Library, Inc., New York, New York.

17. Quoted in Merle Miller, *Plain Speaking: An Oral Biography of Harry S. Truman* (New York: Berkley Publishing Co., 1974), p. 11. Used with permission of Berkley Publishing Corporation.

18. For more information, see Richard Fenno, *The President's Cabinet* (Cambridge, Mass.,: Harvard University Press, 1959).

19. *The Imperial Presidency* by Arthur M. Schlesinger, Jr., pp. 222–23. Copyright © 1973 by Arthur M. Schlesinger, Jr. Reprinted by permission of Houghton Mifflin Company.

20. *New York Daily News*, 14 September 1971.

21. Philippa Strum, *Presidential Power and American Democracy* (Pacific Palisades, Cal.: Goodyear, 1972), pp. 51–52.

22. *The Imperial Presidency* by Arthur M. Schlesinger, Jr., p. 381. Copyright © 1973 by Arthur M. Schlesinger, Jr. Reprinted by permission of Houghton Mifflin Company.

23. For additional information, see Thomas E. Cronin and Sanford D. Greenberg, eds., *The Presidential Advisory System* (New York: Harper & Row, 1969).

24. *Newsweek*, 27 August 1973, p. 11.

25. Theodore H. White, *The Making of the President 1972* (New York: Atheneum), p. 193. Copyright © 1973 by Theodore H. White.

26. See Arthur M. Schlesinger, Jr., "Is the Vice-Presidency Necessary?" *The Atlantic*, May 1974, pp. 37–44.

27. *The Imperial Presidency* by Arthur M. Schlesinger, Jr., p. x. Copyright © 1973 by Arthur M. Schlesinger, Jr. Reprinted by permission of Houghton Mifflin Company.

28. Arthur Schlesinger, Jr., "Presidential War: 'See if You Can Fix Any Limit to His Power,'" *New York Times Magazine*, 7 January 1973, p. 24.

29. James MacGregor Burns, "The Presidency at the Crossroads," in Hans J. Morgenthau, ed., *The Crossroads Papers: A Look into the American Future* (New York: W. W. Norton, 1965), p. 197.

30. Henry Steele Commager, "Misuse of Power," *The New Republic*, 17 April 1971, p. 20.

7 Into the Legislative Labyrinth

W_{hen} it comes to influencing policy, Senators and Representatives would seem to be in enviable positions. As members of Congress, they share a unique responsibility for enacting, or blocking, legislation affecting the health and well-being of millions of Americans. Indeed, to many who seek political power, Congress has the allure of an exciting arena in which bills, amendments, and appropriations are in a never-ending state of creation. The men and women in Congress are seen as active participants in a dynamic process in which they share a great opportunity to translate their dreams into political reality. Undoubtedly, it is this vision that compels many citizens to try to influence their Senator or Representative, to sway his or her vote on pending legislation.

A Sense of Impotency

Yet, in some ways, such a vision of creative potential is deceptive, obscuring both the difficulties Congress has experienced in serving as a productive law-making body and the obstacles many members have faced in trying to achieve even modest political goals. One finds, in fact, that how one views power in Congress depends greatly on which Senators and Representatives one chooses to examine. If one looks at those committee chairmen who serve as the spokesmen for wealthy and powerful interests—the oil companies, the banking lobby, or the military—then the opportunities for influence may seem boundless. But if one examines instead those members who come to Washington ostensibly to work on behalf of people without strong representation and leadership—such as the poor and elderly—then the chances of achieving meaningful goals in Congress may appear more remote. In other words, while some Representatives and Senators—notably those chairing important committees—often enjoy extensive power, such is not the case for most members of Congress. As newly elected members soon discover, Congress does not provide immediate gratification of the thirst for power or desire for reform that may have been the driving force behind their campaigns. "A new Congressman," Rep. Shirley Chisholm has written, "faces a lot of disappointments. One most freshman House members share is the discovery that, while getting elected made him a big man back home, Washington has seen green representatives arrive by the thousands and is not very impressed. Then, unless he has had legislative experience, he will be frustrated to learn that his plans for laws that will solve the problems of the country, whatever he deems them to be, are doomed because he is a very junior member of a rather large group."[1]

Nor are such frustrations confined to freshmen members. Even seasoned congressional veterans can find their efforts blocked. With committees that decentralize decision making, complex procedures, and the inordinate influence of special interests, Congress can be a source of irritation even to those familiar with its ways. Members seeking solutions to social problems complain time and again that Congress is a difficult place in which to assume a constructive role. Explaining why he chose to retire from the House in 1974 after serving fourteen years, one Representative snapped, "It's the system. I can't do anything unless I'm chairman of an important committee—and I could wait forever for that."[2]

Even Senators occasionally feel drowned. While they may have the advantage over House members of enjoying greater prestige, having a six-year rather than two-year term, and serving in a smaller body with less rigid rules and procedures, each remains only one voice among many. Even if a Senator wins the support on a bill of all 100 members of his own chamber, he still must contend with the 435 members of the House.

Also, members of Congress cannot count on basking in the warmth of public adulation once they have reached this lofty position. Based on past congressional failures, the attitude of citizens is often skeptical and cynical toward Congress members' claims of noble intentions. Indeed, Senators and Representatives would have to go to considerable lengths to restore public confidence in their law-making abilities. According to a June 1975 Gallup poll, only 38 percent of Americans interviewed said they approved of the way Congress has been handling its job, as compared with 48 percent who said they disapproved.

In fact, for years, Congress has been chided for lacking the will to confront social problems and for serving as an obstacle to reform. Generations of commentators, satirists, and cartoonists have decried what the nineteenth-century writer, Alexis de Tocqueville, once described as its "vulgarity and its poverty of talent." Even the venerable satirist Mark Twain had scathing things to say about Congress:

It could probably be shown by facts and figures that there is no distinctly native American criminal class except Congress.

I . . . was a reporter in a legislature two sessions and the same in Congress one session—and thus learned to know personally three sample-bodies of the smallest minds and the selfishest souls and the cowardliest hearts that God makes.

. . . those burglars that broke into my house recently . . . are in jail, and if they keep on they will go to Congress. When a person starts downhill you can never tell when he's going to stop.

While most Americans today may be amused by Mark Twain's iconoclastic views of Congress, many also harbor similarly negative feelings. They hear tales of Senators and Representatives accepting bribes for political favors, attending cocktail parties when they should be legislating, or traveling abroad on "pleasure junkets" at taxpayers' expense. But perhaps the most widespread feeling is that Congress remains unresponsive to people's needs. Crime still rages in the streets, prices continue to skyrocket, millions of elderly citizens go on living in run-down tenements—while members of Congress just coast along making promises that are rarely fulfilled.

Some reform-minded members were, of course, heartened by Congress's recent efforts to modernize its legislative machinery, as evidenced by the assaults on seniority as the traditional means of deciding committee assignments. With the possibility that a more democratic power structure was developing in Congress, hope was rekindled that Congress would respond more decisively to the nation's social and economic ills. Moreover, in the wake of Watergate, some members hoped Congress would permanently regain some of the powers lost or abandoned to the White House. Congress seemed to move in this direction when it placed new restrictions on the President's war powers and assumed greater control over federal spending. Some members hoped that the reassertion of congressional power might ultimately filter down to each Representative and Senator, giving each a greater role to play in policy making. However, whether such grand visions are ever realized will depend on how Congress handles its responsibilities in the years ahead.

To better understand the action potential of serving on Capitol Hill, we will examine some of the powers and responsibilities of Senators and Representatives. We will also look at the evolving power structure in Congress—especially how that structure may or may not be suitable to the goals of individual members. Obviously, those of us who desire to feed our own ideas into the legislative labyrinth also need to know what our Representative and Senator can, or cannot, do for us—what sort of obstacles we as citizens can expect to face.

The Tools of Congressional Influence

An incredible diversity of responsibilities and opportunities for influence remains the most striking feature of a congressional career. On any given day, a Senator or Representative may wield the crucial vote on a foreign policy bill, chair an important committee hearing on bureaucratic waste, help trim or fatten the federal budget, or sponsor legislation to protect consumer rights. Although it is in practice almost impossible to separate the powers and responsibilities of Congress members into tidy little segments, for the purpose of understanding the range and potential of a legislator's job we will look at how each of these powers and responsibilities may be exercised.

The Legislative Gambit

As we would suspect, the greatest potential for political power enjoyed by members of Congress is the opportunity to forge new domestic and foreign policies. Because the Constitution plainly declares that "all legislative powers herein granted shall be vested in a Congress of the United States," each Senator and Representative may introduce and help pass legislation designed to promote the general welfare of the country (or at least some special group). Each year members of the House and Senate may collectively consider as many as twenty thousand new pieces of legislation, out of which perhaps a few hundred eventually are signed by the President into law.

However, it is important to remember that the actual amount of influence on policy making varies with each member. Some Senators and Representatives are clearly more or less ambitious than others and expect, or refuse, to wield the maximum power they can draw from their positions. Moreover, the hurdles of Congress can at times seem insurmountable. Since most policy making, for example, takes place in committees, a member may find it difficult to push through legislation unless the proper committee shares his concerns. Not only may the committee not share his concerns, but many other bills may be competing for its attention. After all, Congress receives legislative proposals from a grab-bag of sources: lobbyists pushing pet causes, left-over bills not passed earlier, as well as individual policy brainstorms of powerful committee chairmen and budding presidential hopefuls. And, since the President has been handed the responsibility to set Congress's legislative agenda, a Senator or Representative may find his or her own pet project placed on the back burner while the President's policy recommendations receive priority.

Thus, while constituents at home dash off letters urgently pleading for legislation to cure society's ills, the policy maker in Congress struggles with the legislative machinery. Despite pressures emanating from home, few members of Congress, especially those with little seniority in the large House of Representatives, actually succeed each year in getting important new legislation passed. Although some members remain indebted to special interests and could not care less about serving constituents, others find their dreams of legislative knighthood vaporized. As one Representative lamented, "I came here thinking I would immediately share in the drafting of legislation. As all of us soon discover, the likelihood of first or second termers, and particularly minority members, doing any major drafting of legislation that passes is slim if not completely unknown."[3]

Nor does the average member of Congress wield tremendous influence with his or her vote on the floor. Although voting is regarded as one of a member's most important legislative responsibilities—after all, it is through voting that a Senator and Representative theoretically expresses the will of constituents—few members perceive their votes as decisive on most pieces of legislation. This is particularly the case in the larger House of Representatives with its 435 voting members. "Since I've been here," one Representative has proclaimed, "only one major bill has been decided by a single vote. If you try to evaluate your incremental impact, you have to decide that, unless you're Speaker, chairman of an important committee, or part of the House leadership, you just can't have much impact on normal Congressional operations."[4]

However, as we will see, a member can wield significant influence in committee where a single vote can be decisive in determining the life or death of a bill. The question then becomes: how to decide what bill to support or reject. One standard view is that members of Congress ultimately are "delegates" of their constituents and should honor constituents' wishes. As one Representative has stated, "You cannot buck district sentiment on certain issues. In my area, oil, coal, and mining are extremely important, and if you're 'right' on these things you have a much easier time of it. But you are opening yourself up to criticism if you vote against the district often."[5]

Supporters of the ruling-elite theory insist, of course, that most members of Congress remain ultimately "delegates" of powerful local elites. They point out that Representatives and Senators tend to have far greater communication with active special interests in their home districts and states than with the great majority of their constituency who are ignorant of congressional activities. This means that in a district whose chief industry is coal mining, the key and relevant constituency will be those who dominate that industry. However, whether the interests of the local elite necessarily conflict with the interests of a majority of the legislator's constituency is another question. Conceivably, a majority of the local populace may feel that congressional policy benefiting local industry also benefits them in terms of jobs and other economic services.

In any event, how can legislators know what the majority of their constituents want on most issues? Although tools are available to sample opinions—including polls and mailed questionnaires—they are impractical on an issue-by-issue basis. As John Kennedy discovered when he served in Congress, "In Washington

Senator Muskie and constituents.

Donald Patterson, Stock, Boston

I frequently find myself believing that forty or fifty letters, six visits from professional politicians and lobbyists, and three editorials in Massachusetts newspapers constitute public opinion on a given issue. Yet in truth I rarely know how the great majority of the voters feel, or even how much they know of the issues that seem so burning in Washington."[6] Indeed, such doubts have convinced many legislators that they are ultimately "trustees" of the people, and must make their own decisions as to what is to their district's best advantage. "The voters selected us," Kennedy concluded, "because they had confidence in our judgment and our ability to exercise that judgment from a position where we could determine what were their own best interests, as a part of the nation's interests."[7]

In practice, the views of most members of Congress toward law making vary from policy to policy. One finds that on issues not specifically pertaining to their districts—such as foreign aid— lawmakers often will act in response to their own sentiments. But on matters closer to home—such as economic issues—they often will try to vote more in keeping with the views of constituents. As one survey of Congress members discovered, 28 percent tended to regard themselves primarily as "delegates" of their districts, 23 percent as "trustees," and 46 percent as a combination of both.[8]

The Mail from Home

Although Senators and Representatives face interesting challenges in legislating for the nation, they are not solely lawmakers. Since they know their jobs can slip away at the polls, they must also attend to constituent mail.

The pressure to respond to such mail weighs heaviest on members of the House, who receive the bulk of personal requests for aid. Even though most of the mail pouring into the office is handled by a hired staff, the average Representative, as Table 7-1 shows, spends more than 30 percent of his or her time receiving visitors, answering letters, and responding to requests from constituents.

As the federal bureaucracy expands its influence over people's lives, Representatives must spend an increasing amount of time helping constituents cut red tape or correct bureaucratic injustices. Perhaps an elderly constituent has not received his monthly social security check; or perhaps a teacher wants a visa to visit China or the Soviet Union. As one Representative discovered, "Much of the work that comes across a Congressman's desk has absolutely no relationship to legislation. All of these casework problems probably could not easily be sent elsewhere. Certainly the people don't know where else to take them. But the fact is that having to deal with these matters takes vital time that a Congressman should be devoting to government and requires him to do a lot of housekeeping things for constituents."[9]

One common complaint among Congress members is that much of this "casework" can be trivial and ridiculous. They may suddenly be imposed upon to help with an income tax return, fix a

---

Table 7-1. A Representative's Use of Time

Tasks	Hours	Percent of Time
On the floor	15.3	25.8
Legislative research and reading	7.2	12.1
In committee	7.1	12.0
Answering mail	7.2	12.1
Handling constituent problems	5.1	8.6
Visiting with constituents	4.4	7.4
Committee work outside of committee	3.5	5.9
Leadership or party functions	2.4	4.0
Writing chores and speeches	2.7	4.6
Meeting with lobbyists	2.3	3.9
Press work, radio, and television	2.1	3.5

Source: Adapted from Donald G. Tacheron and Morris K. Udall, *The Job of the Congressman*, 2d ed. (New York: Bobbs-Merrill Company, 1970), pp. 303–04.

parking ticket, or attend a wedding anniversary celebration. One Representative even received a letter in the 1950s from a constituent who collected spoons. "She had read," the legislator exclaimed, "that Vice-President Nixon was going to Russia to see Krushchev, and she wanted me to phone him and ask him to bring a spoon back for her. Now I couldn't phone Nixon and ask him in the middle of all his important duties to get a spoon for that woman."[10]

Occasionally, constituents' letters can be nasty. Although members of Congress usually prefer to be diplomatic in such cases, diplomacy sometimes evaporates. In one famous incident in 1934, Rep. John Steven McGroarty of California wrote back to a constituent: "One of the countless drawbacks of being in Congress is that I am compelled to receive impertinent letters from a jackass like you in which you say I promised to have the Sierra Madre mountains reforested and I have been in Congress two months and haven't done it. Will you please take two running jumps and go to hell."[11]

Still, most Senators and Representatives place great importance on their constituent-service function. They believe their continuation in office depends in large part on satisfying those who request personal assistance. Even though most voters may not be familiar with the work of their legislators, few Congress members are willing to alienate those who do contact them—especially when those people belong to an organized group. In the opinion of one Representative, "Unless you can keep constantly in contact with your people, serving them and letting them know what you are doing, you are in a bad way. My experience is that people don't care how I vote on foreign aid, federal aid to education, and all those big issues, but they are very much interested in whether I answer their letter. . . ."[12]

In Chapter Nine, we will consider this point further, taking a look at the constituent-service function of Congress members from the point of view of citizens who write the letters.

Investigating

Over the years, members of Congress have been able to broaden their influence through the use of an "implied power" not spelled out in the Constitution. The right to hold committee hearings and conduct investigations has evolved over time as a legitimate part of their law making responsibilities. Senators and Representatives have come to rely on hearings and investigations to serve several crucial functions: (1) to gather information on proposed bills; (2) to haul up existing policies for review; (3) to oversee the executive branch; and (4) to inform the public on contemporary issues and problems. When bills of an important or controversial nature are being considered, hearings and investigations can last for weeks or months, during which testimony may be obtained from a variety of experts, lobbyists, and citizens.

Adding teeth to their power to investigate is their right to subpoena—that is, to force the appearance of witnesses or delivery of documents—as well as to cite an uncooperative witness for contempt. "Contempt of Congress" may be punishable by a fine of at least one hundred dollars and imprisonment from one to twelve months. The now-defunct House Un-American Activities Committee, for example, issued close to one hundred contempt citations in the 1950s against individuals being investigated for alleged "communist activities."

Two of the most sensational congressional investigations in recent years were those conducted by the Senate Watergate Committee in the summer and fall of 1973 and by the House Judiciary Committee in the spring of 1974. The Senate Watergate Committee first riveted national attention on the scandals that eventually led to President Nixon's fall from office. Chaired by Senator Sam Ervin, a seventy-six-year-old constitutional law expert from North Carolina, the committee (known officially as the "Senate Select

Committee on Presidential Campaign Activities") set out to investigate the break-in at the Democratic party headquarters in the Watergate office and apartment complex during the 1972 presidential campaign. Its ostensible purpose was to uncover the part played in the burglary by the Committee for the Reelection of the President (CREEP) and to recommend legislation preventing future campaign abuses. In the process, the committee heard weeks of televised testimony by key Nixon aides—most notably by John Dean, who implicated President Nixon in the subsequent cover-up of the affair. As its final official action, the committee in July 1974 released a ponderous three-volume report spelling out some recommendations for reform. Among them were the suggestions that an independent Federal Election Commission be created to supervise the laws on campaign contributions and that a permanent public prosecutor's office be established to investigate any campaign misconduct by future administrations.

Equally sensational were the deliberations of the House Judiciary Committee a year later. The thirty-eight-member Judiciary Committee, headed by raspy-voiced Peter Rodino, was delegated the historic responsibility, in Rodino's words, "to investigate fully and completely whether sufficient grounds exist for the House of Representatives to exercise its constitutional power to impeach Richard Milhous Nixon, President of the United States of America." After months of research, hearings, and heated debate, the committee in July 1974 played out its final five days of deliberations over network television. As cameras panned along the long mahogany bench to capture the "aye" or "no" vote of each member, the committee handed down the first recommendation for the impeachment of a President since 1868. In a strong bipartisan vote, the committee approved three articles of impeachment charging Nixon with "obstruction of justice" in the Watergate cover-up, "abuse of power" in his dealings with governmental agencies, and "contempt of Congress" through his defiance of congressional subpoenas. (See section on Impeachment, page 207.)

One significant aspect of these two committee investigations was that they were watched on television and discussed by more people than perhaps any other investigations in history. Indeed, the televised coverage of the committees may have done more to elevate public interest in congressional activities—normally overshadowed by those of the President—than anything else undertaken by Congress during the past several decades.

Congressional investigations have not always been highly praised, of course. Many critics have complained that Senators and Representatives—notably Senator Joseph McCarthy in the early 1950s—have used investigations to intimidate and smear private citizens or to seek personal publicity (a charge some people made even against the Watergate Committee). Columnist Walter Lippmann many years ago characterized some congressional investigations as a "legalized atrocity . . . in which Congressmen, starved of their legitimate food for thought, go on a wild and feverish manhunt, and do not even stop at cannibalism."[13] Of course, the threat that legislators will abuse the investigatory process is perhaps not as great today as it was in the past. The Supreme Court declared in 1957 that all witnesses in a congressional hearing are allowed to have counsel and that issues being investigated should be specifically related to proposed legislation.

Others complain, nevertheless, that committee hearings and investigations are often used as a "political cop-out," as a smoke screen for inaction. Some Representatives and Senators, eager to appear deeply concerned about a problem—such as Indian rights or housing conditions in urban slums—hold public hearings, even though the information already is abundant and the problem cries for immediate solution. In the opinion of Rep. Shirley Chisholm, "Most Congressional hearings are ridiculous. They are held to impress the public, to get someone's name in the papers and on television. . . . Witnesses come in and earnestly testify about something they know and care about, hoping that the committee will be moved. They think if they give Congress the truth, they will get justice in return. Then their testimony is printed in book after book of hearing records, which are piled on shelves to gather dust."[14]

Raising and Spending Money

Many members of Congress feel that a great deal of their power rests with their constitutional authority to regulate the flow of money to executive agencies. Although the President draws up elaborate budget recommendations each fiscal year, members of Congress ultimately determine where the money will come from (such as taxes and government bonds) and how much will be spent. In other words, without their authorization, no money can be doled out for foreign aid, salaries for army generals, or paper clips for bureaucrats.

Interestingly enough, members of the House of Representatives, and not Senators, exercise most financial control. If the President needs money for defense or some other purpose, a bill must be introduced in the House authorizing and appropriating such funds. By custom, the fifty-five-member House Appropriations Committee (which has the primary authority over spending) is the first to review the President's budget requests. It then passes on its recommendations to the Senate Appropriations Committee, which may add amendments. Furthermore, members of the House also have the sole constitutional authority to initiate revenue bills (see Article I, section 7). This means that all tax bills—as well as bills pertaining to social security and medicare—must go first to the House Ways and Means Committee, whose thirty-seven members consider the "ways and means" money shall be raised. Only after a tax bill winds its way through this committee and the House will it reach its Senate counterpart, the Finance Committee, for review.

To get an idea of the power of the Ways and Means Committee, one only has to be aware of the ways even Presidents court its favor. In a recent critical study of Congress, the writers tell of an illustrative incident involving President Johnson and the committee's former chairman, Wilbur Mills. "When, in 1967, LBJ began to take Mills for granted," they recount, "he quickly got put in his place. Mills' committee unceremoniously quashed Johnson's proposed tax increase at a closed committee session, leaving Treasury Secretary Fowler, who had come to make a presentation he never gave, spluttering in anger. Johnson then had to court Mills by White House and Texas ranch dinners and by the promise of reduced federal spending, to get back in his good graces."[15]

Despite the apparent influence of the Ways and Means Committee, however, controversy has raged over how Congress's power of the purse affects its relations with the White House. Some observers believe Congress's control over raising and spending money has suffered a decline as sharp as that over military policy. Ever since the Bureau of the Budget (now the Office of Management and Budget) was created in 1921, members of Congress have had less overall view of spending needs, making only slight alterations in a budget sent over by the White House. Yet, it is also true that control over the purse strings provides Representatives and Senators with their greatest influence over the executive branch. Since few of the President's policies can succeed without funds, a decision to increase or reduce his budget requests can drastically affect his administration's performance. Moreover, in June 1974, Congress passed a bill consolidating congressional spending procedures by establishing new Budget Committees in the House and Senate. The new bill allows Congress to make its own assessments of what the total of governmental spending should be each year. That is, instead of looking piecemeal at the spending and tax revenue proposals offered by the President, Congress would establish overall target figures for governmental spending and revenues—a change that in time could permanently alter the balance of power between the White House and Congress in economic policy making.[16]

Another important feature of the 1974 budget reform bill was a provision to stop presidential impoundments. This provision coincided with a series of court cases in which cities and states brought suit against the federal government for not spending appropriated funds. Ever since Thomas Jefferson's reign, Presidents have occasionally balked at spending money appropriated by Congress. When the House and Senate in 1972, for example, authorized $25 billion to clean up the nation's waterways, President Nixon vetoed the bill in an effort, he said, to hold down federal spending. Then, after Congress overrode his veto, Nixon simply impounded $6 billion by ordering that it not be spent. He argued that as Chief Executive he had the constitutional authority to impound any funds allotted by Congress. Many members of Congress objected, however, that under the Constitution the President may veto a bill only in its entirety; he may not item veto specific appropriations. "The power of the purse," Senator Sam Ervin argued, "is one of the most basic powers of the legislative branch, and if it is not exercised in a decisive and fiscally responsible manner, the Congress itself may rightfully be accused of abrogating its role under the separation of power doctrine."

Providing "Advice and Consent"

Although members of the House have an edge over Senators in revenue matters, Senators have the sole constitutional authority to oversee the White House by reviewing the President's appointments and treaties. Just as the President can veto bills passed by Congress, so can Senators "veto" his appointments and treaties.

The Constitution stipulates that the President's appointments of federal officers—including his Cabinet, ambassadors, the director of the FBI, the chairman of the Atomic Energy Commission, and Supreme Court Justices—are subject to the "advice and consent" of a simple majority of Senators present and voting. Members of the House do not share this duty with the Senate, except when a President (under the Twenty-fifth Amendment) must pick a new Vice-President. When President Nixon in the fall of 1973 selected Gerald Ford as his new Vice-President to replace Spiro Agnew, and when President Ford a year later selected Nelson Rockefeller as his Vice-President, both houses of Congress were called upon to give formal approval by a majority vote.

Although most presidential appointments are confirmed without difficulty, Senators on occasion do exercise a veto. Both Lyndon Johnson and Richard Nixon saw two of their Supreme Court nominees snubbed by the Senate. Presidents must bear in mind that, even though Senators will give them considerable freedom to appoint federal officers (only eight Cabinet nominees since 1789, for example, have been rejected), it is still wise to clear prospective nominees with key Senators—especially those from the state in which the appointee is to serve—before making an appointment.

The same is generally true for treaties—which, unlike appointments, require the approval of *two-thirds* of Senators present and voting. The possibility that the Senate may reject a treaty compels the President to seek the support of key Senators in advance, especially those on the powerful Foreign Relations Committee. Although Senators historically have approved more than 90 percent of the treaties submitted, they occasionally have withheld support. In 1919, Woodrow Wilson made the disastrous mistake of not compromising with the Senate Republican leadership on the Treaty of Versailles, and thereby helped doom the League of Nations. Of course, as we saw in the preceding chapter, the response of Presidents to the risk of treaty rejection has been simply to rely on executive agreements, that do not require the Senate's concurrence.

Impeachment

Perhaps the most formidable and dramatic power that can be exercised by Senators and Representatives—albeit its use is rare—is the impeachment and removal from office of all federal officers, from the President on down (only military officers and fellow members of Congress are exempt). The framers of the Constitution provided for impeachment—with the President at the top of their minds—after having revolted from an unimpeachable king. They feared that a President who could not be removed from office might become a tyrant. "No point is of more importance," George Mason declared at the Constitutional Convention, "than that the right of impeachment should be continued. Shall any man be above justice? Above all, shall that man be above it who can commit the most extensive injustice?"

Technically, impeachment amounts to a formal accusation similar to a grand jury indictment. If any member of the House of Representatives formally accuses a federal official, such as the President or a judge, of wrongdoing, the charges typically go to the House Judiciary Committee which studies the charges and reports its findings and recommendations to the floor. If a simple majority of the House votes to indict the official, a final bill of impeachment is sent to the Senate spelling out his alleged offenses. The House then picks "floor managers" to direct the prosecution, while the entire Senate sits as the jury hearing the evidence in the case. Usually, the presiding officer in the trial is the Vice-President, unless the President is the one who has been impeached; in that event, the Chief Justice of the United States presides. This arrangement is specified by the Constitution since the Vice-President would have an obvious personal stake in the outcome of the trial. If two-thirds of the Senators present find the official guilty of any of the charges, he is removed from his post and disqualified from holding further office. In the opinion of most legal scholars, there is no appeal.

One of the problems relating to impeachment is the uncertainty of what constitutes an impeachable offense. The Constitution states only that an official "shall be removed from office on impeachment for, and conviction of, treason, bribery, or other high crimes and misdemeanors." While the definitions of treason and bribery are clear, the meaning of high crimes and misdemeanors is not. Perhaps the broadest interpretation of the phrase was volunteered by Gerald Ford during his 1970 crusade as a member of the House to impeach Supreme Court Justice William O. Douglas. "An impeachable offense," Ford boasted, "is whatever a majority of the House of Representatives considers it to be at a given moment in history." This suggests that impeachment is as much a political tactic as a legal decision, and that if Congress becomes intensely opposed to a President or Supreme Court Justice, it may initiate impeachment proceedings on very narrow legal grounds.

Indeed, there is substantial support for the view that the broadest case for impeachment rests not necessarily on any criminal act, but on an "abuse of the office." "Start with the proposition that impeachment is a removal process," argues Professor Philip B. Kurland. "If a President spent a term fishing, it wouldn't be criminal; but it would be an abuse of office and he would be subject to removal."[17]

Since the ratification of the Constitution in 1789, impeachment proceedings have been initiated more than sixty times in the House, although only twelve cases have ever reached the Senate for trial. And of the twelve persons impeached by the House—including one President, one Supreme Court Justice, one U.S. Senator (whose case was dismissed "for lack of jurisdiction"), a Secretary of War, and eight lower court judges—only four were convicted by the Senate and removed from office. All four were federal judges.

The most celebrated Senate trial was that of President Andrew Johnson in 1868. Although Johnson was impeached—that is, formally indicted by the House—the Senate fell one vote short of the two-thirds majority needed for conviction. He was charged with violating the Tenure of Office Act (later ruled unconstitutional) by firing his Secretary of War without Senate approval and with making inflammatory speeches against Congress. Most scholars agree the charges against him were largely politically motivated, fueled by "radical reconstructionists" who resented his conciliatory attitude toward the post–Civil War South.

In addition to the case against Andrew Johnson in 1868, formal resolutions have been introduced in the House to impeach at least five other Presidents: John Tyler (1843); Grover Cleveland (1896); Herbert Hoover (1932); Harry Truman (1952); and Richard Nixon (1973). Beginning in the fall of 1973, Richard Nixon clearly faced the strongest call for the impeachment of a President in more than one hundred years. Following a year and a half of Watergate-related revelations in the press and the courts, demands swelled for a congressional investigation into his possible complicity in the Watergate break-in and cover-up. By January 1974, the House Judiciary Committee had opened its inquiry into the matter, and within six months it had approved three specific Articles of Impeachment. Article I accused Nixon of "obstruction of justice" on nine counts, including lying to investigators, withholding evidence, and misusing the Central Intelligence Agency. Article II charged him with "abuse of power" for, among other things, employing confidential Internal Revenue Service files against political opponents, directing the improper surveillance of private citizens, and interfering with the operations of the Justice Department. And Article III accused him of "contempt of Congress" for his refusal to hand over tapes and documents subpoenaed by the Judiciary Committee. Two additional articles—charging him with purposely concealing from Congress the facts about the secret bombing of Cambodia and with misusing governmental funds to improve his personal property—were rejected by the committee. Although Nixon's aides tried to undercut the committee as a "kangaroo court," public support for his impeachment grew substantially during this period, to the point where two-thirds of those surveyed favored a Senate trial. But such a trial never materialized. In August 1974, after confessing he had concealed vital information and after being told by his closest aides that his fate was sealed, Nixon resigned his office—becoming the first President to do so in the history of the Republic.

Amending the Constitution

Finally, members of Congress command the power to amend the Constitution—a power that may be used to revamp virtually the entire federal system. The Founding Fathers believed that no Constitution could remain unchanged for all time, and so provided four amending procedures (two ways to propose and two ways to ratify) for modifying the original document. (See Article V of the Constitution.)

Usually, a constitutional amendment has to be proposed by a two-thirds vote of both the House and Senate (although it may also be proposed by a national convention called by Congress at the request of two-thirds of the states). Any amendment passed by both houses must then be approved by three-fourths of the state legislatures. This method has been followed for all twenty-six existing amendments, except the Twenty-first repealing prohibition: it was ratified in 1933 by specially called conventions in three-fourths of the states. A Twenty-seventh Amendment (banning discrimination on the basis of sex) also was passed by Congress in 1972, but as of this writing it is still making the rounds of the states. Usually, Congress places a seven-year time limit on ratification; only a few amendments passed by Congress so far have failed to be ratified.

A striking aspect of this amending procedure is that the President has no legal power to veto. In fact, not even the Supreme Court can overturn an amendment. An amendment ratified by the states becomes part of the written Constitution; and in no way can the Court declare part of the document itself "unconstitutional." This means that members of Congress can use the amending power either to bypass a presidential veto (which was done in 1947 to limit all Presidents to two terms) or to reverse a Supreme Court ruling. Congress did overturn the Court, for example, with the Sixteenth Amendment (establishing the federal income tax) after the Court in 1895 had declared such a tax unconstitutional.

This amending power remains limited, however, not only by the reluctance of Congress members to take such a bold step, but also by the need to secure the approval of three-fourths of the states. Considering the difficulties involved, it is not surprising that only eleven amendments have been passed and ratified during the past one hundred years.

Recruitment to Congress

If one concludes that a congressional career is desirable from the standpoint of political action, the immediate concern becomes: Who is most likely to attain the post? The Constitution stipulates only a few legal qualifications for election to Congress: that Representatives (who serve two-year terms) must be at least twenty-five years old and Senators (who serve six-year terms) must be at least thirty; that the former must be American citizens

Table 7-2. *Characteristics of the 94th Congress (1975–1977)*

	House	Senate	Total
Sex and Race			
Men	417	100	517
Women	18	0	18
White	419	99	518
Black	16	1	17
Prior Occupations			
Agriculture	31	10	41
Business or banking	140	22	162
Educator	63	8	71
Engineering	2	2	4
Journalism	24	5	29
Labor Leader	3	0	3
Law	220	66	286
Law enforcement	2	0	2
Medicine	5	1	6
Minister	5	0	5
Scientist	2	0	2
Veteran	306	73	379
Religion			
Baptist	45	10	55
Episcopal	51	15	66
Jewish	20	3	23
Methodist	64	16	80
Presbyterian	50	17	67
Roman Catholic	109	15	124
Other	96	24	120

Source: Data from the *Congressional Quarterly Weekly Report*, 18 January 1975.

for at least seven years and the latter for at least nine; that they must reside in the states in which they were elected; and that they may not hold any other civil office while serving their terms.

However, although most Americans may legally qualify to serve in Congress, neither the House nor Senate truly reflects a cross section of the populace. As ruling-elite theorists are quick to point out, the vast majority of those serving on Capitol Hill are white, male, Protestant, native-born, at least fifty years of age, and either lawyers, businessmen, or bankers. As Table 7-2 shows, women are remarkably underrepresented in Congress; although they comprise more than 50 percent of the population, they account for only 3 percent of the 94th Congress (1975–1977), with a total of eighteen members. A similar underrepresentation of most racial and ethnic minorities also prevails; although 12 percent of the U.S. population is black, for example, the 94th Congress includes only seventeen black members—a total of less than 3 percent. Most other minorities, including Chinese, Spanish, and Indian, have few or no members in either the House or Senate.

Congress probably will never reflect a true cross section of the population in every respect (obviously, it is not surprising that lawyers predominate in a law-making body); however, it is difficult to justify such underrepresentation of women and prominent minorities. Such underrepresentation not only perpetuates disillusionment with the governing process but probably encourages a neglect of social problems that many Senators and Representatives simply do not identify with or understand. How broader representation can be achieved, however, remains a perplexing question. Certainly the prejudices of voters, the inequalities of campaign financing, and many additional roadblocks are as responsible for the underrepresentation as is Congress itself.

The Structure of Power: Implications for Action

Although the ability of Senators and Representatives to gain significant political influence has much to do with their talents and ambitions, ultimately it depends on the position they attain in the congressional power structure. Like most organizations, Congress is not a body of equals. Its internal rules, procedures, and customs do not encourage equal access to policy making by all its members. Some Senators and Representatives, by virtue of their committee assignments and leadership roles, can attain a position of power to which other members can only aspire.

Indeed, as already stated, many newly-elected Senators and Representatives are shocked to find how little influence they can exert on policy making and how often Congress can tear apart meaningful legislation. They discover not only that the procedures and power structure in Congress can be quite foreboding, but that a handful of legislators can impede or permanently block bills supported by a majority of members and the public. While the seniority tradition, Senate filibuster, and other hallowed procedures have recently been the targets of reform, disturbing questions about the responsiveness of Congress remain.

Many historians have pointed out, of course, that the Framers of the Constitution never intended Congress to be a particularly responsive institution. The fact that they created a bicameral (two-house) legislature composed of an often competitive and mutually hostile House and Senate (the latter originally not even directly elected by the voters) suggested a willingness to allow delay and deadlock in its law making. As we will see in the following chapter on the Supreme Court, many of the Founding Fathers were apprehensive about creating a national legislature that might respond too speedily to the changing moods of future majorities.

In this section, therefore, let us consider some of the main features of the congressional power structure—features that can often frustrate those hoping to see constructive policies emerge from the legislative labyrinth.

The Committees

With rare exceptions, all legislative craftsmanship in the House and Senate takes place in committees. Each bill introduced on Capitol Hill is referred to a committee for consideration; and it is in the committee, not on the floor, that its fate usually is determined. After being ushered into the House and Senate galleries, tourists often are amazed to see perhaps only a dozen or so members on the floor, speaking eloquently to rows of empty seats. Unless an important vote is about to take place, most members probably will remain in their offices or attend to the business of their committees.

Congress relies on committees to divide the workload and to enable each member to specialize in a few fields. (It is common today for most members to serve on only one or two standing committees.) With as many as twenty thousand bills introduced each year on Capitol Hill, few Senators or Representatives can become familiar with the details of each bill. As a result, each committee in the House and Senate (comprising anywhere from seven to fifty-five members each) has jurisdiction over a certain broad area, such as foreign relations, education, or agriculture.

At present, there are nineteen permanent or "standing" committees in the Senate and twenty-two in the House. Because each standing committee is supposed to mirror the party composition of the entire body, each is bipartisan with its seats distributed according to the relative strength of the two major parties. For most of the past forty years, a majority on each committee in both the House and Senate—as well as *all* committee chairmen— have been drawn from the majority Democratic party. Obviously, some committees carry greater prestige and more important responsibilities than others, and thus positions on them are more highly coveted. As we can see in Table 7-3, one scholar some years back ranked most of the committees by groups according to their prestige and importance.

Senior members with high status have been more likely to sit

Table 7-3. Standing Committees (ranked in groups, by order of importance)

Senate Committees	*House Committees*
1. Appropriations (26 members)	Rules (15 members)
Foreign Relations (17)	Appropriations (55)
Finance (17)	Ways and Means (37)
2. Armed Services (15)	Armed Services (43)
Judiciary (16)	Judiciary (38)
Agriculture and Forestry (13)	Agriculture (36)
Commerce (18)	Interstate and Foreign Commerce (43)
	International Relations (40)
	Government Operations (40)
3. Banking, Housing and Urban Affairs (16)	Banking, Currency and Housing (39)
Labor and Public Welfare (16)	Education and Labor (38)
Public Works (14)	Interior and Insular Affairs (41)
Interior and Insular Affairs (13)	Science and Technology (30)
	Public Works and Transportation (39)
4. Post Office and Civil Service (9)	Post Office and Civil Service (26)
Government Operations (16)	Merchant Marine and Fisheries (39)
	Veterans Affairs (26)
5. District of Columbia (7)	District of Columbia
Rules and Administration (9)	House Administration (26)

Source: Adapted from Stephen K. Bailey, *The New Congress* (New York: St. Martin's Press, 1966), pp. 54–55.

on and chair such top-ranking committees as Appropriations and Armed Services, whereas new members (especially in the House) frequently have had to settle for the less important committees like Administration and District of Columbia. To most of the men and women in Congress, their committee assignment is of crucial importance; it is in their committee, not on the floor, that they will have the best chance to guide legislation and establish their reputations. Although Senators and Representatives normally are assigned to committees that reflect their interests or the concerns of their constituents, new members (particularly in the House) occasionally have been placed on committees having little to do with their concerns. In 1969, Rep. Shirley Chisholm was shocked to find herself assigned to the House Agriculture Committee. She objected vehemently to the appointment, insisting that service on that committee was an absurd way for her to represent her urban and mostly black district in Brooklyn. "Apparently, all they know here in Washington about Brooklyn," she commented sarcastically, "is that a tree grew there."[18] Her committee assignment was eventually changed.

The major standing committees are themselves broken down into hundreds of smaller subcommittees to handle specialized subjects. The House Judiciary Committee, for instance, has sub-committees on Civil and Constitutional Rights, Crime and Monop-olies, and Commercial Law. Congress also utilizes "conference committees" to iron out differences in bills passed by both houses, as well as "select committees" to conduct special investigations. An example of the latter was the Senate Watergate Committee, chaired by the now-retired Senator with the dancing eyebrows, Sam Ervin.

Needless to say, a great deal of criticism has been levied against the committee system. One major complaint is that much of what Congress *does not do* is determined by the committees. Because committees have the power to change drastically or refuse consider-ation of bills, only a small fraction of bills introduced (about 5 or 10 percent) ever show up on the floor for a vote (see Table 7-4). When a bill is referred to a committee, Woodrow Wilson once remarked, it "crosses a parliamentary bridge . . . to dim dungeons of silence whence it will never return."[19]

Although many bills undoubtedly deserve this fate, important bills having wide public and congressional support sometimes are killed in committee by a small number of lawmakers. Indeed, few Representatives and Senators (not to mention concerned citi-zens) have escaped the disappointment of seeing a desired bill destroyed by a handful of hostile committee members. In October

Table 7-4. Passing a Law (bills may be introduced first in either chamber or simultaneously in both)

Senate

Bill Introduced: A bill is introduced by a Senator, perhaps as suggested by the President. It is given an identification number by the Clerk, and then referred by the Vice-President (or by whomever is presiding) to the proper standing committee.

Committee Considers: If the committee does not kill the bill outright (which usually happens), it may refer the bill to a subcommittee and hold hearings, After the bill wins a majority vote in the committee (possibly with amendments), it is scheduled for debate on the floor.

Floor Action: After the bill is debated and passed by a majority vote of the entire Senate (possibly with additional amendments), it is sent to the House of Representatives where it must clear similar hurdles.

House

Bill Introduced: The bill is sent to the Speaker, who refers it to the proper standing committee in the House.

Committee Considers: Again, if this committee does not kill the bill outright, it also may add amendments. After the bill wins a majority vote in the committee, it is sent to the Rules Committee which determines if and when the bill will arrive on the floor of the entire House (only appropriations and revenue bills usually bypass the Rules Committee).

Rules Committee: If the Rules Committee decides not to kill the bill, it determines *when* the bill will be heard on the floor, *how long* debate on it may last, and *whether* it can be amended on the floor.

Floor Action: Finally, after the bill is debated and wins a majority vote of the entire House, it may be sent either (1) directly to the President for his signature or veto, (2) back to the Senate for approval of amendments added in the House, or (3) to a conference committee of both Senate and House members, where the differences may be hammered out (in which case, another vote on the bill must take place in both chambers).

1972, for instance, the House Judiciary Committee, under pressure from the gun lobby, quashed a bill by Senator Birch Bayh to ban cheap handguns called "Saturday night specials"—the type of weapons used to kill Senator Robert Kennedy and cripple Alabama Governor George Wallace. The bill already had passed the Senate and, according to opinion polls, had the support of a majority of Americans. Although controversy still rages over gun legislation, the fact remains that a handful of legislators—not a majority in Congress—determined the fate of Senator Bayh's bill.

In fact, even if a Senator or Representative succeeds in propelling a bill through both houses, the bill may still become useless because of an appropriations committee's actions. This is because any bill approved by Congress—especially one setting up a new federal program—is only an "authorization" for the program; money still has to be raised to put it into effect. To get that money, the Appropriations Committees in the House and Senate must support a new bill allotting the funds. Historically, many programs have never been given full funding simply because the House Appropriations Committee happened not to support them. Rep. Donald Riegle noted that in 1970 his House Appropriations Committee refused to allocate $8.5 billion that already had been earmarked for expenditure.[20] This meant that those who sat on the committee had the awesome power to dilute and potentially destroy programs already approved in principle by a majority of both houses.

However, it is not only members of Congress who may find their will obstructed by committees. Ordinary citizens may be similarly affected. Because the destiny of most bills is decided in committee, special-interest groups—oil companies, labor unions, the gun lobby, or banking interests—can concentrate their pressures on a handful of committee members known to support their concerns. If they wish to bury a bill favored by a majority of the public, such as the one banning cheap handguns, the support of a simple majority of members on the right committee can do the trick. The diffusion of power among committees—each virtually monopolizing policy decisions in a given area—makes Congress particularly susceptible to the pressures of well-organized interests. Such interests can have considerably greater impact on legislation than if they had to deal with the entire membership of Congress— often to the detriment of an unalerted public.

Moreover, the presence of committees encourages an inequality of representation among the electorate. Those of us fortunate enough to reside in a district served by a member who sits on, or possibly even heads, a powerful House committee like Appropriations or Ways and Means can sometimes count on more immediate return for our votes than those living in a district served by a junior Representative with little experience or position. Although a working relationship (if any) between citizens and their Representative depends on many conditions, a Representative who has been relegated to a minor committee and who commands little influence imposes a handicap on those seeking an effective political voice. Some citizens may find their ability to help move legislation through Congress will be considerably less than that of citizens whose Representative shares their concerns and wields considerable clout.

In fact, it has been said that how much constituents benefit from legislation depends greatly on how long their Representative has served in Congress and on what position he or she holds. Chairmen of committees can be especially effectual in catering to the economic interests of constituents and local industry alike, helping to channel funds into their districts for such projects as military installations and veterans' hospitals. Congress-watchers noted that during Mendel Rivers' reign as chairman of the House Armed Services Committee from 1965 to 1970, more military funds were pumped into his South Carolina district than it knew what to do with. Meanwhile, other districts went hungry.

Rules Committee

Perhaps the most striking example of committee influence on legislation can be found in the procedures of the House Rules Committee. Because the House of Representatives has more than four times as many members as the Senate (435 as compared with 100), more bills are introduced in that body each year. To save the members from drowning in endless pieces of legislation, most bills approved by a standing committee must pass through the Rules Committee on their way to the House floor. The committee determines (1) what bills are to be considered or rejected, (2) the sequence in which bills will be taken up by the entire House (they do not have to be reported out in the order they come in from other committees), (3) how much time will be allotted to each Representative for debate, and (4) whether amendments can be offered on the floor.

Although these functions appear necessary, the Rules Committee has been lambasted for lacking objectivity and for occasionally wielding life-or-death power over legislation. Members of the Rules Committee can insist that a bill be amended as the price for permitting it on the floor (which often kills a bill right there), and can even substitute an entirely new bill for the one originally proposed. In fact, if a majority of the fifteen-member Rules Committee decide to delay or table a bill, it will probably die—even though it might be favored by most House members and the public at large. A majority of members can petition to "discharge" the bill from the committee, but such action is rare. One reason is that few members are willing to antagonize the committee that may eventually decide the fate of *their* own bills.

Filibuster

Although the Senate functions without a Rules Committee, it has its own procedures that can obstruct the will of the majority of

Senators and their constituents—most notably the filibuster. Because the Senate, unlike the larger and more unwieldy House, permits almost unlimited discussion on a bill, any Senator can try to stop a bill through continuous talking or other procrastinating means (such as asking for endless roll-call votes and points of order). A Senator, once having gained the floor, can speak as long as his voice holds out and yield to anyone he pleases. To filibuster, all he must do is remain standing and keep talking; the subject does not have to be even remotely relevant to the bill at hand. A Senator may entertain colleagues with Mother Goose nursery rhymes, recipes from a cookbook, or selections from *Sherlock Holmes*. The Civil Rights Act of 1957, for example, was delayed by Senator Strom Thurmond who bored the Senate for more than twenty-four hours by reading editorials in southern newspapers and the opinions of former Chief Justice Taft on jury trials in contempt cases.

However, since individual Senators cannot rely on iron vocal cords to carry them through, the most effective strategy is for a group of Senators to follow one another in succession. When one Senator tires, he can simply yield to a colleague who continues the "debate." Then, while one or two Senators take turns on the floor, the other members of the group can rest or sleep. Such a group filibuster may drag on for days or even weeks. The longest group filibuster in the Senate's history was staged by a coalition of southern Senators who tried unsuccessfully to block passage of the 1964 Civil Rights Act; their filibuster lasted more than eighty-three weary days.

Interestingly enough, the Senate in March 1975 made a historic change in the filibuster by revising the time-honored cloture rule for cutting off debate. Under the old rule, if two-thirds of the Senators on the floor supported a petition to restrict debate, all further discussion on a bill would be limited to one hour per Senator. The revised cloture rule reduces the number of Senators needed to stop a filibuster from two-thirds of those present to a permanent "constitutional" three-fifths of the total Senate membership. This means that, with no vacancies in the Senate, sixty votes would be required at all times to end debate. The only exception is that the two-thirds requirement must be retained for cutting off filibusters involving proposals to change Senate rules.

The new cloture rule is the end product of a long, twenty-year campaign led by Senate reformers to soften the two-thirds-vote requirement. The reformers had complained that the old two-thirds rule made it extremely difficult to cut off a filibuster. Indeed, prior to the 1975 revision, the cloture rule had been used successfully only a few times—although success had become more frequent during the past few years. Out of the 101 cloture votes taken between 1917 and February 1975, only 22 succeeded.

The revised cloture rule, however, actually represents a watered-down compromise. Reformers originally had wanted a straight three-fifths vote of Senators *present* to limit debate, but they could not muster enough support to put it through. As a result, the new rule will not always make it easier to stop a filibuster. If the number of Senators present should be less than ninety (which is typical), then the new three-fifths requirement (sixty votes minimum at all times) would actually make cutting off debate harder than under the old rule.

But why should a filibuster pose a threat at all? Why should Senators be afraid of seeing a colleague monopolize the floor for an extended period of time? The major reason is that as long as a filibuster continues, they will be unable to enact other legislation. A filibuster can be enormously effective in the closing days of a session (in December) when time is running short and members have pet projects they wish to pass. This was the basic strategy behind the one-man filibuster staged by Senator James Allen in December 1973 against the Senate campaign financing amendment. The amendment would have provided for governmental financing of presidential election campaigns. But because it was attached to an emergency debt ceiling bill just before Christmas vacation, the Senate felt compelled to give in to the filibuster and drop the amendment.

The filibuster has been denounced, therefore, for permitting small groups in the Senate to thwart the wishes of the majority. Under most circumstances, even when most Senators support a bill, they have a difficult time trying to muster either a three-fifths or two-thirds majority to stop a minority talkathon. A handful of Senators can bury dozens of popular bills, simply by gaining the floor and refusing to yield until their demands are met. Self-proclaimed liberal Senators have been especially critical of the filibuster since it has been used by southern conservatives to block civil rights legislation. However, many of the same liberal Senators also have relied on the device and frequently have voted against motions of cloture to cut off debate.

Even though the filibuster can be severely criticized, then, many Senators continue to champion its use. One reason is that it allows control over legislation by a Senator who, although greatly affected by a bill, had not been part of the crucial legislative machinery. By filibustering, a Senator can stop a bill that could be disastrous for his state. In addition, the filibuster may sometimes be used by a majority against a minority. It may be employed as a "holding action" by one or two Senators to prevent the minority party from passing legislation while many majority party members are not present. Whether these justifications, however, surmount the criticisms of the filibuster remains a matter of dispute.

Committee Chairmen

We should also consider the special powers of committee chairmen. Although their style and influence may vary from committee to committee, most chairmen exercise considerable control over policy making. For one thing, because hundreds of bills may be brought before a committee, they have the authority to determine the order in which bills will be inspected, and can occasionally even refuse to consider bills they oppose. They also appoint the members of most subcommittees, and thereby can seal a bill's fate by putting it into the hands of a group known to be hostile toward it. Furthermore, when hearings on a bill are held, the committee chairmen can decide who will testify and how much time each member has to cross-examine. And, in rare cases, they can even kill a bill outright simply by refusing to schedule any hearings at all. When Emanuel Celler, chairman of the House Judiciary Committee in 1958, was asked how he stood on a particular bill, he replied angrily: "I don't stand on it. I am sitting on it. It rests four-square under my fanny and will never see the light of day."[21]

Until recently, committee members had done little to change matters. As we will see, only during the past few years has the autocracy of committee chairmen been challenged through an assault on the seniority tradition. For most of Congress's history, the decisions of committee chairmen have tended to prevail. They have been able to veto policy—preventing or stalling majority action—and to push through their own pet projects irrespective of majority sentiment. As former Representative Clem Miller noted scornfully, "There are all sorts of ways to get things done in Congress. The best way is to live long enough to get to be a committee chairman."[22]

The Tradition of Seniority

This brings us then to the seniority rule—a controversial, long-standing tradition that only recently has come under heavy assault. For the past sixty years, members of each party have been ranked according to their length of uninterrupted service in the House or Senate. Power and position have been determined not by expertise, intelligence, or party loyalty but primarily on the basis of time spent on the same committee. This has meant that whenever a member dies, resigns, or is defeated at the polls, everyone remaining moves up a step on the seniority ladder. As a member rises in seniority, his or her chances of being heard, introducing legislation, and heading a subcommittee, increase. And the member of the majority party who has served longest on the committee almost automatically becomes its chairman.

One might ask why this custom has prevailed. What could justify the selection of chairmen on the basis of their longevity? One popular argument in favor of seniority has been that it promotes internal harmony in Congress by providing a peaceful route to power. If the heads of committees were selected by other means, such as by election, more dissension and bitterness might result. As former Vice-President Alben Barkley once proclaimed, without the seniority rule "the element of personalities and favoritism would come into play. . . . Jealousies, ambitions, and all the frailties of human nature would crop out in the electioneering methods of men who wanted to be chairmen of committees."[23] Of course, this justification may be inconsistent with the fact that other important positions in Congress, such as the Speaker of the House and the floor leaders, have been filled through elections.

Others defend seniority by arguing that it encourages the selection of experienced and able chairmen. It rewards those who know firsthand the technicalities of legislation and who have had long exposure to the subject matter of the committee. In the inimitable words of Emanuel Celler, "Here you have a man who starts from the bottom and he climbs the greasy pole, as it were, and in the process he gathers expertise and knowledge and acquaintances with the idiosyncrasies and the views of his fellow members of the committee, and he finally reaches the top, and he is somewhat of an expert with reference to the work of his committee."[24] The main drawback, however, has been that seniority does not reward experience gained by younger members. "A man can come to Congress when he's thirty-five," Rep. Donald Riegle has complained, "serve here twenty years and emerge, at age fifty-five, as the ablest man on his committee. But because he has to wait for all the members ahead of him to either retire or die, he may have to wait another twenty years—until he's seventy-five—before he becomes a chairman."[25]

Table 7-5. Standing Committees of the 94th Congress (1975–1977)

Senate Committee	Chairman	State	Age
Aeronautical and Space Sciences	Frank Moss	Utah	63
Agriculture and Forestry	Herman Talmadge	Ga.	61
Appropriations	John McClellan	Ark.	78
Armed Services	John Stennis	Miss.	73
Banking, Housing and Urban Affairs	William Proxmire	Wis.	59
Budget	Edmund Muskie	Maine	61
Commerce	Warren Magnuson	Wash.	69
District of Columbia	Thomas Eagleton	Mo.	45
Finance	Russell Long	La.	56
Foreign Relations	John Sparkman	Ala.	75
Government Operations	Abraham Ribicoff	Conn.	64
Interior and Insular Affairs	Henry Jackson	Wash.	62
Judiciary	James Eastland	Miss.	70
Labor and Public Welfare	Harrison Williams	N.J.	55
Post Office and Civil Service	Gale McGee	Wyo.	59
Public Works	Jennings Randolph	W.Va.	72
Rules and Administration	Howard Cannon	Nev.	62
Small Business	Gaylord Nelson	Wis.	59
Veterans Affairs	Vance Hartke	Ind.	55

House Committee	Chairman	State	Age
Agriculture	Thomas Foley	Wash.	45
Appropriations	George Mahon	Tex.	74
Armed Services	Melvin Price	Ill.	70
Banking, Currency and Housing	Henry Reuss	Wis.	62
Budget	Brock Adams	Wash.	48
District of Columbia	Charles Diggs	Mich.	52
Education and Labor	Carl Perkins	Key.	62
Government Operations	Jack Brooks	Tex.	52
House Administration	Wayne Hays	Ohio	63
Interior and Insular Affairs	James Haley	Fa.	76
International Relations	Thomas Morgan	Pa.	68
Interstate and Foreign Commerce	Harley Staggers	W.Va.	67
Judiciary	Peter Rodino	N.J.	65
Merchant Marine and Fisheries	Leonor Sullivan	Mo.	71
Post Office and Civil Service	David Henderson	N.C.	53
Public Works and Transportation	Robert Jones	Ala.	62
Rules	Ray Madden	Ind.	82
Science and Technology	Olin Teague	Tex.	64
Small Business	Joe Evins	Tenn.	65
Standards of Official Conduct	John Flynt, Jr.	Ga.	61
Veterans Affairs	Ray Roberts	Tex.	61
Ways and Means	Al Ullman	Ore.	60

Although many members of Congress have been inclined to support the seniority rule in one form or another, others have been strongly critical of the practice. In the words of one group, "Even the 'law of the jungle' operates on a higher level than the 'law' of seniority; the first works to assure the survival of the fittest: the latter operates only to assure the survival of the oldest."[26]

Because of the seniority tradition, Congress has been reproached for being dominated by a "council of elders." While the accuracy of this criticism has varied according to the age of the membership, most standing committees have been headed by members well into their sixties (see Table 7-5). Of course it is not age by itself that has been the great issue. "If the ancient fools of Congress were weeded out," Robert Sherrill has exclaimed, "there is no assurance that they would be replaced by young whizbangs, nor any assurance that some of the wise old men wouldn't be replaced by young asses."[27] Rather, the concern has been that long tenure in Congress breeds committee chairmen who are insulated from the contemporary problems of society. Just as a President may become insulated within the White House, Senators and Representatives serving long terms in Congress may become insensitive to changing social conditions.

Of equal concern has been the tendency of the seniority tradition to favor members from certain states and districts. To gain sufficient seniority to head a committee, members usually have had to be continually reelected from "safe" districts where there is little stiff opposition from the other major party. Because two-party competition has been weakest in the Democratic-dominated South, there has been a tendency for Senators and Representatives from southern states to get a disproportionate share of the chairmanships whenever the Democrats have dominated Congress. At the start of the 94th Congress (1975-1977), eleven of the twenty-two standing committees in the House were headed by southern Democrats (with Texas alone accounting for four of the chairmen). This meant that eight southern states chaired half the major House committees, while the other forty-two states had to divide the rest. Neither California nor New York—the two most populous states in the country—had a chairman of a standing committee in the House or Senate in 1975. Thus, the seniority rule has acted to encourage unequal representation, depriving voters in the largest industrial states of having a Senator or Representative who heads a committee.

Finally, critics have charged that reliance on seniority further splinters party responsibility and makes Congress less internally democratic. If chairmen are not selected on the basis of party loyalty or service, they cannot be held accountable to other committee members or to the elected party leadership. As long as their power derives from just staying alive and getting reelected, they can do almost as they wish on legislation. They can continue to wield power in autocratic fashion with little fear of being removed.

Thus, it is not surprising that critics of the seniority tradition applauded the actions of the House Democrats in January 1975. In a major break with the seniority tradition, the House Democratic caucus (comprising all the Democratic members of the House) voted to strip the committee chairmanships from three senior Democrats: eighty-one-year-old Wright Patman of Banking, seventy-three-year-old F. Edward Hebert of Armed Services, and seventy-five-year-old W. R. Poage of Agriculture. All three were removed in a wave of resentment among young and liberal members, many of whom were swept into the House in the 1974 Democratic landslide. Just a few weeks earlier, the once indominable Wilbur Mills had been ousted from the chairmanship of the powerful Ways and Means Committee, following a series of highly publicized escapades with a local strip-tease artist affectionately known as the "Argentine Firecracker."

A number of changes in the established House rules during the preceding four years had paved the way for this assault on the seniority tradition. In 1971, the Democrats in the House had adopted a resolution stating that any ten members of a committee could demand a vote before the entire party caucus on the status of their committee chairman. There was such a challenge in 1971 against John MacMillan, head of the District of Columbia committee; however, he clung to his post by a vote of 126 to 96. Then, at the close of the 1972 session of Congress, the Democrats approved a system by which all chairmen must garner a majority vote of the full party caucus every two years to retain their positions. Interestingly enough, when the first such vote was taken in January 1973, all the existing chairmen survived by wide margins. The third major reform came in late 1974 when the House Democratic caucus stripped the Democratic members of the Ways and Means Committee of their power to make committee assignments for other Democrats and transferred it to the Steering Committee, a select panel of the top elected leaders. It was this Steering Committee that in January 1975 first voted to recommend the ouster of the incumbent chairmen eventually removed by the Democratic caucus.

Many reformers predicted that the defrocking of the committee chairmen in 1975 signalled a greater "democratization" of the power structure. By directly assaulting the seniority tradition, the Democratic caucus jarred the committee leaders into a new awareness: in the future they would have to be more responsive to the party majority and the elected leadership if they wished to retain their posts.

It should be pointed out, of course, that seniority was not entirely abandoned. Most of the newly elected chairmen were members with many years of congressional service. The new head of Armed Services, for example, was seventy-year-old Melvin Price who had thirty years of tenure in the House. Moreover, in the Senate the seniority tradition was at least momentarily preserved, since all the present chairmen kept their posts. Senate Democrats did catch the fever of reform, however, by voting to select committee chairmen in 1977 by secret ballot—a move many reformers expected would warn all potentially autocratic chairmen that their positions would no longer be guaranteed by seniority.

Elected Positions

Finally, power tends to be allocated unequally in Congress not only through the committee system and other internal procedures but through its elected leaders. The most powerful and prestigious elected positions in Congress—such as Speaker of the House and floor leaders—are held by a handful of Senators and Representatives selected by their party to keep other members in line and provide policy leadership. Although they may be chosen in part by seniority, other factors—such as political philosophy, integrity (contrary to Mark Twain, it occasionally surfaces), and legislative experience—determine who gets the plum positions. (Lyndon Johnson, for example, was chosen as Senate Democratic Leader in 1953, even though he had served only four years in the Senate.) Let us then consider some of these elective offices, starting with the Speaker of the House.

Speaker of the House

The Speaker of the House commands the rostrum as the presiding officer of the House of Representatives. He is elected by the entire body every two years and is always a member of the majority party (presently the Democrats) due to a straight party-line vote.

The Speaker historically has been the most powerful elected leader on Capitol Hill. During the nineteenth and early twentieth centuries, men like James Blaine, "Czar" Thomas Reed, and "Uncle" Joe Cannon virtually dictated the priorities of legislation. They not only appointed members to all the committees in the House but chaired the powerful Rules Committee as well. As Speaker Thomas Reed reportedly boasted to a colleague in 1892,

"I have been 15 years in Congress and I never saw a Speaker's decision overruled, and you will never live to see it either." Actually, his prophecy did not hold true. In 1910, a coalition of Democrats and Republicans stripped away several of the Speaker's powers, including the right to chair the Rules Committee.

Despite the loss of some power, however, the House Speaker continues to wield enormous influence. Although he no longer heads the Rules Committee, the Speaker can nominate its Democratic members as a result of the reforms passed by the House Democratic Caucus in late 1974. With the power to recognize members on the floor and rule on points of parliamentary procedure, the Speaker can also control debate. Moreover, unlike the Vice-President in the Senate, he not only may vote but can step down from the rostrum to join in debates on the floor. He can refer bills to committees and appoint members to all select and conference committees. And, although the crisis has never occurred, the Speaker may even assume the Presidency if both the President and Vice-President die or become disabled.

In the final analysis, the extent of the Speaker's power depends on his style and personality. While some Speakers (like Sam Rayburn, who ruled during the 1940s and 1950s) have used their position as leader of the majority party in the House to great advantage—serving effectively as their party's "contact" with the President, deciding who gets the best committee seats, and so on—other Speakers (including Carl Albert, who became Speaker in 1971) have used their position to far less political advantage.

President Pro Tempore

The President Pro Tempore, who presides over the Senate in the Vice-President's absence, wields considerably less clout than the Speaker of the House. This is a prestigious, but largely powerless, position usually bestowed on an elder member of the majority party. In fact, as one indication of the job's insignificance, the President Pro Tempore frequently does not even preside over the Senate when the Vice-President is absent. Instead, the job falls to a junior Senator who takes a turn wielding the Senate gavel.

The Majority Leaders

Actually, it is the House and Senate Majority Leaders who each enjoy one of the most powerful elected positions. The Majority Leader in the Senate, for example, is usually regarded as the most influential member of that body; when held by a forceful individual like Lyndon Johnson, the position may rank equally with the Speakership in overall influence. The Senate Majority Leader's preeminence stems from his role as chief strategist of the majority party in the Senate—a position somewhat akin to that of the Speaker of the House. The Majority Leader's main duty is to mobilize the party behind bills the leadership decide are in the party's best interests.

Naturally, in view of the decentralized, undisciplined character of American parties, this is quite an ambitious task. Generally, the Majority Leader strives to achieve as much party unity as possible. To this end, he pushes for the committee assignments of newly elected members of his party, works with the Minority Leader to determine the sequence in which bills are debated on the floor, and serves with the Speaker as his party's liaison with the President. The Majority Leader's success ultimately depends, however, on his persuasiveness—his ability to cajole, bribe, flatter, even threaten other Senators in the party. A leader who is weak and unpersuasive will have little lasting success in keeping other party members, especially powerful committee chairmen, in line.

Although not as influential as his Senate counterpart, the Majority Leader in the House faces similar travails. While performing many of the same duties, he serves principally as the Speaker's assistant, helping him to bargain with committee chairmen and reconcile disputes between party members. One significant aspect of the job, however, is that it frequently serves as a stepping stone to the Speaker's post, as when Carl Albert rose from House Majority Leader to Speaker in 1971.

The Minority Leaders

The Minority Leaders in the House and Senate provide a kind of leadership for the Republican party similar to that provided by the Majority Leaders for the Democrats. They help manage the legislative programs of their parties, direct party strategy, and work closely with the Majority Leaders and the President to iron out differences on bills. During the Nixon administration, for example, both the Senate Minority Leader, Hugh Scott, and the then House Minority Leader, Gerald Ford, carried the major responsibility for pushing Nixon's legislative programs through a Democratic-controlled Congress.

The Party Whips

Finally, both parties in the House and Senate have a party Whip to assist the floor leader. The party Whip—a post recently held in the Senate by Edward Kennedy—is responsible for communicating the wishes of the floor leader to other party members. The Whip also rounds up party members for important votes on the floor, and thus can determine the potential party strength on legislation. (The title "Whip," incidentally, comes from the term "whipper-in," used in Britain to describe the person assigned during fox hunts to prevent the dogs from straying.)

Evaluation: Strengthening Congress

The feelings of impotency and frustration that overcome some of the men and women in Congress largely reflect the difficulty in getting Congress as a whole to move. As the country's primary lawmaking body, Congress has not been adept at fulfilling its responsibilities. Although the recent 93rd Congress (1973–1975) made a significant mark in American history by limiting the President's war powers, voting in a sweeping campaign financing reform act, nearly impeaching a U.S. President, and approving two successive Vice-Presidents under the Twenty-fifth Amendment, it still failed to confront the major social problems facing the country. Crime and double-digit inflation continued on the rampage, poverty and environmental pollution still ravaged the nation, while people in increasing numbers cast a weary and cynical eye on government.

Advocates of congressional reform have argued that the rules and customs of Congress frustrating many members—such as the seniority rule, the Senate filibuster, and the gross inequalities of committee influence—also have interfered with Congress's ability to fulfill its lawmaking responsibilities. Even when a major social problem has reared its ugly head, Congress has been too splintered by internal bickering, too much under the control of conservative committee chairmen indebted to special interests, and too encumbered by an antiquated, slipshod organization to do much about it. "Clumsy, unresponsive, controlled in large part by its most ordinary members," says Warren Weaver, Jr., "the national legislature blunders on, facing nuclear problems with colonial procedures, insisting all the while that nothing is wrong."[28] Thus, many believe Congress urgently needs—in addition to the complete elimination of the seniority rule and other outworn procedures—improved ways to obtain and analyze information, a way to clamp down on corruption and the undue influence of special interests, and even a new perception of its own policy-making role.

Corruption has been an especially persistent concern. When a scandal involving a member of Congress becomes public—such as the bribery charges against former Senator Daniel Brewster in 1972—people have no way of knowing whether such a case is exceptional or whether corruption is commonplace but simply undetected or unpublicized. In the wake of the Watergate disclosures, when the public's faith in government is at an all-time low, many consider it imperative for Senators and Representatives to prevent and expose wrongdoings that might further weaken people's confidence in Congress. Apart from the campaign-financing reforms discussed in Chapter Five, some believe the best preventive would be a further reduction of secrecy in committee meetings. Although Congress in recent years has taken steps to encourage open meetings, influential committees (particularly those dealing with appropriations) have continued to conduct a significant portion of their business behind closed doors. Each year, a dozen different subcommittees slice up more than $300 billion, authorizing expenditures for military hardware, governmental subsidies, and projects within the members' own districts. Advocates of reform insist all such allocations—including those for the CIA—should be made openly, in full view of the public and media. After all, how Senators and Representatives respond to bills in committees—and their reasons—may reveal more about their views and fidelities than how they vote on the floor.

Another problem pointed out by congressional critics has been inadequate staff services. Despite the passage of the Legislative Reorganization Act of 1970, which authorized each committee to employ up to six professional experts, members of Congress have continued to experience difficulties in overseeing the executive branch. They often have been unable to compete with the thousands of experts and enormous technical resources of the executive bureaucracy (not to mention the Pentagon and industry), and thus have been unable to prevent irresponsible policy decisions. Senator Walter Mondale complained that when he held a hearing to argue against more aircraft carriers, it was a case of "myself and one college kid versus the U.S. Navy and everybody who wanted to build a carrier."[29]

Moreover, members of Congress have been chided for relying

on nineteenth-century equipment that cannot possibly match the banks of computers, operations specialists, and retrieval systems of the executive branch. Their outdated computers and other equipment, one critic declared, have had the "capability, roughly, of the First National Bank of Kodoka, South Dakota." With the tremendous growth in industry, population, and social services, Senators and Representatives require modern tools to retrieve and analyze complex statistics thrown at them by an increasingly powerful executive bureaucracy. As Rep. Wayne Owens complained, "It is impossible for Congress to meet its Constitutional responsibilities to govern intelligently without independent sources of information and information evaluation. We are thirty years behind the technology because, to use a popular phrase around here, the Congress is 'penny wise and pound foolish.'"[30]

Of course, one might argue that a larger and more professional staff and computer system may only create additional woes. One negative result already of a growing congressional bureaucracy is the increasing insulation of Congress members from their constituents. As we will see in the final chapter, citizens often find it difficult to communicate directly with their Representatives and Senators, who must rely on a squad of caseworkers to handle constituents' problems.

Moreover, improved staff services and computers may not be sufficient to strengthen the role of Congress in policy making. As more of the vital policy decisions have been made by the President and his aides, Senators and Representatives have found themselves on the sidelines, waiting to accept or reject the legislative packages tossed to them from the White House. During both the Johnson and Nixon administrations, members of Congress found they were kept in the dark about many important policy questions. Even with improved staffing and modern equipment, Congress members still would require added support in providing policy leadership. Yet, some critics charge that many Senators and Representatives simply lack the will to exert strong leadership. In the caustic opinion of Rep. Donald Riegle, "Congress is really a body of followers, not leaders, and it's often necessary to build a significant public mandate to get Congress to move. Congress usually won't face up to a problem until it has to, before it's forced to."[31]

This does not mean that the prognosis for Congress has been entirely pessimistic. Many have hoped that the lessons of Watergate and the growing distrust of presidential power will result in a permanent reassertion of congressional leadership. With the election in 1974 of many younger, reform-minded members of the House, there has been an expectation of an increased congressional hand in the economy, foreign affairs, environmental protection, and social services. As Senate Democratic Whip Robert Byrd affirmed following the 1974 elections, "We've gone through a dreadful period in which the legislative branch has been trying to regain the powers we've allowed to erode, and we will continue to be assertive. We won't fall back into the old ways."[32]*

Other observers remain doubtful, however. Many ruling-elite theorists insist that the ability of Congress to respond to social problems depends on more than the reform of its procedures. They argue that the very goals of Congress are shaped and limited by the power structure of the society in which it thrives. Congress simply mirrors the prevailing inequities of the political and economic system, serving as an instrument of elite interests to the detriment of most Americans. "As long as Congress reflects the distribution of economic power in the wider society," one writer argues, "it is not likely to change much even if liberals in both houses manage to gain control of the major committees, and even if the cloture rule is changed to enable the Senate to rid itself of the filibuster, and even if the Rules Committee is deprived of its arbitrary powers, and even if seniority is done away with. For what remains is the entire system of organized corporate power with its elitist institutions, business-controlled media and mass propaganda, organized pressure groups, high-paid lobbyists and influence-peddling lawyers, campaign contributions and bribes—all of which operate with such telling effect on legislators, including most of the professedly liberal ones."[33] Such a view implies that changes in the entire economic fabric of our society may be required before meaningful improvements in the responsiveness of Congress are realized—a view not without far-reaching implications.

Recommended Reading

Chisholm, Shirley. *Unbought and Unbossed.* Boston: Houghton Mifflin, 1970.

Clapp, Charles L. *The Congressman: His Work As He Sees It.* Washington, D.C.: Brookings Institution, 1963.

Davidson, Roger H. *The Role of the Congressman.* Indianapolis: Pegasus, 1969.

Green, Mark J.; Fallows, James M.; and Zwick, David R. *Who Runs Congress?* New York: Bantam, 1972.

Harris, Joseph P. *Congress and the Legislative Process,* 2d ed. New York: McGraw-Hill, 1972.

Huitt, Ralph K., and Peabody, Robert L. *Congress: Two Decades of Analysis.* New York: Harper & Row, 1969.

Riegle, Donald. *O Congress.* New York: Doubleday, 1972.

Tacheron, Donald G., and Udall, Morris K. *The Job of the Congressman,* 2d ed. New York: Bobbs-Merrill, 1970.

Weaver, Warren, Jr. *Both Your Houses: The Truth About Congress.* New York: Praeger, 1972.

Wright, Jim. *You and Your Congressman.* New York: Coward-McCann, 1965.

1. *Unbought and Unbossed* by Shirley Chisholm, p. 100. Copyright © 1970 by Shirley Chisholm. Reprinted by permission of Houghton Mifflin Company.   *Notes*

2. From the copyrighted editorial, "Dropout's Lament," in *U.S. News & World Report,* 25 March 1974, p. 96.

3. Quoted in Charles L. Clapp, *The Congressman: His Work As He Sees It* (Washington, D.C.: Brookings Institution, 1963), p. 426. © 1963 by the Brookings Institution, Washington, D.C. Used with permission of the Brookings Institution.

4. Donald Riegle, *O Congress* (New York: Doubleday, 1972), p. 65. © 1972 Doubleday & Company, Inc. Used with permission of Doubleday & Company, Inc.

5. Quoted in Charles L. Clapp, *The Congressman: His Work As He Sees It* (Washington, D.C.: Brookings Institution, 1963), p. 377. © 1963 by the Brookings Institution, Washington, D.C. Used with permission of the Brookings Institution.

6. John F. Kennedy, *Profiles in Courage* (New York: Harper & Row, 1955), p. 18. Used with permission of Harper & Row, Publishers, Inc.

7. Ibid., p. 16.

8. Roger H. Davidson, *The Role of the Congressman* (Indianapolis: Pegasus, 1969), pp. 117–19.

9. Quoted in Charles L. Clapp, *The Congressman: His Work As He Sees It* (Washington, D.C.: Brookings Institution, 1963), p. 54. © 1963 by the Brookings Institution, Washington, D.C. Used with permission of the Brookings Institution.

10. Ibid., p. 70. © 1963 by the Brookings Institution, Washington, D.C. Used with permission of the Brookings Institution.

11. Quoted in John F. Kennedy, *Profiles in Courage* (New York: Harper & Row, 1955), p. 10. Used with permission of Harper & Row, Publishers, Inc.

12. Quoted in Charles L. Clapp, *The Congressman: His Work As He Sees It* (Washington, D.C.: Brookings Institution, 1963), p. 52. © 1963 by the Brookings Institution, Washington, D.C. Used with permission of the Brookings Institution.

13. Walter Lippmann, *Public Opinion* (New York: Harcourt, Brace, 1922), p. 289.

14. *Unbought and Unbossed* by Shirley Chisholm, p. 104. Copyright ©️ 1970 by Shirley Chisholm. Reprinted by permission of Houghton Mifflin Company.

15. Mark J. Green, James M. Fallows, and David R. Zwick, *Who Runs Congress?* (New York: Bantam Books, 1972), pp. 71–72.

16. For more evaluation of the budget reform, see the *Congressional Quarterly Weekly Report,* 7 September 1974.

17. Philip B. Kurland, quoted in *Time,* 4 February 1974, pp. 30–31. Reprinted by permission from *Time,* the weekly Newsmagazine, Copyright Time Inc.

18. Quoted in Mark J. Green, James M. Fallows, and David R. Zwick, *Who Runs Congress?* (New York: Bantam Books, 1972), p. 56.

19. Woodrow Wilson, *Congressional Government* (New York: Meridian Books, 1956), p. 63. Originally published 1885.

20. Donald Riegle, *O Congress* (New York: Doubleday and Co., 1972), p. 171. ©️ 1972 Doubleday & Company, Inc. Used with permission of Doubleday & Company, Inc.

21. Quoted in Jim Wright, *You and Your Congressman* (New York: Coward-McCann, 1965), p. 134. With permission of Coward-McCann.

22. Clem Miller, *Member of the House: Letters of a Congressman* (New York: Charles Scribner's Sons, 1962), p. 39.

23. Quoted in the *Congressional Quarterly Weekly Report,* 6 January 1973.

24. Ibid.

25. Donald Riegle, *O Congress* (New York: Doubleday & Co., 1972), p. 141. ©️ 1972 Doubleday & Company, Inc. Used with permission of Doubleday & Company, Inc.

26. House Republican Task Force on Congressional Reform, *We Propose: A Modern Congress* (New York: McGraw-Hill, 1966), p. 26.

27. Robert Sherrill, *Why They Call It Politics,* 2d ed. (New York: Harcourt Brace Jovanovich, 1974), p. 117.

28. Warren Weaver, Jr., *Both Your Houses: The Truth About Congress* (New York: Praeger, 1972), p. 4. With permission of Praeger Publishers Inc.

29. Senator Walter Mondale, quoted in *Time,* 15 January 1973, p. 16. Reprinted by permission from *Time,* the weekly Newsmagazine, Copyright Time Inc.

30. *Congressional Quarterly Weekly Report,* 21 April 1973.

31. Donald Riegle, *O Congress* (New York: Doubleday, 1972), p. 66. ©️ 1972 Doubleday & Company, Inc. Used with permission of Doubleday & Company, Inc.

32. Robert Byrd, quoted in *Newsweek,* 18 November 1974, p. 33. Copyright Newsweek, Inc., 1974; reprinted by permission.

33. Michael Parenti, *Democracy for the Few* (New York: St. Martin's Press, 1974), pp. 205–6.

8 *"Politicians in Black Robes":*
The Judicial Approach

There appear to be many Americans who, essentially disgusted with politicians and bureaucrats, retain a certain reverence for the judicial process, as exemplified by the Supreme Court. In contrast to members of Congress, Presidents, and lobbyists who appear to be locked forever in partisan battle, the robed judges who sit on the high bench—while certainly not immune to controversy—seem to tower above the usual pettiness and strife of political ambition. If public opinion polls are to be believed, the Justices of the Supreme Court have enjoyed greater prestige than any other officials in national or state government.[1]

Yet, while the popular image of Supreme Court Justices may suggest an aloofness from partisan politics, the Justices are as much practitioners of political art as any other elected or appointed officials. Indeed, they must be viewed in much the same light as Senators and Presidents: as individuals who have achieved a position of power and who exercise that power in terms of their own personal values and priorities. Once appointed to the Supreme Court, Justices do not relinquish their claims to personal opinion, nor forego prejudice and political ambition. As former Justice James McReynolds once stated, a Supreme Court Justice does not become an "amorphous dummy, unspotted by human emotions."

One writer many years ago poked fun at the popular image of Justices as impartial and dispassionate beings, in an irreverent little piece entitled the "Song of the Supreme Court."

Some have cynically suggested that the Justices enjoy high prestige because of the public's overall ignorance of their activities. If people knew more about how Justices are appointed and understood the motivations for their rulings, such respect would be no greater than for other practicing politicians. Whatever the merits of this observation, social scientists have discovered that

---

Song of the Supreme Court

We're nine judicial gentlemen who shun the common herd,
Nine official mental men who speak the final word.
We do not issue postage stamps or face the microphones,
Or osculate with infants, or preside at corner-stones.
But we're the court of last resort in litigation legal.
(See: Case of Brooklyn Chicken *versus* Washington Blue Eagle.)
We never heed the demagogues, their millions and their minions,
But use *this* handy yardstick when in doubt about opinions:

Chorus

If it's In The Constitution, it's the law,
For The Constitution hasn't got a flaw.
If it's In The Constitution, it's okay,
Whether yesterday, tomorrow, or today—
Hooray!

If it's In The Constitution, it must stay!
Like oysters in our cloisters, we avoid the storm and strife.
Some President appoints us, and we're put away for life.
When Congress passes laws that lack historical foundation,
We hasten from a huddle and reverse the legislation.
The sainted Constitution, that great document for students,
Provides an airtight alibi for all our jurisprudence.
So don't blame us if now and then we seem to act like bounders;
Blame Hamilton and Franklin and the patriotic founders.

Chorus

If it's In The Constitution, it's the law, *etc.*

Source: Arthur L. Lippman, *Life* magazine, August 1935; reprinted in Glendon Schubert, *Constitutional Politics* (New York: Holt, Rinehart and Winston, 1960), pp. 11–12. Used with permission of Henry T. Rockwell.

an overwhelming majority of Americans scarcely know what the Court is doing. Few can name more than a handful of the Court's nine Justices, describe its procedures, or recount the nature and history of its role in the political system. And, apart from a few highly controversial cases—such as those concerning busing and prayer in the public schools—most Court decisions stir little public interest. One study revealed that more than 55 percent of American adults could not describe any recent Supreme Court rulings.[2]

The Court's press coverage, of course, has not been as extensive as that of the President and Congress, and many of the Court's decisions have abounded in legal technicalities that defy most people's understanding. Moreover, most Americans have neither the opportunity nor the desire to become intimately acquainted with the Court's activities. They do not write letters to the Justices, are unable to penetrate the secrecy in which much of the Court's work is accomplished, and have few of the required resources to bring an injustice to the Court's attention. Some scholars, such as the ruling-elite theorists, aptly conclude that among the various governmental institutions in this country, the Supreme Court remains one of the least open to citizen scrutiny and the least accessible to individual influence—a conclusion that, if shared by most Americans, may indeed inhibit understanding and awareness.

The Power To Nullify "Law"

The widespread ignorance of Supreme Court activities should not obscure the enormous power the nine Justices command in the political system. Nor should it obscure the occasional storms of controversy accompanying their decisions. During the past few decades alone, the Justices have handed down opinions of far-reaching significance affecting the very fabric of American society.

From the standpoint of political action, for example, the role of the Justices has been profound. Their decisions have ranged over a wide area of political expression, touching on voting rights, freedom of speech, freedom of the press, and freedom of association. Their rulings in the 1960s on the issue of what constitutes permissible acts of public protest carried broad implications for those seeking constitutional protection for political expression. In response to widespread civil rights and anti-Vietnam War protests, the Justices confronted federal, state, and local laws restraining public speech and assembly. In 1963, for example, the Court upheld the right of almost two hundred students to demonstrate on the South Carolina state capitol grounds, ruling that the students were exercising "basic constitutional rights in their most pristine and classic form."[3] Similarly, in 1966, the Court upheld a sit-in by five black adults protesting the segregationist policies of a regional library.[4] However, in a number of cases, the Court also came down hard against political protest. In 1967, it sustained the convictions of two hundred college students demonstrating against a segregated county jail on the grounds that the jail was not on public property.[5] And, in 1968, it upheld the convictions of four persons who had burned their draft cards in violation of federal law.[6]

The basis for these and other controversial rulings is the Justices' sweeping power to exercise "judicial review." By law and tradition, the nine Court Justices can overturn decisions of Congress, the President, state legislatures, and lower courts that in their opinion conflict with the Constitution. Although state and lower federal court judges also wield this power, and while the President and members of Congress continually interpret the Constitution through their actions, Supreme Court Justices usually have the final word in interpreting the document's meaning. As former Chief Justice Charles Evans Hughes stated bluntly in 1907, "We are under a Constitution, but the Constitution is what the judges say it is."

Take one recent and dramatic example. In July 1974, the Supreme Court Justices, acting under a provision permitting direct appeal of cases "of such imperative public importance as to . . . require immediate settlement," held an extraordinary midsummer hearing on whether President Nixon had to surrender sixty-four White House tape recordings sought by Special Prosecutor Leon Jaworski. Titled *The United States of America* v. *Richard M. Nixon*, the case marked the first appearance of the Watergate scandal in the highest court. In their historic decision, the Justices ruled against President Nixon, upholding a previous order by District Court Judge John Sirica requiring the President to hand over the tapes as evidence in the Watergate cover-up trial of six former Nixon aides.

Simply stated, the Justices rejected Nixon's sweeping assertion that only a President can decide what White House materials can be used as evidence in criminal proceedings. The doctrine of separation of powers and the need for confidential communications within the executive branch, the Justices ruled unanimously, does not give the President absolute privilege to withhold material from the courts. In a criminal case such as the cover-up trial, where the claim of confidentiality is not based on grounds of military or diplomatic secrecy, the President's assertion of "executive privilege" must yield to the need for evidence.

Clearly, the case represented one of the most significant disputes over governmental powers in American history, and strongly bolstered the Court's position relative to that of the President in the area of law. Nixon's compliance to the ruling reaffirmed the Court's preeminence among the three branches of government in interpreting the Constitution.

One of the most important facts about judicial review, however, is that the Constitution does not specifically authorize Supreme Court Justices to exercise it. Although Article III stipulates that the Justices may consider "all cases, in law and equity, arising under the Constitution," this provision does not clearly empower them to strike down acts they consider to be unconstitutional. However, many historians point out that the use of judicial review had been anticipated before the Constitution was written and that many state courts already had invalidated acts that conflicted with state constitutions. Furthermore, many members of the Constitutional Convention in 1787 had championed judicial review as one of the vital functions of the Court.[7] An early study by historian Charles Beard revealed that at least seventeen of the twenty-five most influential members of the Convention were "on record in favor of the proposition that the Judiciary would in the natural course of things pass upon the constitutionality of acts of Congress." And of the less prominent members, Beard found, six were on record who "understood and approved" the doctrine.[8]

Moreover, in *The Federalist*, a series of essays promoting ratification of the Constitution by the states, Alexander Hamilton pleaded for the right of the judicial branch to decide whether legislative acts were constitutional. "The complete independence of the courts of justice is peculiarly essential in a limited constitution," he argued, and such a limited constitution "can be preserved in practice no other way than through the courts of justice, whose duty it must be to declare all acts contrary to the manifest tenor of the Constitution void. Without this, all the reservations of particular rights or privileges would amount to nothing."[9] In fact, in the Judiciary Act of 1789, Congress handed Supreme Court Justices the power to nullify state court decisions. By doing so, many historians contend, Congress implied that the Justices could overturn laws contradicting the federal Constitution.

But because the Constitution was silent on the Court's right to review congressional or presidential acts, the Justices gradually acquired this power through their own interpretations of the document. The celebrated case of *Marbury* v. *Madison* (1803) was especially important in this regard, since it set the precedent for reviewing acts of Congress. The case developed in 1801 when John Adams, just before stepping down from the Presidency, hurriedly appointed a number of Federalist party judges—among them William Marbury as justice of the peace in the District of Columbia. When Thomas Jefferson, Adams's Republican successor, discovered that Marbury's commission had not been delivered to him in time, he decided to appoint someone else. Marbury, evidently disappointed and angered by Jefferson's refusal to honor his appointment, appealed the matter directly to the Supreme Court. He insisted that the Justices should force Jefferson to deliver the commission. He based his appeal on the fact that Congress, in the Judiciary Act of 1789, had stated that requests for a "writ of mandamus" (an order demanding a public official to do his duty) could be taken directly to the Supreme Court; that is, such requests were part of the Court's "original jurisdiction."

Clearly, the Justices were placed in an uncomfortable position. On the one hand, if they tried to order Jefferson to deliver the commission to Marbury, Jefferson probably would just ignore the order and thereby humiliate the Court. But, on the other hand, if they refused to support Marbury, they would be admitting the Court's weakness.

Chief Justice John Marshall's majority opinion was a masterpiece of strategy. He admitted that Marbury should be given his commission, but stated that the Justices did not have the power to help him get it. This was because the section of the Judiciary Act authorizing them to honor direct requests for writs of mandamus in the first place was unconstitutional. Congress had no authority, Marshall said, to enlarge the Court's original jurisdiction outlined in the Constitution by handing the Justices the added authority to issue such writs. The Court's original jurisdiction is limited by the Constitution and cannot be enhanced by Congress. It applies only to cases involving diplomats or disputes between states. And because Marbury was neither a diplomat nor a state, the Justices had no authority to issue a writ of mandamus to Jefferson on his behalf. Thus, even though Marbury did not benefit by this decision, the Justices and the Court clearly did. By ruling that a section of the Judiciary Act was unconstitutional, they avoided a confrontation with Jefferson and simultaneously established the Court's authority to interpret the constitutionality of congressional acts.

Ironically, in the years since the Marbury decision, Supreme Court Justices have not overturned many other acts of Congress;

only about one hundred such acts have been declared totally or partially unconstitutional. Most of the Court's judicial review power has been directed instead against the states. One estimate is that more than one thousand state and local acts have been invalidated by the Court. In the opinion of some observers, in fact, the power to review state acts has been even more important than the power to review legislation of Congress. Without the power to interpret state acts, there would be little to prevent the states from going their independent legal ways to the detriment of the federal Constitution. As former Justice Oliver Wendell Holmes concluded, "I do not think the United States would come to an end if we lost our power to declare an act of Congress void. I do think the Union would be imperiled if we could not make that declaration as to the laws of the several states."[10]

Justifications for Judicial Review

What possible justifications can we find for allowing Supreme Court Justices to wield judicial review? Why should nine robed judges who never face the voters command the awesome power to overturn the decisions of popularly elected legislators and exec-utives? Such power, according to ruling-elite theorists, would ap-pear to be at variance with the "democratic" ideal that no group—particularly an elite appointed for life—should determine policy for a majority of society.

One justification is that our political system is based on more than majority rule, that it ultimately rests on a foundation of constitutional law. As Alexander Hamilton wrote in *Federalist* No. 78 and as Chief Justice John Marshall ruled in *Marbury* v. *Madison* (1803), the Constitution must be regarded as the supreme law of the land, superior to any acts of Congress, the President, lower courts, or state legislatures. And, because the responsibility of the courts is to interpret the law, Supreme Court Justices must be the ultimate interpreters of the Constitution. They must determine whether any legislation passed by Congress or other legislative body is in accord with it. If the Justices should find a conflict between such legislation and the Constitution, it is their duty to declare that legislation invalid.

Related to this legal justification is the more obvious fact that many of the Founding Fathers were never willing to put full trust in the majority or their elected representatives. They feared that the majority might trample on the rights of those individuals or minorities who happen to offend the prevailing prejudices of the times. And, because every citizen is likely to be a member of some minority at one time or another, no individual might be spared persecution by the many. "It is of great importance in a republic," James Madison warned in *Federalist* No. 51, "not only to guard the society against the oppression of its rulers, but to guard one part of the society against the injustice of the other. . . . If a majority be united by a common interest, the rights of the minority will be insecure." Thus, in the opinion of many of the Founding Fathers, it would be unrealistic to entrust members of Congress or state legislatures with the sole responsibility to draw either the boundaries of their own authority or the rights of individuals and minorities. These bodies are elected by temporary majorities whose prejudices and passions at any moment might be unleashed against unpopular groups. (Consider some of the studies discussed in Chapter Three.) Only Supreme Court Justices, who are not elected directly by the voters and who serve for life, have sufficient independence to protect individual rights guaranteed by the Constitution.

Naturally, this does not mean that Supreme Court Justices have always provided such protection. As we will see, constraints have been imposed on the Court to prevent the Justices from challenging the majority will for long periods of time. In fact, Supreme Court Justices even have aided the repression of individual rights at various times in history. In *Dred Scott* v. *Sanford* (1857) they ruled that descendants of slaves were not United States citizens and that Congress could not halt the expansion of slavery into the territories. In *Plessy* v. *Ferguson* (1896) a majority of the Justices supported the concept of "separate but equal" facilities for different races. And in *Korematsu* v. *United States* (1944) a similar

Elliott Erwitt, Magnum Photos

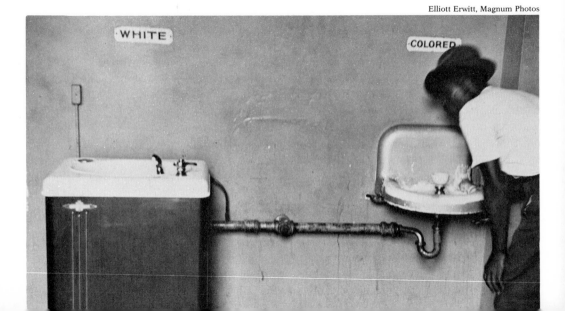

majority upheld President Roosevelt's order placing thousands of loyal Japanese-Americans in makeshift detention camps during World War II. While these rulings may be regarded as exceptional in the Court's history, they offer little reassurance to those expecting judicial "knights in shining armor" always to wield their swords of judicial review to defend the rights of individuals in distress.

History of the Court

The exercise of judicial review by Supreme Court Justices has had an interesting, and somewhat mixed, history. The rulings of the Court during the past 180 years reveal that the orientations of the Justices have tended to shift quite remarkably, reflecting changes in both social concerns and legal perspectives. It is possible, in fact, to distinguish several periods in the Court's history during which certain issues dominated the Justices' attention.

1789–1865

During the initial period of the Court's history, from 1789 until the Civil War, the Justices were primarily involved in power disputes between the federal government and the states. Under the reign of John Marshall, who served as Chief Justice from 1801 to 1835, they labored not only to establish the Court as the supreme interpreter of the Constitution[11] but to strengthen the authority of the federal government. They ruled in *McCullock* v. *Maryland* (1819), for instance, that the states could not interfere with the authority of Congress to create a national bank by the use of their taxing power, and declared in *Gibbons* v. *Ogden* (1824) that Congress, not the states, had the ultimate authority to regulate interstate commerce. Because the federal government, Marshall stated, is "emphatically, and truly, a government of all the people," its decisions must prevail.

Even with Marshall's death in 1835, the Justices continued to be preoccupied with the nation-state issue. However, under Roger B. Taney, who served as Chief Justice from 1836 to 1864, they retreated from the strong support previously given to the claims of the federal government and gave greater (although not exclusive) support to the claims of the states. They asserted that the

Chief Justice Roger B. Taney

two levels of government were basically coequal and that powers delegated to the federal government were clearly limited by the powers reserved to the states in the Tenth Amendment. The reputation of the Taney Court was badly tarnished, however, by the *Dred Scott* v. *Sanford* decision in 1857 that Congress had no right to exclude slavery from the new territories. This decision greatly undermined the Court's prestige in the North for more than a generation and may even have helped precipitate the Civil War.

1865–1941

From the Civil War until the New Deal in the 1930s, the Justices turned their attention from the nation-state issue and became preoccupied with guarding capitalist industrial development from governmental regulation. Although previous Justices under Marshall and Taney had been concerned with business and property rights as well, most of the Justices during this second period were business-oriented, and they condemned almost all attempts by government to regulate free enterprise. Under a succession of

Chief Justices, the Court held that a provision of the Fourteenth Amendment (ratified in 1868) prohibiting the taking of a person's property without "due process" also protected business enterprises from governmental interference. It ruled that a corporation was a "person," and that employers and employees had a right to bargain in any way they wished. In due course, it struck down the federal income tax in 1895,[12] overturned legislation curbing child labor in 1918,[13] and repealed minimum wage laws for women in 1923.[14] These and similar rulings were condemned by Progressives who viewed the Justices as merely defenders of industrial "robber barons."

Interestingly, the Great Depression in the 1930s brought the Court's probusiness orientation into direct conflict with Franklin Roosevelt's New Deal. Maintaining a laissez-faire philosophy, the Court declared more than eleven major New Deal policies unconstitutional. President Roosevelt sharply attacked their destruction of his policies and vowed revenge. In a message to Congress in 1937, he asked for legislation to increase the Supreme Court's size from nine to fifteen Justices and thereby ensure a majority sympathetic to the New Deal. Although this "Court-packing" plan failed to win support in Congress, the President's determination eventually sparked some changes. Several of the Justices switched their positions ("The switch in time that saved nine"), and vacancies on the bench finally allowed Roosevelt to appoint new Justices who favored his policies. As a result, the Court upheld both the Social Security Act and the National Labor Relations Act as valid federal legislation.

1941–1969

Following the entrance of the United States into World War II, the major concern (and controversy) facing the Justices began to involve, not business-government relations, but the issue of equal rights and due process. And, during this twenty-eight-year period, a majority of Justices were found on both sides of the issue. During the reigns of Chief Justice Harlon Stone (1941 to 1946) and Chief Justice Fred Vinson (1946 to 1953), the Court generally refused to challenge the federal government's repressions of individual rights. Not only did the Justices, in *Korematsu v. United States* (1944), uphold the infamous order incarcerating thousands of Japanese-Americans in detention camps during World War II, but they also, in *Dennis v. United States* (1951), upheld the Smith Act prohibiting freedom of speech for certain political groups and refrained from interfering with the persecution of private citizens by Senator Joseph McCarthy and the House Un-American Activities Committee.

Not until the Court came under the direction of former California Governor Earl Warren in 1953 did it actively employ judicial review to extend the protections of the Bill of Rights. The Warren Court ruled that the procedural protections of the Bill of Rights (applying mainly to Congress) also applied to the states via the "due process" and "equal protection" clauses of the Fourteenth Amendment. This meant that the states had to recognize and uphold the provisions of the Fourteenth Amendment and that state laws violating these provisions were unconstitutional. (The Supreme Court, in *Gitlow* v. *New York*, 1925, had already ruled that freedom of speech and of the press—protected by the Fourteenth Amendment from abridgment by Congress—also were not to be restricted by the states). Thus, although by no means unwavering in its support for individual rights, the Warren Court struck down state laws supporting racial segregation in the public schools,[15] required the states to furnish an attorney for any defendant who could not afford one,[16] and prohibited state prosecution of criminal *suspects* not notified of their rights or provided with counsel during interrogations.[17] These rulings won favorable notice from many Americans who felt the Justices had performed a valuable service for individual rights too long ignored or resisted by other agencies of government. But they also won a surprising amount of criticism from those who thought the Justices had moved too fast and too far.

1969–Present

Many observers contend that Richard Nixon's appointment to the bench of four so-called judicial conservatives, beginning in 1969, initiated a new period for the Supreme Court. Under Chief Justice Warren Burger, the Court appeared to reverse the tendency of its immediate predecessor to interpret broadly the Constitution and extend legal protections for individual rights. Although the Burger Court continued to battle for individual rights in such significant areas as busing, abortion, and the famous Pentagon Papers case, it also weakened the rights of criminal suspects,[18] made it easier for state and local officials to define and crack down on "pornography,"[19] and upheld the Bank Secrecy Act allowing governmental officials broad access to citizens' banking records.[20]

The new direction of the Court was evidently welcomed by those who had criticized the Warren Court for making policy decisions they felt belonged to the elected branches of government; they had argued that Supreme Court Justices should keep their hands off social problems and not substitute their own social values for statutes passed by Congress and state legislatures. Taking a similar view, President Nixon had promised to appoint only "strict constructionists" who would interpret the Constitution according to the precise meaning of its words. "It is my belief," he declared, "that it is the duty of a judge to interpret the Constitution and not to place himself above the Constitution or outside the Constitution. He should not twist or bend the Constitution in order to perpetuate his personal political and social values."[21] Thus, Nixon expected his appointments of Warren Burger, Harry Blackmun, Lewis Powell, and William Rehnquist would force the Court to conform to his standards of judicial conservatism and not make sweeping changes in existing law.

Table 8-1. Supreme Court, 1976

	Age	Appointed by	Date
Chief Justice:			
Warren E. Burger	66	Nixon	1969
Associate Justices:			
John Paul Stevens	55	Ford	1975
William H. Rehnquist	51	Nixon	1972
Lewis F. Powell, Jr.	68	Nixon	1972
Harry A. Blackmun	67	Nixon	1970
Thurgood Marshall	67	Johnson	1967
Byron R. White	58	Kennedy	1962
Potter Stewart	60	Eisenhower	1958
William J. Brennan, Jr.	69	Eisenhower	1956

Of course, as many scholars have pointed out, such labels as "strict constructionist" and "judicial conservative" are oversimplifications. Certainly many of the Burger Court's decisions—notably the 1973 ruling striking down state laws against abortions—reflect as broad an interpretation of the Constitution as any decision handed down by the Warren Court. Few Justices are likely to pass up the chance to apply their own values to legal interpretations, or to ignore completely their unique opportunity to influence American life. In fact, the vagueness of key phrases in the

Constitution compels the Justices to apply their own criteria, to choose among alternative and competing values. "Throughout the 184 years of the Court's history," Chief Justice Warren Burger recently stated, "you see the Justices struggling repeatedly to define phrases such as 'due process of law,' 'establishment of religion,' 'freedom of speech,' 'equal protection,' or 'probable cause' for arrest, search, or seizure. By their very nature, these concepts are general words that must be applied to real-life situations."[22]*

Thus, whether Supreme Court Justices are considered liberal or conservative, they tend to apply their own brands of judicial activism and judicial conservatism in interpreting the Constitution. For example, one writer notes, "Liberal Justices Douglas and Black were a great team of strict constructionists of the First Amendment. When the Constitution says, 'Congress shall make no laws . . . abridging the freedom of speech, or of the press,' they judged it to mean just that—*no law*, and that includes no laws against pornography, for example. Is this what Nixon meant, too?"[23]

Most critics of the Court also have voiced different opinions of its actions at various times in history. While many so-called conservatives lambasted the frequent use of judicial review by the Warren Court in the 1950s and 1960s, they applauded its use in the 1930s when an earlier Court overturned many of Franklin Roosevelt's New Deal policies. Similarly, while many self-proclaimed liberals were gratified to see the Warren Court flex its judicial review muscles, they were strongly critical of such displays by more conservative, probusiness Courts in the past. In view of such changes of opinion, it is clear that the major issue has not been the Supreme Court's activism or restraint, but rather the substantive nature of its decisions. To put it more bluntly, support or rejection of the Court's activist role has often depended merely on whose ox is being gored by its rulings.

Constraints on Judicial Action

Although ruling-elite theorists and others may consider the Supreme Court one of the nation's most elitist institutions, the Justices remain under considerable constraint. The President, Congress, even ordinary citizens can employ weapons against the Justices to circumvent their judicial rulings. Let us first consider Congress.

*Excerpts from "The Chief Justice Talks About the Court." Used with permission from *Reader's Digest*, February 1973.

Congress

If members of Congress become sufficiently upset over the decisions of Supreme Court Justices, they have several alternative weapons to employ. For one, they may impeach a Justice in an attempt to intimidate or remove him for actions they consider offensive. When Gerald Ford was House Minority Leader in 1970, he introduced a resolution to impeach Justice William O. Douglas. Ford apparently disliked the "radical" political views expressed in Douglas's book *Points of Rebellion*, excerpts of which surfaced in an issue of *Evergreen* magazine featuring photographs of nudes. Ford's threat to impeach the reputable Justice was based on the elusive constitutional provision that judges "shall hold their offices during good behavior," as well as Ford's own remarkable view that "an impeachable offense is whatever a majority of the House of Representatives considers it to be at a given moment in history." (See Chapter Seven.) However, Ford's efforts to impeach Douglas fizzled when the House Judiciary Committee concluded that no sufficient grounds for impeachment existed. Actually, impeachment has never been a potent weapon against Supreme Court Justices. Although four lower federal court judges have been removed by Congress, not a single member of the Supreme Court has been deposed. The only Supreme Court Justice who has been impeached—that is, formally accused of an offense by the House—was Samuel Chase, who was accused in 1805 of making seditious public statements about the Jefferson administration; but the Senate did not find Chase guilty.

Members of Congress also have the constitutional power to take away the Justices' appellate jurisdiction in certain kinds of cases. Article III states that, except for original jurisdiction in a few areas, the Court's right to hear appeals on federal questions is subject to "such exceptions, and under such regulations as the Congress shall make." Although Congress has not exercised it in more than one hundred years, this power remains a potentially significant threat to the Court's independence.

If members of Congress are reluctant to impeach Court Justices or strip them of their appellate jurisdiction, they can always try instead to change the Court's size in order to alter its philosophical complexion. In fact, Congress seriously considered this tactic in 1937 when President Roosevelt threatened to pack the Court with six additional members after the Court invalidated some important New Deal policies. However, Congress declined to accept the Court-packing scheme and has not seriously considered such a move since.

Probably the most effective way for members of Congress to keep Supreme Court Justices in line is to pass constitutional amendments reversing their decisions. As we saw in Chapter Seven, the Constitution empowers Congress to amend the Constitution if it can muster the support of three-fourths of the state legislatures. In 1909, for example, Congress passed the Sixteenth Amendment (ratified by the states in 1913) establishing the federal income tax. This amendment directly overturned an earlier Court ruling that such a tax would be unconstitutional.[24] Although this and other procedures have not been resorted to often, the threat of congressional retaliation always exists.

The President

Supreme Court Justices must be concerned about the challenges of the President as well as of Congress. While the President's weapons may not be as dramatic as those of Congress, his influence tends to be more immediate and direct. For one thing, he can alter the philosophy of the Court by appointing new Justices. Although some Presidents have had little opportunity to place new Justices on the bench (Calvin Coolidge, for example, appointed only one), others have appointed sufficient numbers to affect the Court's judicial orientation. Richard Nixon, for example, by filling four vacancies on the Court, considerably shifted the Court's judicial philosophy during his five and a half years in office.

Equally significant is the President's command of the federal bureaucracy that enforces the law. Because Supreme Court Justices can boast no police or army of their own—that is, no independent enforcement machinery—they ultimately must rely on the President and Justice Department to carry out their decisions. If they were to make a decision strongly offensive to the President (as well as to Congress and most other Americans), they might find themselves in a helpless position. When President Lincoln suspended the writ of habeas corpus during the Civil War, for instance, the Court could not even muster the courage to scold him for his actions until after Lincoln had died. And, when the Court ruled in 1954 that racial segregation in the public schools was unconstitutional, schools throughout the country remained—and still remain—segregated. Little or no effort was made by President Eisenhower or by state officials to enforce the Court's ruling. As the Governor of Texas stated flatly in 1956, "The Supreme Court passed the law, so let the Supreme Court enforce it."

The People

Indeed, the Justices' reliance on public support can significantly constrain their power. In the opinion of many scholars, Supreme Court Justices must remain sensitive to the changing climates of opinion or run the risk of sacrificing the Court's legitimacy. Because the Justices ultimately depend on the President and the cooperation of the public to enforce their rulings, they cannot afford to make too many decisions running counter to the political mainstream of the times. In the words of the late Justice Felix Frankfurter, "The Court's authority—possessed neither of the purse nor the sword—ultimately rests on sustained public confidence in its moral sanction." This means that even the Justices' support of individual rights can never extend too far beyond the tolerance of majority opinion. If it did, the public could ignore their decisions or encourage Congress to supersede the Justices' authority through a constitutional amendment.

In recent years attempts have been under way to measure the impact of Supreme Court decisions by determining the extent of public compliance with its rulings.[25] One conclusion is that although most Court decisions are obeyed—especially those requiring the compliance of only a few officials, such as a ruling on the death penalty—other decisions directed toward major social reform have been more difficult to enforce. On matters of racial discrimination, for example, Justices have found their decisions on desegregating public schools, busing of school children, and open housing ignored by a large segment of the population. These decisions have aggravated deeply ingrained prejudices and necessarily depend for their effectiveness on the cooperation of millions of people.

The Justices Themselves

Finally, Supreme Court Justices observe their own restrictions on judicial review. Because their jurisdiction is primarily appellate, they cannot take the initiative. They must wait for a case to be appealed to the Court before they can pass judgment. And, even when such an appeal surfaces, at least four of the Justices must agree on the legal importance of the case before it can be accepted for consideration.

Furthermore, Justices tend to fashion their own doctrine of "judicial restraint." Although Justices are not likely to pass up every temptation to exercise the powers of their office, they know such temptations must be restrained by political realities. They must at least retreat from cases that might jeopardize the Court's independence. Most Justices have been reluctant, for example, to interfere with presidential decisions in foreign and military affairs, even when those decisions have raised serious constitutional questions. In 1970, the Massachusetts state legislature filed a suit challenging the constitutionality of United States involvement in Vietnam. The suit requested the Justices to declare American participation "unconstitutional in that it was not initially authorized or subsequently ratified by Congressional declaration." But a majority of the Justices refused to review the suit, just as they refused to entertain suits challenging the legality of the draft in an undeclared war and the right of President Nixon to send troops into Cambodia without formal congressional authorization. Unlike Justice William O. Douglas (who would likely have brought the Court directly into the Vietnam War controversy) most of the Justices decided to skirt the issue. Given the long-standing public concern about "national security"—as well as the fear that the President would ignore the Court's ruling anyway—little serious consideration was given to challenging executive authority in military matters.

One effect of this reluctance has been to frustrate many citizens who earnestly have looked to the Court for help in defeating foreign policy and other decisions with which they disagree. Their attempts to gain access to the Court have been shadowed by the practical political considerations that may influence the Justices' decision whether to hear a case, regardless of the case's constitutional implications. Because the Justices either may refuse to consider the constitutionality of certain governmental policies or may be unable to enforce their decisions, citizens have faced innumerable challenges in trying to confront existing laws and practices through the Court.

Approaching the Bench

Since judicial review can be exercised only after a case is brought before the Court, we should consider some of the ways a case may reach the Court and be decided. Occasionally we hear people proclaim defiantly that they will fight an issue "all the way to the Supreme Court." What these people may not realize is that, even if they could afford to spend thousands of dollars to appeal a case to the highest court, there is no assurance the case would be heard. Apart from political considerations weighed by the Justices, a case will not be heard unless it raises constitutional questions having greater significance than the outcome of a single dispute. The kinds of cases typically reaching the Court involve issues affecting a large segment of society.

In fact, the Justices severely limit the number of cases they review each year, despite the enormous quantity of petitions pouring in. Unlike members of Congress, Supreme Court Justices have no committee system to divide the workload; they must all help to decide each case. In 1973, for example, they received petitions to hear more than 4,600 cases—an increase of 2,000 cases during the preceding decade. If they had been required to rule on all the petitions in 1973, they would have had to decide more than 15 cases a day! Instead, they ruled on only about 200 cases that year, which meant that more than 95 percent of the appeals were dismissed.

This does not imply that citizens face impossible odds in winning a Supreme Court hearing. In exceptional cases, individuals with little money and legal support have successfully brought civil rights and criminal justice cases before the Court. In the early 1960s, a prisoner in Florida named Clarence Gideon sought a review of his conviction by submitting a handwritten letter asking the Court for a writ of habeas corpus—an order freeing him on the grounds that he was illegally imprisoned. According to federal statues, persons too poor to pay the usual costs of a court appeal may proceed "in forma pauperis" (in the manner of a pauper). Thus, although Gideon had little money and had drafted his petition in pencil on lined paper, the Justices accepted his case. They eventually ruled in his favor, finding that, because he did not have the benefit of an attorney in his original trial, his conviction was invalid—thus establishing the landmark decision *Gideon* v. *Wainwright* (1963).[26]

Jurisdiction of the Court

Essentially two principal ways exist to gain access to the Supreme Court. The first is to rely on the Court's "original jurisdiction" which, as described in the Constitution, permits a case to be brought directly before the Court. Since the Supreme Court is the final arbitrator or umpire of the federal system, it has the original jurisdiction to settle major disputes between various levels and branches of government. However, the Court normally will hear such disputes only when they involve "Ambassadors, other public Ministers and Consuls," or when they involve controversies between two or more states, residents of different states, or a state against the federal government. In fact, such "original" cases have been quite rare, having been settled by the Court only about 150 times. A frequently cited example is the 1963 dispute between Arizona and California over water rights in the Colorado River.

A more common path to the Court is through its "appellate jurisdiction," as established by Congress. The Supreme Court often will entertain an appeal from an ordinary citizen whose case raises a substantial federal question (such as a potential violation of the Bill of Rights). An appeal usually is made by the losing party in a lower-court case who claims the judge wrongly interpreted the Constitution. Although the Supreme Court has a basic obligation to accept certain kinds of appeals—for example, when a state court overturns an act of Congress, or when a federal court strikes down a state law—most of the cases reaching the Court do so through a petition for a writ of *certiorari* (Latin for "to be made more certain"). Essentially, such a petition is a request by the losing party that the Supreme Court order a lower court to send up the records of the case for review. Normally, the Justices will agree to issue such a writ (to hear the case) only when at least four of them feel the issue at stake involves a serious constitutional question or falls within the Court's jurisdiction. This means that even though the Court may be flooded by thousands of petitions for a writ of certiorari each year, the Justices will grant only a few hundred; the decision as to which cases to accept is entirely up to them.

Deciding the Cases

How then do the nine Justices process the cases they agree to hear? Usually, they hear cases in open court two weeks each month during the October-June term, scheduling the other two weeks for research and opinion writing. On the Mondays through Thursdays when open court sessions are held, the Justices march into the marble-columned courtroom at precisely 10:00 A.M. dressed in flowing black robes. (No wigs will be worn, however, since they do not mimic this aspect of the British judicial costume.) As they pull up their chairs behind a huge mahogany bench, the "crier of the Court" pounds his gavel and shouts:

Oyez, Oyez, Oyez! All persons having business before the Honorable, the Supreme Court of the United States are admonished to draw near and give their attention, for the Court is now sitting. God save the United States and this Honorable Court!

After dispensing with administrative chores, the Justices read their decisions on previously heard cases. The Chief Justice then calls for the first case of the day, to be presented by opposing attorneys seated at the counsel tables in front of the bench. Although the Justices already will have reviewed the written briefs of all sides of the case, they will allow the lawyers to present brief oral arguments. They usually allow only thirty minutes for each side, although in some important cases they will allot more time. To the chagrin of the lawyers, the Justices may interrupt their speeches to ask questions or contradict their arguments. At times, the Justices may even talk among themselves, scribble notes, or, as in the exceptional case of Oliver Wendell Holmes, who frequently had already made up his mind, take a nap.

But, as imposing as these public sessions may be, the real work of the Justices takes place behind the scenes. Each Justice spends most of his time researching and studying cases alone or with law clerks. Then, every Friday morning, the Justices assemble in an ornate conference room to decide which new petitions for writs of certiorari to accept, and to vote on the cases already presented in chamber. These conferences may last all day and are totally confidential—not even law clerks or stenographers are allowed to attend. The junior Justice (the last member appointed to the Court) usually acts as the "guardian of the door," occasionally dashing from the conference table to accept or deliver messages.

Although it is difficult to learn what goes on in these secret meetings, we do know the Chief Justice presides and usually begins each meeting by summarizing the cases and how he feels they should be decided. For example, on a petititon for a writ of certiorari he might argue "this is a very compelling issue . . . but we cannot improve on the decision made by the Court of Appeals. So I suggest we deny the petition." He then yields to the senior Associate Justice, with discussion proceeding down the line in order of seniority until each Justice has voiced an opinion. When they are ready to vote—sometimes after heated debate—the junior Justice votes first and the Chief Justice last. Unless a case receives four affirmative votes, review is denied.

When a case has been accepted, presented in chamber, and voted on—with at least five Justices agreeing—a majority opinion

"My dissenting opinion will be brief:
'You're all full of crap!'"

must be drafted explaining the Court's decision. If the Chief Justice sides with the majority, he will assign the job either to himself or to another Justice who supported the same view; otherwise, the senior Associate Justice in the majority will make the assignment. Usually, the drafting of an opinion is an intricate process taking weeks or even months to complete. An initial draft will likely circulate among the Justices for many rewritings until it is approved by everyone in the majority. Those Justices who disagree with the majority view may, of course, write a dissenting opinion. Sometimes, Justices writing a dissenting opinion can persuade their colleagues to change their minds before the final decision is read in open court.

Ironically, some observers see this practice of dissenting as weakening the prestige of the Court by revealing its internal divisions. The fact that many important Court decisions have been split five to four or six to three convinces some critics that the Court often cannot provide a definitive solution to a legal controversy.

Yet, many powerful legal expressions have been voiced in dissent-ing Court opinions—especially in those by Oliver Wendell Holmes, Louis Brandeis, and Hugo Black. In fact, many dissenting opin-ions eventually become the Court's majority opinion, reflecting both changes in the times and new perspectives on legal issues. (Indeed, since 1789, the Supreme Court has reversed itself at least 140 times.)

The Chief Justice

It should be understood that judicial influence is not shared equal-ly by all nine Justices. Just as some members of Congress exert a disproportionate influence on policy making, some Justices, by virtue of their superior legal skills, exert considerably greater in-fluence on judicial decisions.

The role of the Chief Justice is extremely important in this regard, for if he is an especially forceful individual, he can stamp his own character on the Court. The Chief Justice gains special authority by presiding over open court sessions and by directing the secret Friday conferences, in which he usually presents his views first and votes last. Although having only one vote, he has the power to set time limits on debate, establish ground rules for discussion, and assign the writing of Court opinions. In addi-tion, he is the Court's symbolic head and holds in some respects the highest governmental office next to that of the President. By virtue of his prestige, he may guide the Court toward making a profound and lasting imprint on national policy.

Recruitment to the High Court

As we would expect, a major influence on judicial decision making is the background of each person appointed to the Court. Yet, while the Constitution outlines legal requirements for other politi-cal offices—the President, for example, must be at least thirty-five years old and born in the United States, and a Senator must be at least thirty years old and an American citizen for a minimum of nine years—it is silent about the qualifications of a Supreme Court Justice. As far as the Constitution is concerned, a Justice could be foreign born (and not even a United States citizen), too young to vote, and totally without legal training.

In fact, the Constitution does not even specify how many Justices there should be. This responsibility was handed to Congress. In the beginning, the Court was composed of only six members; but this number was changed half a dozen times until Congress finally settled on nine Justices in 1869.

However, although the Constitution does not specify any legal qualifications to be a Supreme Court Justice, other, informal qualifications have tended to prevail. The backgrounds of Justices have been similar to those of Presidents and members of Congress in that they have not been representative of the general population. Most have been Protestant, financially independent, and fifty to fifty-five years of age at the time of their appointment. Only about 10 percent have been Catholic or Jewish; only one has been black; and so far, none has been a woman. (It might be noted that some of President Ford's aides in the summer of 1975 did tout a woman candidate for the Court—Carla Hills, Secretary of Housing and Urban Development—before Ford finally picked yet another man, John Paul Stevens, to replace the retired William O. Douglas.)

Interestingly enough, although every Supreme Court Justice has been a lawyer, few have had prior experience as a judge. Out of the 101 Justices in the Court's history, at least 60 have had no prior judicial training. This includes some of the Court's most eminent members, such as John Marshall, Louis Brandeis, Felix Frankfurter, and Earl Warren. Generally speaking, Justices do not reach the Supreme Court by advancing up through the lower federal or state courts.

The Role of the President

Although a seat on the high bench is a top prize for those seeking political influence, it cannot be campaigned for like a seat in Congress or won through a public popularity contest. Like other federal judgeships, a Supreme Court seat must be filled by presidential appointment, subject to Senate approval. Article II of the Constitution, dealing with the executive branch, states that the President "shall nominate, and by and with the Advice and Consent of the Senate, shall appoint . . . Judges of the Supreme Court."

Historically, Presidents have tended to select Justices who reflect their own political and judicial philosophies, using the appointive process to augment their political influence. Because rulings of the Supreme Court can greatly affect national policy, the appointment of Justices is a prime way for Presidents to implant their own ideas on the Court's judicial decisions. As Richard Nixon once stated, "There is probably no more important legacy that a President of the United States can leave in these times than his appointments to the Supreme Court. . . . You will recall, I am sure, that during my campaign for the Presidency I pledged to nominate to the Supreme Court individuals who shared my judicial philosophy."[27] Given this perspective, it should not be surprising that approximately 90 percent of all Supreme Court Justices appointed between 1789 and 1975 have belonged to the same party as the appointing President.

Table 8-2. Supreme Court Nominations Not Confirmed by the Senate

From 1789 through 1970, 27 Supreme Court nominations have failed to receive Senate confirmation. Of these, 11 have been rejected outright and the remainder withdrawn or allowed to lapse when Senate rejection appeared imminent. Following is the complete list of nominees failing to receive confirmation:

Nominee	President	Date of Nomination	Senate Action	Date of Senate Action
William Paterson	Washington	Feb. 27, 1793	Withdrawn	(Later renominated and confirmed)
John Rutledge (for Chief Justice)	Washington	July 1, 1795	Rejected (10-14)	Dec. 15, 1795
Alexander Wolcott	Madison	Feb. 4, 1811	Rejected (9-24)	Feb. 13, 1811
John J. Crittenden	John Quincy Adams	Dec. 17, 1828	Postponed	Feb. 12, 1829
Roger Brooke Taney	Jackson	Jan. 15, 1835	Postponed	March 3, 1825 (Later nominated for Chief Justice and confirmed)
John C. Spencer	Tyler	Jan. 9, 1844	Rejected (21-26)	Jan. 31, 1844
Reuben H. Walworth	Tyler	March 13, 1844	Withdrawn	
Edward King	Tyler	June 5, 1844	Postponed	June 15, 1844
Edward King	Tyler	Dec. 4, 1844	Withdrawn	
John M. Read	Tyler	Feb. 7, 1845	Not Acted Upon	
George W. Woodward	Polk	Dec. 23, 1845	Rejected (20-29)	Jan. 22, 1846
Edward A. Bradford	Fillmore	Aug. 16, 1852	Not Acted Upon	
George E. Badger	Fillmore	Jan. 10, 1853	Postponed	Feb. 11, 1853
William C. Micou	Fillmore	Feb. 24, 1853	Not Acted Upon	
Jeremiah S. Black	Buchanan	Feb. 5, 1861	Rejected (25-26)	Feb. 21, 1861
Henry Stanbery	Andrew Johnson	April 16, 1866	Not Acted Upon	
Ebenezer R. Hoar	Grant	Dec. 15, 1869	Rejected (24-33)	Feb. 3, 1870
George H. Williams (for Chief Justice)	Grant	Dec. 1, 1873	Withdrawn	
Caleb Cushing (for Chief Justice)	Grant	Jan. 9, 1874	Withdrawn	
Stanley Matthews	Hayes	Jan. 26, 1881	Not Acted Upon	(Later renominated and confirmed)
William B. Hornblower	Cleveland	Sept. 19, 1893	Rejected (24-30)	Jan. 15, 1894
Wheeler H. Peckham	Cleveland	Jan. 22, 1894	Rejected (32-41)	Feb. 16, 1894
John J. Parker	Hoover	March 21, 1930	Rejected (39-41)	May 7, 1930
Abe Fortas (for Chief Justice)	Lyndon Johnson	June 26, 1968	Withdrawn	
Homer Thornberry	Lyndon Johnson	June 26, 1968	Not Acted Upon	
Clement F. Haynsworth Jr.	Nixon	Aug. 18, 1969	Rejected (45-55)	Nov. 21, 1969
G. Harrold Carswell	Nixon	Jan. 19, 1970	Rejected (45-51)	April 8, 1970

Source: Library of Congress, Congressional Research Service *Congressional Quarterly*, 1973.

The very process of selecting a Justice can be remarkably political. While federal district judgeships are usually filled on the recommendations of state party organizations or Senators from each state, vacancies on the Supreme Court are filled after the President has received recommendations from a variety of sources. Members of Congress, lobbyists, judges, and other interested persons may be asked for their lists of personal favorites long before a final selection is made. There is usually an effort to maintain some religious, ethnic, and geographic balance on the Court to help legitimize its decisions and gain political support from influential groups. However, as we have seen, such considerations have not applied to most minority groups and to women, who generally have been excluded from the appointive process.

Naturally, the ability of Presidents to shape the Court to their own philosophies is limited by the necessity of winning Senate approval. For example, Richard Nixon saw both of his southern nominees, Clement Haynesworth, Jr., and G. Harold Carswell, rejected by the Senate in 1969 and 1970. The record for rejections, however, is held by John Tyler, who saw four of his nominees turned down. Although the Senate does not customarily resist presidential nominations in such fashion, at least one of every five has been either postponed, rejected, or not acted on at all (see Table 8-2).

Presidents sometimes also make mistakes and discover that their appointees take positions contrary to what they expected. Supreme Court Justices can become quite independent once they reach the bench, especially since they are appointed for life. President Eisenhower, for example, was less than happy to find Earl Warren—a Republican whom he had appointed Chief Justice in 1953—leading one of the most activist Courts in American history. The appointment of Warren, Eisenhower reportedly lamented, was "the biggest damnfool mistake I ever made." As we will see, some critics suggest that Supreme Court Justices, rather than being appointed by the President, should be elected directly by the voters.

Other Courts, Other Judges

Although Supreme Court Justices stand at the pinnacle of the federal judicial structure, the rulings of lower federal and state court judges also can have tremendous political and legal significance. Without the diligence of District Court Judge John Sirica. (*Time* magazine's "Man of the Year" for 1973), the Watergate scandal might have attracted considerably less attention. It was Judge Sirica, a Republican who headed the federal district court in the nation's capital, who presided at the trial of the seven Watergate burglars and who broke open the case by agreeing to review their penalties if they talked—as James McCord eventually did. Not only did the disclosures in Judge Sirica's courtroom help elevate the original burglary into a national scandal, but it was there that the White House, the Senate Watergate Committee, and the special prosecutor battled over possession of the elusive White House tapes. It was Judge Sirica, not the Justices of the Supreme Court, who first pitted the judicial branch against the President of the United States by ordering Richard Nixon to turn over the tapes for court inspection. Even a President, Sirica ruled, must respond to subpoenas for evidence in criminal cases; the court, not the President, must decide whether claims of executive privilege to withhold such evidence are valid.

Judge John Sirica

Given the latent political importance and legal power of judges like Sirica in the American judicial system, we should consider the nature of their duties and the structure of their courts. Article III of the Constitution specifies that "the judicial power of the United States shall be vested in one supreme Court, and in such inferior Courts as the Congress may from time to time ordain and establish." This means that although the Constitution specifically provides for the Supreme Court, it gives Congress the sole authority to determine the number and jurisdiction of other federal courts. Beginning with the Judiciary Act of 1789, which established the first federal district and circuit courts, Congress has been creating an increasing number of federal courts to meet the country's growing size and judicial workload.

Federal District Courts

The largest number of federal courts are those at the base of the federal judicial system, the district courts. At present, there are eighty-nine federal district courts in the United States, plus one in the Commonwealth of Puerto Rico. Containing anywhere from one to twenty-four judges each, these district courts settle all civil disputes between citizens of different states in which more than $10,000 is at stake, resolve federal questions arising under the Constitution, federal laws, or treaties (such as the constitutional controversy surrounding the White House tapes), and conduct trials for all violations of federal law (such as counterfeiting, illegal immigration, and fraud). These district courts have original jurisdiction only, and do not hear cases on appeal.

The work of these district courts has received a great deal of attention in recent years, not only as a result of the original Watergate revelations in Judge Sirica's courtroom but as a result of the trials of several former Nixon associates—including Attorney General John Mitchell, White House chief of staff H. R. Haldeman, and presidential assistant John Ehrlichman. These trials, as much as anything, underscored the Watergate issues and helped bring down the Nixon administration.

Courts of Appeals

Because the rulings of district court judges are occasionally controversial or imprecise, the federal judicial system also provides eleven different courts of appeals to review their decisions. Each of these courts of appeals serves one of the eleven judicial circuits into which the country has been divided and contains anywhere from three to fifteen permanent judgeships. They have the responsibility not only to hear appeals from lower district courts but occasionally to review decisions of the federal regulatory agencies, such as the Federal Communications Commission and the Civil Aeronautics Board. Because these courts hear cases only on appeal, they do not use juries; instead, three judges normally sit as a panel to hear each case.

It may be recalled that the federal courts of appeals also received publicity from the Watergate scandal, especially in 1973 when the seven-member court of appeals in Washington, D.C., upheld Judge Sirica's order directing President Nixon to hand over the White House tapes. Although Nixon later appealed a similar case to the Supreme Court, he obeyed the ruling of the court of appeals in the first confrontation, establishing a precedent future Presidents may find difficult to ignore. This same court of appeals, incidentally, also attracted national publicity by overturning most of the government's prosecutions of 12,000 demonstrators arrested during the Washington, D.C., May Day protests in 1971.

Special Federal Courts

In addition to the district and appeals courts, a number of other federal courts have been created by Congress to deal with special kinds of cases. Briefly stated, these courts include the United States Court of Claims, Customs Court, Court of Customs and Patent Appeals, Tax Court, Court of Military Appeals, and the Territorial Courts. The judges of these courts, like the judges of the district and appeals courts, are appointed by the President with the consent of the Senate. And the decisions of these courts also may be appealed to the Supreme Court.

State Courts

Finally, we should remember that there are two different sets of courts in the United States—federal and state. Each of the fifty states has its own court system to handle cases not within the judicial power granted to the federal courts by the Constitution and Congress. Theoretically, neither set of courts is inferior to the other, but the state courts must obey the rulings of the United

States Supreme Court even if those rulings conflict with state laws. In fact, the Supreme Court often has used judicial review to overturn decisions of the state courts.

State court judges nevertheless play an extremely important role in the judicial system. Not only do they possess the same judicial review power to interpret acts of state legislatures and other state officials, but they, not federal court judges, try most of the nation's civil and criminal cases. This is because the bulk of criminal and civil laws—such as those covering divorce, negligence, burglary, and homicide—are enacted by the states and not the federal government. Thus, although most Americans probably will never be a party in a federal court case, there are few who have not at least paid for a traffic ticket in a state municipal court.

It might be added that, even though the structure of state courts varies throughout the country, most state courts are organized along a similar hierarchy: municipal and justice courts; superior (or county) courts: district courts of appeals; and a state supreme court. And, in contrast to all federal judges, who are appointed by the President with the approval of the Senate, in about two-thirds of the states the judges are elected at the polls.[28]

Evaluation: Facing Reform

In its long history, the Supreme Court has faced a large number of reform proposals. Some of these proposals have been made by those who strongly support an activist role for the Court but who feel it urgently needs reorganization and streamlining. Still other proposals have been made by those who are strongly critical of the Justices' exercise of power and who wish to see such power severely curtailed. Although the two types of reform proposals overlap in some ways, let us consider an example of each.

Reducing the Workload

The practice of hearing cases for only two weeks each month might seem to give Supreme Court Justices a great deal of time to research and study cases. Yet there have been complaints that their workload has become increasingly hard to bear. As the

Court's annual number of appeals and petitions for certiorari has climbed from about 1,300 cases in the early 1950s to more than 4,600 in the 1970s, concern has been expressed that the Justices have become entangled in too much legal paperwork. With so many cases to consider each year, the Justices have not had enough time properly to oversee the judicial process. And with so many cases competing for the Justices' attention, citizens with legitimate grievances find the opportunities for judicial redress restricted. As Chief Justice Burger asserted in 1971, the greatest challenge facing the Justices in the 1970s would simply be "to try to keep up with the volume of work that ought to come from this Court."[29]

One proposal to meet this challenge was made in 1972 by a study group headed by Harvard Law Professor Paul Freund. This study group, appointed by Chief Justice Burger, recommended the creation of a national court of appeals composed of judges chosen on a rotating basis from the federal courts of appeals. This new court would screen all cases now referred to the Supreme Court for review, and would decide which cases were important enough for the highest court to see. Supreme Court Justices would retain the right to hear any case they wanted, but would be relieved of handling the large volume of mostly trivial and insubstantial petitions. Chief Justice Burger, while not officially endorsing the proposal, urged serious consideration of it, stating that "No person who looks at the facts can rationally assume that nine justices today can process four or five times as many cases as the courts that included Taft, Holmes, Brandeis and Hughes . . . and do the task as it should be done."

However, a number of persons denounced the study group's proposal, on the grounds that Supreme Court Justices would only lose much of their independent authority to decide which new petitions to consider. Former Chief Justice Earl Warren, for instance, felt the creation of a new national court of appeals would do "irreparable harm to the prestige, the power and the function of the Supreme Court." It would simply add to the bureaucracy of justice and impose goals and values conflicting with those expressed by the high Court. Moreover, Justice William O. Douglas asserted, the whole "case for our 'over-work' is a myth" anyway. Not only can most trivial petitions be dismissed quickly, he said, but the actual number of cases resulting in signed opinions has remained substantially the same over the years. "The signed opinions of the Court," Douglas recalled, "totalled 137 in the 1939 term . . . while in the 1971 term we had 129 opinions. . . . So in terms of petitions for certiorari granted and appeals noted and set for argument our load today is substantially what it was 33 years ago."[30] In view of these objections, the proposal to establish an intermediary court of appeals has not been put into effect.

Curbing the Court's Powers

Far more dramatic suggestions for reforming the Court have been offered as a result of repeated criticisms of Court decisions. As we have seen, Supreme Court Justices have had their share of critics who accuse them of usurping undue powers. While some attacked the Justices in the 1930s for obstructing the policies of the New Deal, others criticized the Justices in the 1950s and 1960s for their rulings on school desegregation, police procedures, and prayers in public schools. Such criticisms have given birth to a number of proposals to curb the Justices' powers, such as requiring more than a simple five-to-four majority to render any law or action unconstitutional and narrowing the Justices' appellate jurisdiction.

Perhaps the most dramatic suggestion has been to elect Justices for limited and fixed terms. Critics argue that since the Court plays a major role in policy making, Justices should be elected at the polls instead of appointed by the President for life terms. They contend there is adequate precedent for such a change, since most states currently elect their highest court judges for terms ranging anywhere from six to twelve years. Even though these state court judges also exercise judicial review, the voters still have an opportunity to review their behavior and opinions without resorting to impeachment.

Such a reform proposal, however, has not been vigorously championed, partly because the constraints on the Justices already mentioned have been considered adequate. Many observers insist that the public, through the President and Congress as well as through their own actions, ultimately can circumvent unpopular Court decisions. In addition, many feel reluctant to extend majority control over the Court for reasons discussed earlier. If Justices were required to run periodically for reelection, they might be subject to increased pressures from special interests and no longer would remain sufficiently independent to protect the rights of individuals and minorities from majority prejudices. "The very purpose of having a written Constitution," Chief Justice Burger has stated, "is to provide safeguards for certain rights that cannot yield to public opinion. . . . The Justices' duty is to stand firm in defense of basic Constitutional values, as they see them, even against momentary tides of public opinion."[31]* In any case, as Ruth Ross and Barbara Stone have aptly concluded in their study of California's judicial system, "There are problems with both methods: executive appointment may result in numerous political hacks on the bench, while election assumes that the people are knowledgeable in the area of judicial qualifications and care enough to become informed."[32]

*Excerpts from "The Chief Justice Talks About the Court." Used with permission from *Reader's Digest*, February 1973.

Abraham, Henry J. *The Judiciary: The Supreme Court in the Governmental Process*, 3rd ed. Boston: Allyn and Bacon, 1973.

_____. *The Judicial Process: An Introductory Analysis of the Courts of the United States, England, and France*, 2d ed. New York: Oxford University Press, 1968.

Becker, Theodore L., and Feeley, Malcolm M., eds. *The Impact of Supreme Court Decisions*, 2d ed. New York: Oxford University Press, 1973.

Bickel, Alexander. *The Least Dangerous Branch*. New York: Bobbs-Merrill, 1962.

McCloskey, Robert G. *The American Supreme Court*. Chicago: University of Chicago Press, 1960.

Dean, Howard E. *Judicial Review and Democracy*. New York: Random House, 1966.

Forte, David F., ed. *The Supreme Court in American Politics: Judicial Activism vs. Judicial Restraint*. Lexington, Mass.: D. C. Heath, 1972.

Lewis, Anthony. *Gideon's Trumpet*. New York: Random House, 1964.

Mitau, G. Theodore. *Decade of Decision: The Supreme Court and the Constitutional Revolution 1954–1964*. New York: Charles Scribner's Sons, 1967.

Recommended Reading

1. See, for example, Rober Hodge, Paul Siegel, and Peter Rossi, "Occupational Prestige in the United States, 1925–1963," *American Journal of Sociology*, November 1964, pp. 286–302.

2. Walter F. Murphy and Joseph Tanenhaus, "Public Opinion and the United States Supreme Court," in Joel B. Grossman and Joseph Tanenhaus, eds., *Frontiers of Judicial Research* (New York: Wiley, 1969).

3. *Edwards* v. *South Carolina* (1963).

4. *Brown* v. *Louisiana* (1966).

5. *Adderly* v. *Florida* (1967).

6. *United States* v. *O'Brien* (1968).

Notes

7. See, for example, Edward S. Corwin, ed., *The Constitution of the United States of America: Analysis and Interpretation* (Washington, D.C.: U.S. Government Printing Office, 1953).

8. Charles Beard, "The Supreme Court—Usurper or Grantee?" *Political Science Quarterly*, March 1912, pp. 1–35.

9. *The Federalist*, No. 78.

10. "Law and the Court," *Speeches* (Boston: Little, Brown, 1934), p. 102.

11. *Marbury* v. *Madison* (1803).

12. *Pollock* v. *Farmer's Loan and Trust Company* (1895).

13. *Hammer* v. *Dagenhart* (1918).

14. *Adkins* v. *Children's Hospital* (1923).

15. *Brown* v. *Board of Education* (1954).

16. *Gideon* v. *Wainright* (1963).

17. *Miranda* v. *Arizona* (1966).

18. *Harris* v. *New York* (1971).

19. *Miller* v. *California* (1973).

20. *California Bankers Association* v. *Schultz* (1974).

21. Richard M. Nixon, speech of 21 October 1971.

22. Excerpts from "The Chief Justice Talks About the Court." Used with permission from *Reader's Digest*, February 1973.

23. Robert Sherrill, *Why They Call It Politics*, 2d ed. (New York: Harcourt Brace Jovanovich, 1974), p. 164.

24. *Pollock* v. *Farmer's Loan and Trust Company* (1895).

25. See, for example, Theodore L. Becker and Malcolm M. Feeley, eds., *The Impact of Supreme Court Decisions*, 2d ed. (New York: Oxford University Press, 1973).

26. For more on the case, see Anthony Lewis, *Gideon's Trumpet* (New York: Random House, 1964).

27. Richard M. Nixon, speech of 21 October 1971.

28. For more information, see Henry J. Abraham, *The Judicial Process*, 2d ed. (New York: Oxford University Press, 1968).

29. Quoted in *Congressional Quarterly Weekly Report*, 17 November 1973.

30. Ibid.

31. Excerpts from "The Chief Justice Talks About the Court." Used with permission from *Reader's Digest*, February 1973.

32. Ruth A. Ross and Barbara S. Stone, *California's Political Process* (New York: Random House, 1973), p. 140.

Channels of Citizen Influence

9 Taking On the System:
The Strategies and Pitfalls

As stated at the outset, the question of whether to engage in or retreat from political action looms as a major concern of our time. In view of the many social and political problems facing American society, the call to action places many of us in a dilemma our conscience and reason alone cannot resolve. While we may recognize and lament the problems around us, we may either feel too disgusted with politics to become actively involved or doubt whether any effective means exist to permit meaningful participation.

Of course, not everyone perceives such a dilemma. To some, the desire to work within the system as reformers or as full-time politicians requires little reflection. The driving motivation to obtain political power supersedes any concern about effectiveness and outweighs any consideration of costs. Similarly, to those impatient with the slow progress of reform, commitment to revolutionary action seems a necessary response to the problems of society. The willingness to accept personal sacrifice—based on an optimism that radical political surgery can indeed cure society's ills—requires little debate or self-examination.

But to those who cannot commit themselves to either extreme, the question of whether to take any kind of political action remains problematic. Even if they are not completely disgusted with the political process, they still may wonder whether any of the common tools and strategies for political influence in this country—the vote, the petition, the media, letters to Congress, pressure groups, or direct action (such as demonstrations and strikes) can be employed effectively.

Although the endless variety of circumstances in which political action takes place makes it virtually impossible to answer this question satisfactorily, it is possible at least to explore some of the common promises and pitfalls of each strategy. Assuming a person feels strongly about an issue or problem, what can he or she expect from trying to work within the system to influence policy in a limited, pragmatic, and short-range way?

Guidelines for Action

Obviously, any evaluation of action strategies must first take into account the attitude of an individual toward the political system. Deciding whether to participate at all in politics clearly depends on one's faith in the political process. A person who genuinely believes it is *not* possible to affect policy—that the direction of government cannot be altered by political pressure (whatever the form)—is less likely to participate than someone who maintains an optimistic view.

One often hears that this country boasts a viable "democratic" system offering its citizens numerous ways to influence governmental policy and articulate demands. But many different countries and ideologies are described as "democratic" and have adopted the term as their slogan and justification for being. The concept of democracy is among the most vague and value-laden in all political thought. One scholar estimates there are as many as two hundred separate definitions of the concept.[1] In this country, for example, many people equate democracy with rule by the majority—that is, an electoral process in which a candidate who garners more than 50 percent of the votes represents all the people (including those who did not support him). Yet, a problem with this definition is its failure to suit multiparty elections in which no candidate can win a clear majority. Was democracy discarded in 1968 when Richard Nixon became President, even though more people combined voted for his two opponents, Hubert Humphrey and George Wallace?

To many other people, democracy ultimately implies support for "liberty" and "equality," protection of minority rights, respect for the individual, a fundamental written law, and the availability of choice. To still others, it simply suggests rule in the interests of the people, regardless of the legal and institutional forms. The word itself stems from two Greek roots—*demos* referring broadly to the people and *kratia* connoting rule or authority. Thus, the term implies that rule or authority ultimately is vested in the people.

But definitions should not be our primary concern; the literature on democracy is so exceedingly rich and controversial that we could hardly do full justice to the concept. For the purposes of focusing on citizen action, we might adopt a procedural interpretation of democracy. That is, we might describe a system as democratic if its citizens enjoy a relatively high degree of access to and influence over their leaders. But *relative* is the key word. In no system is there a total absence of public influence over decision makers, and in no system is the influence complete. Hence, the political system in this country may be more or less democratic than another, depending on one's perception of people's ability to affect policy; and that perception will remain controversial.

It is difficult, in fact, to get an accurate estimate of the number of Americans who try to sway political decision making, in part because they tend to exaggerate their involvement. When a sample of Americans were asked in a 1973 Harris survey what political actions they would take to affect policy, 94 percent reported they would go to the polls, 84 percent said they would contact their Representative, 64 percent indicated they would write a letter to a local newspaper, and 72 percent said they would join a citizen-action group.[2] Yet, as shown clearly in Chapter Three, far fewer people resort to any of these political actions. Although 94 percent of the respondents in 1973 said they would go to the polls, actual voter turnout in the 1974 elections was only 38 percent. Although between 65 and 72 percent said they would write letters to their Representative or to newspapers, less than 15 percent have ever done so. In fact, 84 percent of those sampled in a 1966 survey said they had never tried to influence congressional policy, while 79 percent said they had never tried to influence local governmental policy.[3]

Moreover, those who participate may do so for reasons besides wanting to influence policy. They may gain expressive as well as instrumental benefits from their actions, such as letting off steam by firing off letters to a local newspaper. Or perhaps they desire the social contacts stemming from their membership in a political club or organization and enjoy rubbing shoulders with prominent civic officials. Often the opportunity to wield power for its own sake provides sufficient motivation for people to plunge into politics. "To many people in politics," one group of scholars conclude, "the possession of power, in and of itself, is the most desirable goal. It is also a goal which is often underestimated, particularly by those who do not have experience in political affairs, as well as by those at the other extreme who do possess political power but who prefer to disguise their motives in terms of altruism and civic good."[4]

However, despite the different motives and intentions, many do not see any point in becoming politically active. (See Chapter Three.) They do not view the system as ultimately democratic in the sense that they can gain access to and influence over government. Among a sample of Americans polled in 1973, 61 percent agreed with the proposition that "What you think doesn't count much any more."[5] Indeed, many people feel they do not have any control over the affairs of the country, or even over the policies of the city in which they live. Simply being reminded in school or by bumper stickers that "Our system works if you work at it," and "If you're not part of the solution, you're part of the problem," will not compel them to take action. In their view, the political system cannot be made responsive to public demands, so why bother? Although many reasons may account for such feelings of political impotency, some people simply feel overwhelmed by the vast scale and remoteness of government. Each has a sense of being only one among millions and feels that those who make policy decisions are remote and unresponsive. In the words of Herbert Kaufman, "The scale of organization in our society has grown so large that only through large-scale organization does it seem possible to have a significant impact. This impression alone is enough to make individual people feel helplessly overwhelmed by huge impersonal machines indifferent to their uniqueness and humanity."[6]

Obviously, not everyone feels small or impotent. Those living in relatively small communities often voice considerable optimism about affecting local policies. However, negative perceptions of government itself may produce as much pessimism about participation as do any feelings of personal inefficacy. As pointed out in Chapter One, there appears to be an erosion of confidence in government at all levels—an erosion that began well before the Watergate scandal broke in the newspapers and on television. For some people, this erosion of confidence becomes immediately translated into political disinterest and apathy. The intriguing question is: Why do some people who feel estranged from the political system drop out of all political activity while others, similarly estranged, become revolutionaries?[7]

Perhaps another factor inhibiting participation is the knowledge that political influence is unequally shared. Regardless of whether one adopts the pluralist or the ruling-elite view of power distribution, there remains the knowledge that some Americans enjoy considerably more clout than others. As Herbert Kaufman points out, many people "are not mollified by assurances that the characteristics of the system thwarting them also thwart selfish and extremist interests; it appears to them that only the powerful get attention, and that the already powerful are helped by the system to deny influence to all who now lack it."[8] Because such politically relevant resources as wealth, expertise, access to communications, and even time are unequally distributed, some individuals have more opportunities than others to achieve their political objectives. Even the vote is not equally shared; although each American has only one vote, some members of society, by virtue of their prestige or access to the media, have additional opportunities to persuade others how to cast theirs.

Thus, even if one accepts the pluralist view that our political system offers citizens a number of viable routes of influence, one must still examine his or her own resources to determine the chances of affecting political decisions. This means evaluating the time one can devote to a political issue, one's access to means of communication, and one's ability to persuade, cajole, or merely reach those who make the appropriate decisions. Information is a particularly vital resource; the lack of it often is a major stumbling block to effective action. Few people are sufficiently knowledgeable about the procedures of decision making even to know whom to contact or how to exert pressure.

Moreover, any decision to take political action must involve some consideration of costs. This means not only the time and money one can devote to an issue but the extent of frustration and conflict one may be willing to bear. Efforts to change existing policies or to persuade others to adopt one's point of view may meet with failure, rejection, and despair. Although a willingness to persevere on a political problem will sometimes yield tangible returns, no guarantee of that can ever be made. Perhaps those who seek the greatest changes in policy will court the most frustration. The American political system, while flexible, is not too responsive to calls for sweeping reform. But if an individual feels strongly about an issue, and maintains optimism, his or her efforts may be rewarded.

In evaluating the traditional means of political influence offered by the system—the vote, interest groups, the petition, and so forth—it makes sense to choose a strategy that best fits the goal. Those who want to increase social security benefits, for example, are hardly likely to buttonhole a member of the city council. Their efforts must be focused on the national level, where social security policies are enacted. Moreover, their intensity of participation must be determined by what they expect to accomplish. If they desire to change the federal tax structure, it would hardly be worthwhile simply to dash off a letter to the local newspaper.

It should be understood that the strategies we will examine do not exhaust all existing alternatives. We are excluding, for example, consideration of such long-range strategies as running for public office and engaging full-time in reform activity because of their extraordinary demands in personal commitment. However, these and other forms of political activity should be evaluated by those who desire a greater impact on the political fortunes of this country.

Into the Voting Booth

Let us turn first to one of the most common forms of political participation in the United States: voting in elections. There is a long-standing belief in this country that elections are important and that each citizen has a duty to be informed about and vote for the candidates and issues. Even adolescents and teenagers are taught to participate in this activity in school, where they may vote for class president or hold mock elections for gubernatorial candidates. Undoubtedly some would agree with Lyndon Johnson, who proclaimed after signing the 1965 Voting Rights Act, "The vote is the most powerful instrument ever devised by man for breaking down injustice and destroying the terrible walls that imprison men because they are different from other men."

Yet, millions of Americans have not been convinced that casting their ballots is worthwhile. Not only do approximately 40 percent of the voting-age population abstain from voting in presidential elections, but anywhere from 50 to 70 percent of the potential voters shy away from the polls in statewide and local elections. As we discussed earlier, there are many reasons why people fail to participate, including legal obstacles (such as residency requirements), a dislike of the party candidates, an absence of stimulation or time, interpersonal conflicts, or a sense of political impotency and inconsequentiality.

But whatever the personal reasons, some wonder why any sensible person should bother to vote at all. Given the fact that each person is only one of seventy or eighty million voters in the United States, does it make sense to believe his or her participation—his or her one vote—will have any impact on a major election? Simply to raise the question "What if everyone felt the same way?" does not remove the lingering impression that a single person, especially in a national election, is dwarfed by the enormous number of people who do trek to the polls. Indeed, it is likely that the decision of any one of us not to show up would hardly affect the outcome of a major election.

The case for not voting is additionally buttressed by arguments that elections are largely meaningless anyway. As we saw in Chapter Two, supporters of the ruling-elite theory insist that even though voters are given a choice among alternative candidates, their choice is restricted to a narrow range of similar-minded individuals picked by party elites. Elections do not express what most people want or need, nor do they provide guidance for politicians (even if they want it) on what policies to enact. In this view, elections are primarily just rituals that perform a symbolic function for voters. They offer voters a role to play at election time and help tie them to the political system. As one writer scoffs, elections only "quiet resentments and doubts about particular political acts, reaffirm belief in the fundamental rationality and democratic character of the system, and thus fix conforming habits of future behavior."[9]

Still, since most people continue to show their faces at the polls at one time or another, what arguments can be made in favor of voting? One argument is that voting does have significance, if not so much in terms of individual impact, then in putting group pressure on politicians. Because citizens collectively have the power to give or withhold votes, they directly control the tenure of elected officials. Even if the choice is narrowly confined to Tweedledee and Tweedledum, Tweedledee knows that a day of reckoning is fixed by law and that minimally he must strive to avoid displeasing his constituents—or he will lose his job.

There is also the view that an individual can augment his or her impact at the polls by swaying the votes of others. By ringing doorbells, working in a campaign, or just talking to family and friends, one vote can be expanded into many. Such efforts may bring innumerable rewards, considering the number of politicians elected or defeated by razor-thin margins. Lyndon Johnson, for example, launched his political career in 1948 by defeating his rival for the U.S. Senate with less than 800 votes. Similarly, Rep. James Delaney of New York won his House seat in 1956 by only 102 votes, and Rep. Romano Mazzoli of Kentucky squeaked by his opponent in 1970 with just 254 votes. Even more remarkably, in 1974, a controversial Senate race in New Hampshire between Louis Wyman and John Durkin was initially decided by a margin of only 2 votes! The vote was so close that a new election had to be held, with Democrat John Durkin finally emerging victorious. Even some presidential elections have been decided by a small number of votes. If James G. Blaine had garnered an additional 1,200 votes out of the approximately 1 million cast in New York State in 1884, he would have pocketed all the state's electoral votes and defeated Grover Cleveland for President. Moreover, Woodrow Wilson only narrowly defeated Charles Evans Hughes in 1916. If only four thousand people in California had decided instead to support Hughes, Wilson would have lost the election. And, finally, if just one person per precinct in three states in 1968 had backed Hubert Humphrey instead of Richard Nixon, Humphrey would have fulfilled his ambition to be President.

A handful of voters can make a difference particularly at the local level. Although contests for national and state offices attract the largest turnout, the greatest chance for a small number of voters to affect the outcome of an election is in local contests for city council or state legislature. Students at the University of California, for example, played a prominent part in the election of three "radicals" to the Berkeley City Council in 1971, and were influential in electing antiwar critic Ronald Dellums to Congress and environmentalist Kenneth Meade to the State Assembly in 1970. Although they had less success in placing fellow students on the City Council, the election of candidates sympathetic to student concerns resulted in the appointment of students to various city boards and commissions.

But perhaps political efficacy in voting is not the only consideration anyway. As ruling-elite theorists suggest, people do not vote only to influence policy. Millions go to the effort to register and vote for a variety of other reasons as well. Some people may participate just to avoid feeling guilty about not voting. They may have been taught that it is their patriotic duty to vote and that they have no cause to complain about the outcome if they stay at home. Still others may participate to derive satisfaction that they are somehow participants, not just spectators, in an exciting electoral contest. One study found that 71 percent of the respondents interviewed said they got a "feeling of satisfaction" out of going to the polls.[10] Even though their one vote may not be crucial, it nevertheless affirms their role in and support for the political process. Indeed, if one takes this view, it may be irrelevant whether one's vote is ultimately effective; a person votes not only to influence policy in a personal way but to experience the electoral process itself.

However, voting is only one form of political participation confined to fixed intervals. Between elections there are other traditional ways of influencing policy in which the average person can engage at almost any time.

Once Again, There Is Congress

To many who are not satisfied merely with voting as a means of political expression and influence, there is the additional strategy of writing letters to politicians. Public opinion surveys reveal that most Americans have given thought to making use of the pen to express their concerns, although only about 15 percent have ever done so. While letters may be addressed to practically any official—including the President, the mayor, the governor, a judge, or a bureaucrat—the congressional Representative and state legislator are the principal targets for citizen mail.

There are at least two main reasons why people try to get in touch with their Representative. Either they wish to influence legislation or they need assistance with a personal problem. Assuming, first of all, that they want to sway the vote of a member of Congress on a bill, they need to time their letters for the best effect. Probably the best time to write is when a bill is about to reach the House or Senate floor for debate, or when it is pending before a committee. The latter is a particularly crucial time since, as we saw in Chapter Seven, the fate of most bills is sealed in committee. This means that potential letter writers must understand the committee process and keep track of the bill at its various stages. One useful source of information on such matters has been offered by the League Action Service (a service of the League of Women Voters), which keeps a watchful eye on the status of legislation and suggests when action should be taken.

Naturally, those who desire to influence policy must also take into account the committee position held and power commanded by their Representative. If they desire to influence tax policy, for example, and their Representative happens to sit on the Agriculture Committee and is still wet behind the ears, then pressure may have to be directed elsewhere. Indeed, a few letters to the chairman of the Ways and Means Committee may have considerably greater impact than four hundred letters to the young upstart from home. Unfortunately, many people fail to take notice of the position held, talent exhibited, and clout exercised by their Representative before taking action. They also fail to consider the difficulties many members face in seeing their bills enacted into law. By expecting immediate returns for their minimal letter-writing efforts, they ignore the special requirements of an effective citizen campaign.

Many people also are unaware of the impersonal way their letters often will be handled. Their carefully composed letters will not likely reach their Representative directly, but will be read by an administrative or legislative assistant. Typically, only the most important letters are brought directly to a legislator's attention. In fact, most members of Congress do not compose their own replies to constituent letters; rather, an office assistant will type out answers to be signed by the Congress member, giving constituents only the appearance of receiving a personal reply.

Moreover, any letter is bound to be only one among many pouring into a legislator's office. In most instances, a letter from a constituent will not determine how a member of Congress votes on a bill. As we discussed earlier, members of Congress often place greater importance on their own opinions of a bill, especially if they feel they have researched the issue more thoroughly than have their constituents. In such a case, a hapless citizen may simply receive a smug, precomposed reply stating the reasons for the Representative's support or rejection of the bill in question.

Occasionally, notice is taken of constituents' views, especially if many people correspond on an issue. Such was the case in early 1974 when members of Congress were stunned by the enormous volume of spontaneous letters demanding a bill of impeachment against Nixon. In fact, many people believe the only effective way to sway legislators is to trigger a mass letter-writing campaign designed to flood their offices with letters and petitions from home. This strategy is employed to convince legislators that constituents are deeply concerned about an issue and want immediate action.

DOONESBURY   by Garry Trudeau

However, even mass letter-writing campaigns have limitations. An avalanche of correspondence may not be very effective if the letters are not spontaneous and personal. Members of Congress know that in some letter-writing campaigns only a few citizens are behind the effort and that most of the other correspondents have a low commitment to the issue. Such campaigns lose their forcefulness when members learn that letters containing essentially the same information and language are handed to people on the street to sign and mail. "Most experienced Senators and Representatives," Rep. James Wright reflects, "suspect one of these organized campaigns when the first batch of mail begins to hit their desks. The repetition of certain phrases and slogans and the coincidence of several hundred communications in a given day on a certain subject in which little interest previously has been evinced by the constituency almost invariably tip the hand of those who would befuddle the lawmakers with numbers. The design sticks out all over, like a well-developed case of hives."[11] Thus, interest groups often advise their members to state in their own words why they support or reject a bill under debate. Be courteous, they are usually advised, for more flies can be caught with honey than vinegar.

Most people probably will have more success in asking for help with a personal problem. Although they may not obtain such help directly from their Representative (few members of Congress, in fact, personally respond to constituents' requests for aid in most circumstances), they will be assisted by one of the caseworkers in the legislator's office. Each month these caseworkers may accept hundreds of requests for help in retrieving a lost social security check, speeding a relative through immigration, or acquiring information on a bill. Naturally, a person's ability to obtain results depends on the scope of the problem. It is easier to get help from a legislator's office in tracking down a lost social security check, for example, than in trying to stop a new highway from cutting through the neighborhood. Finding a lost social security check may involve little more than a caseworker's convincing an otherwise recalcitrant clerk to thumb through the constituent's records. But halting the invasion of a highway may require cajoling countless high officials into taking appropriate action. In such instances, unless public sentiment runs high against the proposed highway, a simple request for help from a legislator's office probably is doomed to failure.

Furthermore, success often depends on the motivations and talents of the caseworkers. While some respond speedily to a problem and know exactly what strings to pull, others are less committed to constituents and are helpless in cutting through bureaucratic red tape on their behalf.

Still, letters to a legislator's office can have spectacular results. Legislators have on occasion responded to a person's misfortune by introducing new legislation to rectify it. In 1972, an elderly woman wrote to California State Senator Nicholas Petris complaining that, under existing law, she would not be eligible for senior citizens' property tax assistance. She had been denied eligibility because she had been unable to meet her tax obligations the previous fiscal year. Her letter inspired Senator Petris and his caseworker to put together a new bill easing the eligibility requirements. The bill, passed in March 1973, ultimately benefited not only the woman who wrote the letter but countless other elderly citizens who faced a similar problem. In fact, Senator Petris, like most legislators, has introduced a number of important bills in response to constituent letters and phone calls.

Joining with Lobbyists

Since laboring alone to achieve a political goal can be lonely and exasperating, an alternative for many people is to join an interest (or pressure) group working toward similar ends. Politicians and social scientists alike have noted that collective, rather than individual, action offers the greatest promise for affecting governmental policy. In the broadest sense, a pressure group is a collection of people banded together to achieve common objectives, usually by influencing legislation. Although pressure groups carry a negative connotation for many people—conjuring up images of shady characters and back room deals—they may offer a way for a person to feel more effective in influencing policy. By joining a large group having similar goals and working through concerted action, an individual may at least temporarily overcome his or her feelings of political isolation and impotency.

Indeed, as pluralists like to point out, an interest group often can represent an individual in ways that a political party or a legislator cannot. As we may recall from Chapter Four, the Democratic and Republican parties are not strictly issue-oriented; both parties offer only the broadest and vaguest programs in an effort to harvest votes. Furthermore, Senators and Representatives are elected on a geographical basis and are forced to represent districts comprising hundreds of conflicting groups. Under these circumstances, it is difficult to imagine how any individual can feel adequately represented as part of a large, mixed constituency. Interest groups, on the other hand, provide supplementary representation for specific groups by serving their unique occupational or other interests. The American Medical Association, for example, can speak for the interests of thousands of doctors in ways that a party or a legislator alone cannot.

Yet, as ruling-elite theorists are quick to reply, interest groups do not properly serve everyone. With the exception of a few prominent associations, such as the National Welfare Rights Organization, most interest groups speak primarily for middle- or upper-middle-class interests. Many people such as the elderly poor who greatly depend on governmental assistance do not belong to and are unable to benefit from any effective organization that speaks on their behalf. They possess neither the financial resources nor the leadership to pressure the government for policies directly benefiting them.

Furthermore, many who contemplate joining a pressure group are not fully cognizant of the limitations of membership. They do not realize, for instance, that they may still become only small cogs in a large wheel. Not only do many interest groups have thousands of members; they are led by a small cadre of active elites. In many cases, the members of a large interest group elect their leaders from among candidates sanctioned by a dominant or ruling clique—a clique that year after year represents the group in its relations with governmental officials. Thus, while an individual may obtain satisfaction from belonging to a large organization, he or she will be unlikely to have a strong personal influence on its policies and tactics.

Still another limitation is that most powerful interest groups do not press for creative reform. While some do seek major changes in existing policies, the majority of large successful organizations—such as the American Medical Association and the National Rifle Association—are better known for their ability to delay and obstruct policies than to force the enactment of new ones. This is not simply because they desire stagnation, but because, as we saw in Chapter Seven, the legislative process is strewn with obstacles. It is easier to persuade a few prominent committee members to block an undesirable bill than to effect reform by running the gauntlet of numerous centers of decision making. Studies of lobbying techniques reveal that lobbying tends to be most effective when used to reinforce or alter the opinions of a few committee members than to convert a majority of both the House and Senate into taking a new path.

Interest groups do differ widely, of course, in goals, membership, and budgets. While some pursue a broad range of political goals, others specialize and become only marginally entangled in legislative conflicts. And while some interest groups can draw on considerable financial resources, skilled leaders, and large memberships, others are not much more than "letterhead" groups with little money and organization. Even the range and targets of influence vary. Given the many ways government touches the lives of citizens, interest groups approach not only members of Congress and state legislators but also governors, mayors, Presidents, and bureaucrats. They even try to mobilize the public, employing sophisticated propaganda techniques to gain sympathy and rally support.

It might be asked what separates a truly effective lobby from the rest of the pack. Although the answer is difficult to state precisely, success almost invariably demands a lot of people working in concerted action, with the right combination of money and public relations know-how. Certainly one potent weapon in any lobbying arsenal is money. While most groups do not commonly approach politicians with direct illegal bribes, they do need money to contribute to campaigns and to hire able lobbyists, attorneys, and public relations specialists. It is not just coincidental that some of the nation's most powerful interest groups, such as the American Petroleum Institute, the American Bankers Association, and the Teamsters union, have been linked to economic interests. But money alone does not guarantee success. Even though the American Medical Association in 1965 reportedly doled out more than $1 million to block passage of medicare, the act was signed into law (albeit with features that bore the AMA stamp).

Another valuable asset is a large membership. Many successful organizations, including labor unions and veterans' groups, marshall the resources of large segments of the population to influence lawmakers. The National Rifle Association, operating on the premise that nothing shakes a politician like a pile of angry letters from home, has been using its large mailing list to turn aside gun laws since the 1930s. But even size has limitations. Although the National Congress of Parents and Teachers represents one of the largest groups in the country, it has little lasting impact on educational policies. Its members are only loosely associated and share little in common except the broadest goals.

Table 9-1. 25 Top Spenders

The top 25 spenders of the organizations that filed lobby spending reports for 1973 are listed below with the amounts they reported spending in 1973 and 1972.

Organization	1973	1972
Common Cause	$934,835	$558,839
International Union, United Automobile, Aerospace and Agricultural Implement Workers	460,992	no spending record
American Postal Workers Union (AFL-CIO)	393,399	208,767
American Federation of Labor-Congress of Industrial Organizations (AFL-CIO)	240,800	216,294
American Trucking Associations Inc.	226,157	137,804
American Nurses Association Inc.	218,354	109,642
United States Savings and Loan League	204,221	191,726
Gas Supply Committee	195,537	11,263
Disabled American Veterans	193,168	159,431
The Committee of Publicly Owned Companies	180,493	no spending record
American Farm Bureau Federation	170,472	180,678
National Education Association	162,755	no spending record
National Association of Letter Carriers	160,597	154,187
National Association of Home Builders of the United States	152,177	99,031
Recording Industry Association of America Inc.	141,111	88,396
National Council of Farmer Cooperatives	140,560	184,346
American Insurance Association	139,395	82,395
The Farmers' Educational and Co-operative Union of America	138,403	113,156
Committee of Copyright Owners	135,095	no spending record
National Housing Conference Inc.	125,726	77,906
American Petroleum Institute	121,276	38,656
American Medical Association	114,859	96,145
Citizens for Control of Federal Spending	113,659	no spending record
American Civil Liberties Union	102,595	73,131
National Association of Insurance Agents Inc.	87,422	50,924

Source: *Congressional Quarterly Weekly Report,* 27 July 1974.

Thus, in addition to money and size, other desirable resources include prestige, unity, and good leadership. These three attributes have been especially important for professional organizations like the American Medical Association and the American Bar Association, whose influence can be largely traced to the skills and respect commanded by their leadership. Even psychological factors, like hope and confidence, are important, as is the absence of any powerful countervailing group.

One interesting development in recent years has been the proliferation of "citizens' lobbies" organized to promote the "public interest." Many desiring reform and wishing to extend interest group representation to a broader segment of society have put their faith in such groups as the National Committee for an Effective Congress, Ralph Nader's Public Citizen, and Common Cause. Common Cause is perhaps the best-known of these organizations, and is certainly the most well-financed. As Table 9-1 shows, it headed the list of the top declared spenders among all registered interest groups in both 1972 and 1973. (Declared spending, of course, may not necessarily be an accurate index of organization influence. Although ITT, for example, offered a single donation of $400,000 to the Republican National Convention in 1972, it did not appear on the list—nor, for that matter, did any other large corporation.)

Since the inception of Common Cause in 1970, more than a quarter million people—Democrats, Republicans, and Independents alike—have paid membership dues of $15 a year to join its ranks. Common Cause was founded by John Gardner, former Secretary of Health, Education, and Welfare, to press for what it perceives as common public goals: an improved environment, a more equitable tax system, the elimination of the seniority rule in Congress, a more open system for financing political campaigns, and the like. Its members are regularly polled to learn which national and local issues require the most immediate attention.

And it has achieved notable legislative and legal victories. By filing suits in federal courts and by employing the same professional lobbying techniques used by other interest groups, it helped establish the federal Consumer Protection Agency, worked with environmental groups to defeat the supersonic transport (SST), spearheaded the effort to ratify the eighteen-year-old vote amendment, and forced the disclosure of donors who contributed to Nixon's 1972 reelection campaign prior to the April 7 disclosure deadline. It also sponsored a far-reaching California campaign reform act, approved by the voters in 1974.

Yet, even though Common Cause has become a major political force (with a membership exceeding two hundred thousand), it might seem to offer few exciting opportunities for individual action. Apart from paying dues and receiving information on its activities, the individual may regard his or her own contribution as insignificant compared with the efforts of those working directly to influence legislators at the national level. Even volunteer activities often entail doing largely menial chores, such as stuffing envelopes, which, although important, may not satisfy the desire to be directly involved in policy-making decisions. However, since Common Cause has been broadening its scope to press for reforms at the state level, added opportunities exist to work within the organization—to use its resources—for reform in one's own backyard.

Using Communications Media

Another increasingly popular action strategy is to publicize an issue, with the intention of reaching as many people as possible. Because it is generally assumed (except perhaps among hardened supporters of the ruling-elite theory) that policy makers will be more responsive to an issue due to public awareness and concern, many citizens have turned to the communications media (television, radio, newspapers) to broaden the scope of their influence.

This would seem to be a worthwhile action strategy as well, since, with the possible exceptions of gossip and rumor, television and newspapers have the greatest capacity to spread information. As stated in Chapter Five, the Roper Organization found in 1972 that more than 64 percent of American adults said they received most of their political news from watching television. Another large percentage said they received it from reading newspapers. In view of such findings, it might make sense for individuals to find ways to use television, newspapers, and other communications media to their own advantage. Firing off a letter to the editor of a newspaper or magazine is, for many people, the first step. Letter writing can provide a variety of satisfactions, ranging from a feeling that one is performing a public service to expanding one's ego. Many people see letters as a way to get their views before an audience, to bend others to their own point of view. One drawback, however, is that writing a letter to the editor does not guarantee publication. Although no one knows what proportion of letters reach print, it is probably less than one in twenty in most large cities. Besides, letters to the editor are not very effective in stimulating public interest or in pressuring politicians. Although popular with readers, letters are not likely to compel them to translate what they have read into effective political action—even presuming they know how to do so. At best, a letter may attract a few wavering adherents to a cause or provide a relatively inexpensive way to get something off one's chest.

Breaking into television is another alternative. Television has the advantage over newspapers of potentially reaching larger numbers of people, and with more telling effect. If one accepts Marshall McLuhan's thesis, television does not even require as much effort by the viewers. The audience does not have to do something active—such as read—to get the message. (Of course, they may not be mentally attentive to its content, either.) However, getting a message on television is not an easy task; broadcast time is extraordinarily expensive and beyond most people's financial capabilities. To use television, most people have to find either free or relatively inexpensive means of access.

One way to get a message on the air is through a "free speech" message or editorial. The FCC "fairness doctrine," introduced in 1949, requires broadcasters to "afford reasonable opportunity for the discussion of conflicting views on issues of public importance." This means that if a station carries an editorial on an issue such as the death penalty, it must provide air time for "responsible spokesmen" to voice opposing opinions. Although the fairness doctrine does not guarantee equal access for everyone, it can be exploited as a way to obtain free air time, especially if the station has failed to broadcast other points of view.

In fact, rulings by the Supreme Court and federal courts of appeals require stations to allow public access to the airwaves and uphold the citizen's right to challenge the renewal of broadcast licenses. A person who has little power or money but who can come up with a worthwhile community-oriented message may go to a broadcaster to request use of the airwaves. If a station proceeds to throw him into the streets, the individual can write to the Federal Communications Commission and, if the commission agrees with his complaint, make sufficient trouble for the station so that it has to take him seriously.

Assuming a person does succeed in making a brief statement on a local television station, he may reach more than a million people in a large city. Although a thirty-second or one-minute message is unlikely to have tremendous long-term impact on public consciousness, it may attract some support for an issue or publicize a worthwhile event. The impact of such a message can be extended, of course, by supplementing it with other forms of communication in an effort to reach more people.

Some observers note that the growing use of cable television may provide even greater access to the media than is currently available. In a growing number of communities, people are subscribing to the cable system, which eliminates the "noise" and "ghosts" of over-the-air broadcasts and expands the number of available channels. Many communities that give cable operators a franchise to develop a cable system stipulate certain conditions: that they devote a portion of broadcast time to coverage of city council meetings; that they televise adult education courses; that they provide a channel for use by the schools; and that they offer opportunities for local citizens to voice their views on public issues. Most communities, however, have not yet taken full advantage of the opportunities offered by cable television. They have handed out lucrative franchises to cable operators without compelling them to provide maximum service to citizens. But, because of the potential for many channels and two-way response mechanisms, the cable system may eventually provide expanded opportunities for citizen participation and political dialogue.[12]

Doing something newsworthy—something dramatic, new, or of special local interest—is another way to get a message on the air. Television news stations and newspapers will send out eager reporters if an event is sufficiently provocative or unusual. The key, of course, is to know what makes news. Climbing a flagpole or getting arrested would hardly be gratifying if no one showed up to cover the excitement.

However, one does not always have to stage a dramatic event. Television news stations often will respond to a direct request for coverage if an issue causes some local stir. In April 1974, Mrs. Virginia Kerr of Martinez, California, phoned a local television station asking it to cover an impending neighborhood disaster. The sloping hill behind her home was sliding inexorably into her backyard and threatening to destroy her house, as well as those of her neighbors. With the possibility that leaks in the utility pipes and the housing development on top of the hill were causing the slide, she hoped to use the media to pressure city officials into taking action. Mrs. Kerr was pleased, therefore, when the station sent out a reporter and cameras to film the impending disaster. As a result, her problem reached thousands of viewers in a brief two-minute segment on the 6:30 P.M. news.

Unfortunately, the results of the news coverage were minimal;

it brought no response from city officials or the public. She discovered that publicity alone would not guarantee a solution to her problem. Perhaps if her problem had been presented with more controversy—such as by pointing an accusing finger at city officials—and had broken into the news more than once, the response might have been greater.

What, then, can be expected from using the media? Clearly, bending the ear of the public will not always bring about policy changes. After all, what are viewers likely to do once they become aware of an issue? Even though most people are aware of pollution and crime in the streets, they still feel helpless trying to transform that awareness into political solutions. One answer may be that provoking public indignation is less important than threatening elected officials with adverse publicity. Officials may sense that even if constituents do not immediately convey their feelings through letters or other means, adverse publicity may threaten their position next time at the polls. In other words, media publicity may still result in policy changes even though it does not stimulate immediate public outcry.

One final question, however, should be considered. If ruling-elite theorists are correct that the media serve as instruments of an entrenched privileged elite, does this mean that few opportunities exist for citizens to present ideas radically opposed to those of the elite? It would seem that if a ruling-elite remain in control, only those who restrict their complaints to sliding hills, poor governmental administration, or occasional social injustices will find the media open avenues for political expression. Those who seriously intend to challenge the existing order, however, will find the same avenues blockaded, that the media resources granted to others will not be made available. In fact, even if one does not accept the broad tenets of the ruling-elite theory, one may still accuse broadcasters and newspaper editors of not providing an open forum for alternative viewpoints. One only has to recall that, during the Vietnam War, the three major television networks refused to sell time to various citizen groups (including the Democratic National Committee) protesting administration policies on the war.[13]

Yet, the extent to which even those who challenge the existing order can gain access to the media depends on the nature of the access. While so-called revolutionary groups like the Weather underground and the Symbionese Liberation Army (SLA) might find it difficult to present "free speech" messages over local television stations (presuming they would even want to do so), they can and frequently do receive wide network television coverage of their acts. In kidnapping heiress Patricia Hearst in 1974, the SLA called public attention to themselves far out of proportion to their small numbers.

The Litigation Alternative

In the event that the usual media or legislative channels are closed to pressure, another strategy is to challenge the legality of an action or statute in the courts. Many citizens and interest groups have achieved as much success by taking their causes to the courts as by trying to win public support or to pressure legislative and executive officials into taking action. The NAACP, for example, has for years relied on litigation as a tactic to fight school segregation and job discrimination. By persuading the Supreme Court in 1954 to outlaw racial segregation in the public schools (*Brown* v. *Board of Education*), the NAACP won a legal victory as important as any gained through legislation in Congress. (Of course, as we saw in the preceding chapter, the Court's inability to enforce its own rulings may retard the full fruition of victory.)

Even when used by an individual, a lawsuit can achieve wide-ranging political reform. In 1959, a registered voter in Tennessee named Charles Baker brought suit against the state's election officials. Baker charged them with violating his constitutional rights by having failed since 1901 to reapportion the legislative districts to reflect changes in population. Their inaction, he insisted, diluted his vote by permitting rural districts—some with less than four thousand population—to have the same representation as large urban ones, like his own, with more than seventy thousand population. This meant, for example, that in the Tennessee State Senate, 37 percent of the voters controlled more than 60 percent of the senate seats. By winning the case in the Supreme Court three years later (*Baker* v. *Carr*, 1962), Baker opened the way for citizens throughout the country to file similar suits demanding reapportionment of their state legislative and congressional districts.

However, despite this and other dramatic cases, legal tactics are sometimes unreliable. Often the most one can expect from litigation is to win a delay—such as getting a temporary court injunction to halt construction of a high-rise building or a freeway. Many observers have noted that the courts can be more effectively employed to veto actions than to achieve long-term change. Of course, such delaying tactics often reap great rewards. As an example of the many freeway construction revolts in recent years, La Raza Unita and the Sierra Club combined forces in 1971 to block construction of a controversial freeway through Hayward and Union City on the east side of San Francisco Bay. Taking the issue to court, they won an injunction against the project on grounds of detrimental environmental impact and the potential relocation problems of local residents. Such court actions have been similarly effective in San Antonio, Beverly Hills, San Francisco, Washington, D.C., and elsewhere.

Litigation has the additional disadvantage, however, of usually requiring a great deal of time and expense. After months of preparing a case for court, it may be months—or even years—before it is processed and settled. A typical case reaching the Supreme Court, for example, may require anywhere from two to three years of hearings and appeals. In addition, litigation costs money— money to cover attorney's fees, research expenses, and court costs. Unless one can proceed "in forma pauperis" (in the manner of a pauper—see Chapter Eight), a suit may well demand a financial commitment totally beyond the resources of the average person.

One possible exception to this involves a case where a person has suffered job discrimination. Under Title VII of the Civil Rights Act of 1964, the court may appoint a lawyer and assess court expenses and attorney fees against a person or company found guilty of discrimination. This means that a person with little financial support may still bring a legal suit, since a victory will offset all court expenses.

Using the courts is not the only means of taking legal action, however. John Banzhaf, a young attorney from the Bronx, single-handedly forced the television networks to provide equal time for antismoking commercials by writing a short letter to the FCC in 1967. He argued that since the Surgeon General of the United States had determined cigarette smoking to be hazardous to health, cigarette commercials should be considered legally controversial. Because the FCC fairness doctrine requires radio and television stations to air all sides of controversial issues, he wrote, the networks should be forced to present antismoking commercials as well. To Banzhaf's surprise, the FCC agreed with him and ordered the networks to provide time for antismoking ads—an action that moved Congress to pass legislation in 1971 banning cigarette commercials.[14]

Petitions, Initiatives, and Recalls

Another legal tactic is to resort to the initiative. Although most lawmaking is done by legislators elected specifically for that purpose, voters in at least twenty states have the power to pass laws directly without recourse to the legislature. (The states include: Alaska, Arizona, Arkansas, California, Colorado, Idaho, Maine, Massachusetts, Michigan, Missouri, Montana, Nebraska, Nevada, North Dakota, Ohio, Oklahoma, Oregon, South Dakota, Utah, and Washington.) By means of the initiative process, it is possible for a group to force the enactment of laws that legislators have either refused or failed to consider. After securing a sufficient number of signatures on a petition, a group can place a proposition on the state ballot (as well as on many additional local ballots) to be voted on by the people. In this way, they can bypass both the legislature and the governor (who cannot veto or amend an initiative measure).

The initiative is a formidable tool, for a law passed in this way can have as much impact as any single legislative act. In California, for example, the state initiative process has been used to establish the civil service system, daylight saving time, and coastline conservation. In Colorado, voters resorted to the initiative in 1972 to stop the Winter Olympics from being held in their state. In some states, the initiative process can even be used to pass state constitutional amendments, although more citizen support usually is required. A constitutional initiative has the special advantage of becoming part of the state constitution, which means it cannot be overturned by the state courts.

Moreover, voters in at least twenty-two states can employ the referendum to prevent laws passed by the legislature and signed by the governor from going into effect. In most of these states, bills do not become law until at least sixty to ninety days after the legislature adjourns. If a handful of voters can round up enough signatures on a petition during that sixty- to ninety-day interval, a bill can be held in abeyance until the next election. Then, if a majority votes to kill the bill, it is declared void; otherwise it goes into effect as planned. In most states and cities, certain measures such as bond issues and constitutional amendments proposed by the legislature cannot go into effect until they are submitted to the voters for approval. In Oregon, the legislature passed a sales tax measure five different times, only to have it repeatedly rejected by a referendum vote.

Citizens in many states and cities also have the right to recall an elected official before his term officially expires. If enough signatures can be gathered on a petition, a special election must be held to decide whether the official should be booted out and replaced by another candidate. In contrast to initiative and referendum petitions, there usually is no time limit for circulating and filing a recall petition. Nor must the charges be restricted to certain offenses; an official may be removed from office for not parting his hair on the left side. Although successful efforts to recall governors and state legislators have been rare, hundreds of recalls have been effective against mayors and city council members. Voters in Los Angeles, for example, booted out Mayor Frank Shaw in 1938 following charges of corruption. Similarly, in 1973, Berkeley voters dumped D'Army Bailey, one of three "radical" city council members students helped elect in 1971. Bailey's recall—believed by some to be based on his political style rather than misconduct—caused concern among some student groups that the recall process would be used regularly by powerful established interests to thwart student electoral power.

All three of these processes—initiative, referendum, and recall—were established as part of the Progressive movement at the turn of the century. In contrast to most of the Founding Fathers who mistrusted public control over policy making, Progressives in the early 1900s intended the people to exercise more control over legislation and thus neutralize the influence of special interests dominating the state legislatures. In the opinion of many Progressives, these procedures represented the best alternative forms of "direct democracy" available in a large territorial system.

However, growing populations and soaring campaign costs have tended to frustrate these ideals. Although any person today may originate an initiative proposal, many people and a lot of money are needed to organize a successful petition campaign at the state level. To place a proposition on the ballot in most states, it is necessary to obtain a sizable number of valid signatures from registered voters. In the state of Washington, for example, initiative organizers must collect the signatures of voters equal to at least 8 percent of the total votes cast for governor in the preceding election. In California, they must garner at least 5 percent of the votes cast, or roughly one-half million signatures.

Once the proposition appears on the ballot, petition organizers must face the equally arduous task of persuading skeptical voters to support it. Usually this involves a campaign of great expense and organization. Recent history has shown that the most active groups sponsoring or opposing state initiatives have been well-funded special-interest groups, like unions and oil producers, served by skilled public relations experts (who may hire professional "petition-pushers" to circulate petitions and collect the required signatures). Relatively few other people have the organization or financial resources to spread word of a proposition and win support for its adoption. Thus, despite the Progressives' hope that the initiative process would reduce control over government by special interests, it has been special interests—not ordinary citizens—who appear to have benefited most from its use at the state level.

Probably an individual's best chance of effectively using the initiative process is at the local level. Cities throughout the country guarantee citizens the right to originate legislation by means of the initiative. Although used less frequently today than in the past, local initiatives still have the advantage of requiring fewer signatures and less expense than state propositions. A handful of people in a small community can win political victories not obtainable through normal legislative channels. Students at Berkeley, for example, resorted to the initiative process to pass a rent control law in 1972, as well as an ordinance in 1973 decriminalizing the personal possession and use of marijuana. Neither of these initiative measures was a lasting success, however, since both were invalidated by court action. Although the initiative process in Berkeley and elsewhere has yielded mixed results, it will continue to be used by many groups as one of several alternative electoral strategies.

Resorting to Direct Action

Finally, it has been possible for people to bring about changes in public policy through direct action. Direct action embraces a wide variety of both legal and illegal activities, ranging from passive resistance and hunger strikes to mass demonstrations, sit-ins, and boycotts.

Although many people take a negative view of such tactics, several forms of direct action—such as peaceful demonstrations and strikes—have been upheld by the Supreme Court as legitimate expressions of public protest and dissent. As the Court ruled in one important case, the use of the streets and public places "for purposes of assembly, communicating thoughts between citizens, and discussing public questions [is] a part of the privileges, immunities, rights, and liberties of citizens."[15] In fact, even direct action strategies not officially sanctioned by the Supreme Court—such as sit-ins and seizures of property—have played a prominent role in the history of American politics. Recent studies have made a persuasive case that direct action tactics—again, both legal and illegal—are very much a part of our political heritage and that virtually every major social movement has resorted to them at one time or another. This heritage has been seen, for example, in the efforts of workers to achieve union representation, the early black lunch counter sit-ins, the mass demonstrations against the Vietnam War, the seizure of Alcatraz and other territories by American Indian tribes, and the strikes and boycotts by migrant farm workers organized by Cesar Chavez. It even has been witnessed in nationwide strikes by truckers protesting the gasoline shortage and in boycotts by housewives upset over the rising cost of meat.

The reasons for engaging in direct action or protest politics are, of course, practically endless. A variety of personal motivations, ideological assumptions, and strategic considerations may underlie a decision to resort to confrontation. The purpose of such action may be to dramatize an injustice, focus public attention on a social issue, or simply create enough trouble for someone to force a solution to a problem. "Nonviolent direct action," Martin Luther King, Jr., once wrote, "seeks to create such a crisis and establish such creative tension that a community that has constantly refused to negotiate is forced to confront the issue."[16]

Although well-organized and reasonably confident groups have successfully employed direct action tactics in the past, such tactics continue to have special appeal for groups who command little organization and financial resources, and who are less than optimistic about using conventional political channels to achieve their goals. By resorting to boycotts, strikes, and demonstrations, they hope to call attention to injustice and stimulate others to take similar forceful action. Inevitably, they expect that by employing such tactics they will achieve an otherwise unattainable political or legal solution to a problem. One study suggests that, prior to World War II, challenging groups who resorted to direct action to achieve limited goals enjoyed a higher success rate than similar groups who always "played by the rules."[17]

Direct action may also appeal to those impatient with the sluggishness of conventional political strategies—even to the point of engaging in illegal acts. As Robert Sherrill has noted, "Since it took six years under the Highway Beautification Act to get one billboard removed through official channels, it does seem rather reasonable—whatever the morality of the action—for a band of University of Michigan students to make midnight forays with axe and saw and topple dozens of billboards."[18]

The questionable legality of some direct action tactics does, of course, pose problems for many people. At a time of unprecedented political confrontations, few Americans are aware of the rules covering protest tactics—and probably with good reason. Although the First Amendment guarantees "freedom of speech . . . or the right of the people peaceably to assemble, and to petition the government for a redress of grievances," there is no automatic constitutional protection for those wishing to dissent or protest at any time or place. State and city officials are given great latitude to restrict almost any public speech or action they believe might incite violence or disrupt other legitimate interests. As a result, laws dealing even with peaceful demonstrations abound in local variations.

As would be expected, like all other strategies direct action does have limitations. For one thing, it may be disadvantageous for groups seeking wide-based public support. Strikes, sit-ins, and demonstrations run the risk of alienating potentially sympathetic groups who may agree with the goal but reject the methods used to achieve it. While many in our society welcome the correction of injustice, they tolerate only a narrow range of corrective approaches. They reject the use of any tactic that violates their norm of political conduct.

Nor can one guarantee that after much effort has been made to organize a meaningful demonstration or boycott it will accomplish the intended goal. If a protest campaign is designed to persuade other people to join the protest and demand reform, then success would depend on at least gaining television and other media coverage. Tactics and platforms would have to be geared to what those in the communications media consider newsworthy just to gain publicity for the action. Even then, publicity may not compel the public or decision makers to take appropriate measures. To assume simply that awareness of a problem automatically leads to its solution is to belie the conservatism of the political process.

One often finds it difficult, in fact, even to evaluate the gains made through direct action. The domestic protest against the Vietnam War, for example, yielded ambiguous results. Arguably, the wave of protest by students and others succeeded in revealing the deep divisions within the society over the war and in publicizing the war's injustices. But in the eyes of many the protests were a failure. Despite pledges to "close down the government" and "stop the war machine," the war dragged on for more than eight years—longer than World War II and the Korean conflict—in the process killing or maiming millions on both sides.

The civil rights struggle, on the other hand, presents a more convincing case that direct action can work. The sit-ins, freedom rides, and marches in the early 1960s attracted national attention, dramatized the injustices of segregation, and succeeded in winning many local battles against segregation in restaurants, on buses, in churches, hotels, and libraries. They also prompted congressional legislation—notably the 1964 Civil Rights Act prohibiting discriminatory voting qualifications and segregated public facilities—and forced compliance to Supreme Court decisions. Thus, while the effects of direct action tactics are often ambiguous, policy changes can occur. Direct action tactics can modify people's attitudes and pave the way for future reform.

Evaluation: The Measure of Success

Looking at the various strategies we have discussed, we may conclude that the most promising way to affect public policy is through concerted group action. Groups, not single individuals, have become the basic units of influence in our society. Membership in an organization enhances the prospects that an individual will be capable of influencing government and will make an effort to do so.

Yet, ironically, it is difficult for many people to become part of an effective political organization. Their immediate or long-term needs often do not find adequate representation in any established group. Such has generally been the case for consumers, the elderly poor, and those generally ignored in the tussle for political favors. Nor is it easy to put together an effective organization from the ground up. Even when people share a common problem or an enthusiasm for similar goals, tremendous efforts and expenditures in time and money are required to give birth to an effective political machine. Of course, this does not exclude temporarily *using* existing organizations for one's purposes. Often a group can be effectively employed by individuals who are not necessarily connected with it. Thousands of people, for example, have benefited from the services of the Legal Aid Society and the American Civil Liberties Union even though they were not members and their own personal resources were meager.

However, many people simply do not feel comfortable or satis-fied as part of a larger whole; their basic individualism demands that they alone should be able to bring about sweeping policy changes. Compelled to reject any thought of becoming submerged in a larger collective body, they prefer instead that policy makers respond to their personal expectations and demands. But because they cannot achieve a substantial degree of individual impact, they succumb to frustration and drop out.

In this sense, we might say that the measure of success in in-fluencing policy depends greatly on one's expectations. Those who desire as single individuals to achieve immediate and far-reaching solutions to national or local problems may regard anything short of such solutions as worthless. Moreover, as long as they are con-cerned only with their own individual potency, they are likely to ignore the potential rewards of working in concerted action. As we have seen in the preceding chapters, ordinary citizens, members of Congress, and even Presidents occasionally feel de-spair brought on by a sense of personal impotency and lack of control over their political environment. Their expectations of personal importance are such that each unrealized goal becomes a testament to the inflexibility of "the system."

On a final note, we should perhaps not be so obsessed with the pursuit of power that we measure political actions solely in terms of efficacy and success. In many instances, political acts carry moral and symbolic values separate from the expectation of achieving concrete goals. Participating in a demonstration, vot-ing, writing a letter to the editor may all have expressive as well as instrumental benefits. Persons involved in such activities may care less about influencing other people's behavior than about the positive feelings they enjoy from expressing their views.

Indeed, from a philosophical perspective, political acts may even be seen as expressions of human dignity and morality. In protesting a social injustice or in rebelling against authority, a person may be asserting his or her own loyalty to a higher ideal. The fear of failing to achieve a tangible goal may be less important than the need to voice one's commitment to certain values. If a desire exists, for example, to aid the cause of Indian rights or to help ameliorate the deplorable conditions of the elderly poor, then it may be unjust not to become involved simply because one fears failure in the effort. By not participating, the fear of fail-ure becomes a self-fulfilling prophecy, a submission to expediency.

Binstock, Robert H., and Ely, Katherine, eds. *The Politics of the Powerless.* Cambridge, Mass.: Winthrop, 1971.

Burkhart, James, et al. *Strategies for Political Participation.* Cambridge, Mass.: Winthrop, 1972.

Carter, April. *Direct Action and Liberal Democracy.* New York: Harper & Row, 1973.

Golembiewski, Robert T.; Toore, J. Malcolm; and Rabin, Jack, eds. *Dilemmas of Political Participation.* Englewood Cliffs, N.J.: Prentice-Hall, 1973.

Michael, James R., Ralph Nader's Center for Study of Responsive Law. *Working on the System: A Comprehensive Manual for Citizen Access to Federal Agencies.* New York: Basic Books, 1974.

The O.M. Collective. *The Organizer's Manual.* New York: Bantam, 1971.

Pohl, Frederik. *Practical Politics 1972.* New York: Ballantine, 1971.

Ross, Donald K. *A Public Citizen's Action Manual.* New York: Grossman, 1973.

Schwartz, David C. *Political Alienation and Political Behavior.* Chicago: Aldine, 1973.

Wolff, Robert Paul, ed. *Styles of Political Action in America.* New York: Random House, 1972.

Recommended Reading

1. Massimo Salvadori, *Liberal Democracy* (New York: Doubleday, 1957).

2. U.S. Senate, Committee on Government Operations, "Confidence and Concern: Citizens View American Government, A Survey of Public Attitudes," pt. 1 (Washington, D.C.: U.S. Government Printing Office, 1973). See also *Newsweek,* 10 December 1974, pp. 39–48.

3. John G. Robinson, Jerrold G. Rush, and Kendran B. Head, *Measurements of Political Attitudes* (Ann Arbor: University of Michigan, Survey Research Center, 1968).

4. James Burkhart et al., *Strategies for Political Participation* (Cambridge, Mass.: Winthrop, 1972), p. 29.

5. U.S. Senate, Committee on Government Operations, "Confidence and Concern: Citizens View American Government, A Survey of Public Attitudes," pt. 1 (Washington, D.C.: U.S. Government Printing Office, 1973).

6. Herbert Kaufman, "Administrative Decentralization and Political Power," *Public Administration Review,* January-February 1969, pp. 3–15.

7. For one view on this, see David C. Schwartz, *Political Alienation and Political Behavior* (Chicago: Aldine, 1973).

Notes

8. Herbert Kaufman, "Administrative Decentralization and Political Power," *Public Administration Review*, January-February 1969, pp. 3–15.

9. Murray Edelman, *The Symbolic Uses of Politics* (Urbana: University of Illinois Press, 1964), p. 17.

10. Gabriel Almond and Sidney Verba, *The Civic Culture* (Princeton: Princeton University Press, 1963), p. 143.

11. Jim Wright, *You and Your Congressman* (New York: Coward-McCann, 1965), pp. 189–90. Used with permission of Coward-McCann.

12. For a more detailed analysis of the cable system, see Ralph Lee Smith, "The Wired Nation," *The Nation*, 18 May 1970, pp. 582–606.

13. See Robert Cirino, *Don't Blame the People* (New York: Random House, 1971).

14. See Joseph A. Page, "The Law Professor Behind Ash, Soup, Pump and Crash," in Robert Paul Wolff, ed., *Styles of Political Action in America* (New York: Random House, 1972), pp. 124–34.

15. *Hague* v. *C.I.O.* (1939).

16. Martin Luther King, Jr., "A Letter from Birmingham City Jail," 1963.

17. William A. Gamson, "Violence and Political Power: The Meek Don't Make It," *Psychology Today*, July 1974, pp. 35–41.

18. Robert Sherrill, *Why They Call It Politics*, 2d ed. (New York: Harcourt Brace Jovanovich, 1974), p. 316.

The Constitution of the United States

We the People of the United States, in Order to form a more perfect Union, establish Justice, insure domestic Tranquility, provide for the common defence, promote the general Welfare, and secure the Blessings of Liberty to ourselves and our Posterity, do ordain and establish this Constitution for the United States of America.

Article I

Section 1. All legislative Powers herein granted shall be vested in a Congress of the United States, which shall consist of a Senate and House of Representatives.

Section 2. The House of Representatives shall be composed of Members chosen every second Year by the People of the several States, and the Electors in each State shall have the qualifications requisite for Electors of the most numerous Branch of the State Legislature.

No Person shall be a Representative who shall not have attained to the Age of twenty five Years, and been seven Years a Citizen of the United States, and who shall not, when elected, be an Inhabitant of that State in which he shall be chosen.

Representatives and direct Taxes shall be apportioned among the several States which may be included within this Union, according to their respective Numbers, which shall be determined by adding to the whole Number of free Persons, including those bound to Service for a Term of Years, and excluding Indians not taxed, three fifths of all other Persons. The actual Enumeration shall be made within three Years after the first Meeting of the Congress of the United States, and within every subsequent Term of ten Years, in such Manner as they shall by Law direct. The Number of Representatives shall not exceed one for every thirty Thousand, but each State shall have at Least one Representative.

When vacancies happen in the Representation from any State, the Executive Authority thereof shall issue Writs of Election to fill such Vacancies.

The House of Representatives shall chuse their speaker and other Officers; and shall have the sole Power of Impeachment.

Section 3. The Senate of the United States shall be composed of two Senators from each State, chosen for six Years; and each Senator shall have one Vote.

Immediately after they shall be assembled in Consequence of the first Election, they shall be divided as equally as may be into three Classes, so that one third may be chosen every second Year.

No Person shall be a Senator who shall not have attained to the Age of thirty Years, and been nine Years a Citizen of the United States, and who shall not, when elected, be an Inhabitant of that State for which he shall be chosen.

The Vice President of the United States shall be President of the Senate, but shall have no Vote, unless they be equally divided.

The Senate shall chuse their other Officers, and also a President pro tempore, in the Absence of the Vice President, or when he shall exercise the Office of President of the United States.

The Senate shall have the sole Power to try all Impeachments. When sitting for that Purpose, they shall be on Oath or Affirmation. When the President of the United States is tried, the Chief Justice shall preside: And no Person shall be convicted without the Concurrence of two thirds of the Members present.

Judgment in Cases of Impeachment shall not extend further than to removal from Office, and disqualification to hold and enjoy any Office of honor, Trust or Profit under the United States: but the Party convicted shall nevertheless be liable and subject to Indictment, Trial, Judgment and Punishment, according to law.

Section 4. The Times, Places and Manner of holding Elections for Senators and Representatives, shall be prescribed in each State by the Legislature thereof; but the Congress may at any time by Law make or alter such Regulations, except as to the Places of chusing Senators.

The Congress shall assemble at least once in every Year, unless they shall by Law appoint a different Day.

Section 5. Each House shall be the Judge of the Elections, Returns and Qualifications of its own Members, and a Majority of each shall constitute a Quorum to do Business; but a smaller Number may adjourn from day to day, and may be authorized to compel the Attendance of absent Members, in such Manner, and under such Penalties as each House may provide.

Each House may determine the Rules of its Proceedings, punish its Members for disorderly Behaviour, and, with the Concurrence of two thirds, expel a Member.

Each House shall keep a Journal of its Proceedings, and from time to time publish the same, excepting such Parts as may in their Judgment require Secrecy; and the Yeas and Nays of the Members of either House on any question shall, at the Desire of one fifth of those Present, be entered on the Journal.

Neither House, during the Session of Congress, shall, without the Consent of the other, adjourn for more than three days, nor to any other Place than that in which the two Houses shall be sitting.

Section 6. The Senators and Representatives shall receive a Compensation for their Services, to be ascertained by Law, and paid out of the Treasury of the United States. They shall in all Cases, except Treason, Felony and Breach of the Peace, be privileged from Arrest during their Attendance at the Session of their respective Houses, and in going to and returning from the same; and for any Speech or Debate in either House, they shall not be questioned in any other Place.

No Senator or Representative shall, during the Time for which he was elected, be appointed to any civil Office under the Authority of the United States, which shall have been created, or the Emoluments whereof shall have been encreased during such time; and no Person shall be a Member of either House during his Continuance in Office.

Section 7. All Bills for raising Revenue shall originate in the House of Representatives; but the Senate may propose or concur with Amendments as on other Bills.

Every Bill which shall have passed the House of Representatives and the Senate, shall, before it become a Law, be presented to the President of the United States; If he approve he shall sign it, but if not he shall return it, with his Objections to that House in which it shall have originated, who shall enter the Objections at large on their Journal, and proceed to reconsider it. If after such Reconsideration two thirds of that House shall agree to pass the Bill, it shall be sent, together with the Objections, to the other House, by which it shall likewise be reconsidered, and if approved by two thirds of that House, it shall become a Law. But in all such Cases the Votes of both Houses shall be determined by Yeas and Nays, and the Names of the Persons voting for and against the Bill shall be entered on the Journal of each House respectively. If any Bill shall not be returned by the President within ten Days (Sundays excepted) after it shall have been presented to him, the Same shall be a Law, in like Manner as if he had signed it, unless the Congress by their Adjournment prevent its Return, in which Case it shall not be a Law.

Every Order, Resolution, or Vote to which the Concurrence of the Senate and House of Representatives may be necessary (except on a question of Adjournment) shall be presented to the President of the United States; and before the Same shall take Effect, shall be approved by him, or being disapproved by him, shall be repassed by two thirds of the Senate and House of Representatives, according to the Rules and Limitations prescribed in the Case of a Bill.

Section 8. The Congress shall have Power To lay and collect Taxes, Duties, Imposts and Excises, to pay the Debts and provide for the common Defence and general Welfare of the United States; but all Duties, Imposts and Excises shall be uniform throughout the United States;

To borrow Money on the credit of the United States;

To regulate Commerce with foreign Nations, and among the several States, and with the Indian Tribes;

To establish an uniform Rule of Naturalization, and uniform Laws on the subject of Bankruptcies throughout the United States;

To coin Money, regulate the Value thereof, and of foreign Coin, and fix the Standard of Weights and Measures;

To provide for the Punishment of counterfeiting the Securities and current Coin of the United States;

To establish Post Offices and post Roads;

To promote the Progress of Science and useful Arts, by securing for limited Times to Authors and Inventors the exclusive Right to their respective Writings and Discoveries;

To constitute Tribunals inferior to the supreme Court;

To define and punish Piracies and Felonies committed on the high Seas, and Offences against the Law of Nations;

To declare War, grant Letters of Marque and Reprisal, and make Rules concerning Captures on Land and Water;

To raise and support Armies, but no Appropriation of Money to that Use shall be for a longer Term than two Years;

To provide and maintain a Navy;

To make Rules for the Government and Regulation of the land and naval Forces;

To provide for calling forth the Militia to execute the Laws of the Union, suppress Insurrections and repel Invasions;

To provide for organizing, arming, and disciplining, the Militia, and for governing such Part of them as may be employed in the Service of the United States, reserving to the States respectively, the Appointment of the Officers, and the Authority of training the Militia according to the discipline prescribed by Congress;

To exercise exclusive Legislation in all Cases whatsoever, over such District (not exceeding ten Miles square) as may, by Cession of particular States, and the Acceptance of Congress, become the Seat of the Government of the United States, and to exercise like Authority over all Places purchased by the Consent of the Legislature of the State in which the Same shall be for the Erection of Forts, Magazines, Arsenals, dock-Yards, and other needful Buildings;—And

To make all Laws which shall be necessary and proper for carrying into Execution the foregoing Powers, and all other Powers vested by this Constitution in the Government of the United States, or in any Department or Officer thereof.

Section 9. The Privilege of the Writ of Habeas Corpus shall not be suspended, unless when in Cases of Rebellion or Invasion the public Safety may require it.

No Bill of Attainder or ex post facto Law shall be passed.

No Capitation, or other direct, Tax, shall be laid, unless in Proportion to the Census or Enumeration herein before directed to be taken.

No Tax or Duty shall be laid on Articles exported from any State.

No Preference shall be given by any Regulation of Commerce or Revenue to the Ports of one State over those of another: nor shall Vessels bound to, or from, one State, be obliged to enter, clear, or pay Duties in another.

No Money shall be drawn from the Treasury, but in Consequence of Appropriations made by Law; and a regular Statement and Account of the Receipts and Expenditures of all public Money shall be published from time to time.

No Title of Nobility shall be granted by the United States: And no Person holding any Office of Profit or Trust under them, shall, without the Consent of Congress, accept of any present, Emolument, Office, or Title, of any kind whatever, from any King, Prince, or foreign State.

Section 10. No State shall enter into any Treaty, Alliance, or Confederation; grant Letters of Marque and Reprisal; coin Money; emit Bills of Credit; make any Thing but gold and silver Coin a Tender in Payment of Debts; pass any Bill of Attainder, ex post facto Law, or Law impairing the Obligation of Contracts, or grant any Title of Nobility.

No State shall, without the Consent of the Congress, lay any Imposts or Duties on Imports or Exports, except what may be absolutely necessary for executing its inspection Laws: and the net Produce of all Duties and Imposts, laid by any State on Imports or Exports, shall be for the Use of the Treasury of the United States; and all such Laws shall be subject to the Revision and Controul of the Congress.

No State shall, without the Consent of Congress, lay any Duty of Tonnage, keep Troops, or Ships of War in time of Peace, enter into any Agreement or Compact with another State, or with a foreign Power, or engage in War, unless actually invaded, or in such imminent Danger as will not admit of delay.

Article II

Section 1. The executive Power shall be vested in a President of the United States of America. He shall hold his Office during the four Years, and, together with the Vice President, chosen for the same term, be elected, as follows

Each State shall appoint, in such Manner as the Legislature thereof may direct, a Number of Electors, equal to the whole Number of Senators and Representatives to which the State may be entitled in the Congress: but no Senator or Representative, or Person holding an Office of Trust or Profit under the United States, shall be appointed an Elector.

The Congress may determine the Time of chusing the Electors, and the Day on which they shall give their Votes; which Day shall be the same throughout the United States.

No Person except a natural born Citizen shall be eligible to the Office of President; neither shall any Person be eligible to that Office who shall not have attained to the Age of thirty five Years, and been fourteen Years a Resident within the United States.

In Case of the Removal of the President from Office, or of his Death, Resignation, or Inability to discharge the Powers and Duties of the said Office, the Same shall devolve on the Vice President, and the Congress may by Law provide for the Case of Removal, Death, Resignation or Inability, both of the President and Vice President, declaring what Officer shall then act as President, and such Officer shall act accordingly, until the Disability be removed, or a President shall be elected.

The President shall, at stated Times, receive for his Services a Compensation, which shall neither be encreased nor diminished during the Period for which he shall have been elected, and he shall not receive within that Period any other Emolument from the United States, or any of them.

Before he enter on the Execution of his Office, he shall take the following Oath or Affirmation:—"I do solemnly swear (or affirm) that I will faithfully execute the Office of President of the United States, and will to the best of my Ability, preserve, protect and defend the Constitution of the United States."

Section 2. The President shall be Commander in Chief of the Army and Navy of the United States, and of the Militia of the several States, when called into the actual Service of the United States; he may require the Opinion, in writing, of the principal Officer of each of the executive Departments, upon any Subject relating to the Duties of their respective Offices, and he shall have Power to grant Reprieves and Pardons for Offences against the United States, except in Cases of Impeachment.

He shall have Power, by and with the Advice and Consent of the Senate, to make Treaties, provided two thirds of the Senators present concur; and he shall nominate, and by and with the Advice and Consent of the Senate, shall appoint Ambassadors, other public Ministers and Consuls, Judges of the supreme Court, and all other Officers of the United States, whose Appointments are not herein otherwise provided for, and which shall be established by Law; but the Congress may by Law vest the Appointment of such inferior Officers, as they think proper, in the President alone, in the Courts of Law, or in the Heads of Departments.

The President shall have Power to fill up all Vacancies that may happen during the Recess of the Senate, by granting Commissions which shall expire at the End of their next Session.

Section 3. He shall from time to time give to the Congress Information of the State of the Union, and recommend to their Consideration such Measures as he shall judge necessary and expedient; he may, on extraordinary Occasions, convene both Houses, or either of them, and in Case of Disagreement between them, with Respect to the Time of Adjournment, he may adjourn them to such Time as he shall think proper; he shall receive Ambassadors and other public Ministers; he shall take Care that the Laws be faithfully executed, and shall Commission all the Officers of the United States.

Section 4. The President, Vice President and all civil Officers of the United States, shall be removed from Office on Impeachment for, and Conviction of, Treason, Bribery, or other High Crimes and Misdemeanors.

Article III

Section 1. The judicial Power of the United States, shall be vested in one supreme Court, and in such inferior Courts as the Congress may from time to time ordain and establish. The Judges, both of the supreme and inferior Courts, shall hold their Offices during good Behaviour, and shall, at stated Times, receive for their Services, a Compensation, which shall not be diminished during their Continuance in Office.

Section 2. The judicial Power shall extend to all Cases, in Law and Equity, arising under this Constitution, the Laws of the United States, and Treaties made, or which shall be made, under their Authority;—to all Cases affecting Ambassadors, other public Ministers and Consuls;—to all Cases of admiralty and maritime Jurisdiction;—to Controversies to which the United States shall be a Party;—to Controversies between two or more States; between a State and Citizens of another State;—between Citizens of different States;—between Citizens of the same State claiming Lands under Grants of different States, and between a State, or the Citizens thereof, and foreign States, Citizens or Subjects.

In all Cases affecting Ambassadors, other public Ministers and Consuls, and those in which a State shall be Party, the supreme Court shall have original Jurisdiction. In all the other Cases before mentioned, the supreme Court shall have appellate Jurisdiction, both as to Law and Fact, with such Exceptions, and under such Regulations as the Congress shall make.

The Trial of all Crimes, except in Cases of Impeachment, shall be by Jury; and such Trial shall be held in the State where the said Crimes shall have been committed; but when not committed within any State, the Trial shall be at such Place or Places as the Congress may by Law have directed.

Section 3. Treason against the United States, shall consist only in levying War against them, or in adhering to their Enemies, giving them Aid and Comfort. No Person shall be convicted of Treason unless on the Testimony of two Witnesses to the same overt Act, or on Confession in open Court.

The Congress shall have Power to declare the Punishment of Treason, but no Attainder of Treason shall work Corruption of Blood, or Forfeiture except during the Life of the Person attainted.

ARTICLE IV.

Section 1. Full Faith and Credit shall be given in each State to the public Acts, Records, and judicial Proceedings of every other State. And the Congress may by general Laws prescribe the Manner in which such Acts, Records and Proceedings shall be proved, and the Effect thereof.

Section 2. The Citizens of each State shall be entitled to all Privileges and Immunities of Citizens in the several States.

A Person charged in any State with Treason, Felony, or other Crime, who shall flee from Justice, and be found in another State, shall on Demand of the executive Authority of the State from which he fled, be delivered up, to be removed to the State having Jurisdiction of the Crime.

Section 3. New States may be admitted by the Congress into this Union; but no new State shall be formed or erected within the Jurisdiction of any other State; nor any State be formed by the Junction of two or more States, or Parts of States, without the Consent of the Legislatures of the States concerned as well as of the Congress.

The Congress shall have Power to dispose of and make all needful Rules and Regulations respecting the Territory or other Property belonging to the United States; and nothing in this Constitution shall be so construed as to Prejudice any Claims of the United States, or of any particular State.

Section 4. The United States shall guarantee to every State in this Union a Republican Form of Government, and shall protect each of them against Invasion; and on Application of the Legislature, or of the Executive (when the Legislature cannot be convened) against domestic Violence.

ARTICLE V

The Congress, whenever two thirds of both Houses shall deem it necessary, shall propose Amendments to this Constitution, or, on the Application of the Legislatures of two thirds of the several States, shall call a Convention for proposing Amendments, which, in either Case, shall be valid to all Intents and Purposes, as Part of this Constitution, when ratified by the Legislatures of three fourths of the several States, or by Conventions in three fourths thereof, as the one or the other Mode of Ratification may be proposed by the Congress; Provided that no State, without its Consent, shall be deprived of its equal Suffrage in the Senate.

ARTICLE VI

All Debts contracted and Engagements entered into, before the Adoption of this Constitution, shall be as valid against the United States under this Constitution, as under the Confederation.

This Constitution, and the Laws of the United States which shall be made in Pursuance thereof; and all Treaties made, or which shall be made, under the Authority of the United States, shall be the supreme Law of the Land; and the Judges in every State shall be bound thereby, any Thing in the Constitution or Laws of any State to the Contrary notwithstanding.

The Senators and Representatives before mentioned, and the Members of the several State Legislatures, and all executive and judicial Officers, both of the United States and of the several States, shall be bound by Oath or Affirmation, to support this Constitution; but no religious Test shall ever be required as a Qualification to any Office or public Trust under the United States.

ARTICLE VII

The Ratification of the Conventions of nine States, shall be sufficient for the Establishment of this Constitution between the States so ratifying the Same.

Done in Convention by the Unanimous Consent of the States present the Seventeenth Day of September in the Year of our Lord one thousand seven hundred and Eighty seven and of the Independence of the United States of America the Twelfth. In witness whereof We have hereunto subscribed our Names.

[The first 10 Amendments were ratified December 15, 1791, and form what is known as the Bill of Rights.]

AMENDMENT 1

Congress shall make no law respecting an establishment of religion, or prohibiting the free exercise thereof; or abridging the freedom of speech, or of the press; or the right of the people peaceably to assemble, and to petition the Government for a redress of grievances.

AMENDMENT 2

A well regulated Militia, being necessary to the security of a free State, the right of the people to keep and bear Arms, shall not be infringed.

AMENDMENT 3
No Soldier shall, in time of peace be quartered in any house, without the consent of the Owner, nor in time of war, but in a manner to be prescribed by law.

AMENDMENT 4
The right of the people to be secure in their persons, houses, papers, and effects, against unreasonable searches and seizures, shall not be violated, and no Warrants shall issue, but upon probable cause, supported by Oath or affirmation, and particulary describing the place to be searched, and the persons or things to be seized.

AMENDMENT 5
No person shall be held to answer for a capital, or otherwise infamous crime, unless on a presentment or indictment of a Grand Jury, except in cases arising in the land or naval forces, or in the Militia, when in actual service in time of War or public danger; nor shall any person be subject for the same offence to be twice put in jeopardy of life or limb; nor shall be compelled in any criminal case to be a witness against himself, nor be deprived of life, liberty, or property, without due process of law; nor shall private property be taken for public use, without just compensation.

AMENDMENT 6
In all criminal prosecutions, the accused shall enjoy the right to a speedy and public trial, by an impartial jury of the State and district wherein the crime shall have been committed, which district shall have been previously ascertained by law, and to be informed of the nature and cause of the accusation; to be confronted with the witnesses against him; to have compulsory process for obtaining witnesses in his favor, and to have the Assistance of Counsel for his defence.

AMENDMENT 7
In Suits at common law, where the value in controversy shall exceed twenty dollars, the right of trial by jury shall be preserved, and no fact tried by a jury, shall be otherwise reexamined in any Court of the United States, than according to the rules of the common law.

AMENDMENT 8
Excessive bail shall not be required, nor excessive fines imposed, nor cruel and unusual punishments inflicted.

AMENDMENT 9
The enumeration in the Constitution, of certain rights, shall not be construed to deny or disparage others retained by the people.

AMENDMENT 10
The powers not delegated to the United States by the Constitution, nor prohibited by it to the States, are reserved to the States respectively, or to the people.

AMENDMENT 11 [Ratified February 7, 1795]
The Judicial power of the United States shall not be construed to extend to any suit in law or equity, commenced or prosecuted against one of the United States by Citizens of another State, or by Citizens or Subjects of any Foreign State.

AMENDMENT 12 [Ratified July 27, 1804]
The Electors shall meet in their respective states and vote by ballot for President and Vice-President, one of whom, at least, shall not be an inhabitant of the same state with themselves; they shall name in their ballots the person voted for as President, and in distinct ballots the person voted for as Vice-President, and they shall make distinct lists of all persons voted for as President, and of all persons voted for as Vice-President, and of the number of votes for each, which lists they shall sign and certify, and transmit sealed to the seat of the government of the United States, directed to the President of the Senate;—The President of the Senate shall, in the presence of the Senate and House of Representatives, open all the certificates and the votes shall then be counted;—The person having the greatest number of votes for President, shall be the President, if such number be a majority of the whole number of Electors appointed; and if no person have such majority, then from the persons having the highest numbers not exceeding three on the list of those voted for as President, the House of Representatives shall choose immediately, by ballot, the President. But in choosing the President, the votes shall be taken by states, the representation from each state having one vote; a quorum for this purpose shall consist of a member or members from two-thirds of the states, and a majority of all the states shall be necessary to a choice. And if the House of Representatives shall not choose a President whenever the right of choice shall devolve upon them, before the fourth day of March next following, then the Vice-President shall act as President, as in the case of the death or other constitutional disability of the Presi-

dent.—The person having the greatest number of votes as Vice-President, shall be the Vice-President, if such number be a majority of the whole number of Electors appointed, and if no person have a majority, then from the two highest numbers on the list, the Senate shall choose the Vice-President; a quorum for the purpose shall consist of two-thirds of the whole number of Senators, and a majority of the whole number shall be necessary to a choice. But no person constitutionally ineligible to the office of President shall be eligible to that of Vice-President of the United States.

AMENDMENT 13 [Ratified December 6, 1865]
Section 1. Neither slavery nor involuntary servitude, except as a punishment for crime whereof the party shall have been duly convicted, shall exist within the United States, or any place subject to their jurisdiction.

Section 2. Congress shall have power to enforce this article by appropriate legislation.

AMENDMENT 14 [Ratified July 9, 1868]
Section 1. All persons born or naturalized in the United States, and subject to the jurisdiction thereof, are citizens of the United States and of the State wherein they reside. No State shall make or enforce any law which shall abridge the privileges or immunities of citizens of the United States; nor shall any State deprive any person of life, liberty, or property, without due process of law; nor deny to any person within its jurisdiction the equal protection of the laws.

Section 2. Representatives shall be apportioned among the several States according to their respective numbers, counting the whole number of persons in each State, excluding Indians not taxed. But when the right to vote at any election for the choice of electors for President and Vice President of the United States, Representatives in Congress, the Executive and Judicial officers of a State, or the members of the Legislature thereof, is denied to any of the male inhabitants of such State, being twenty-one years of age, and citizens of the United States, or in any way abridged, except for participation in rebellion, or other crime, the basis of representation therein shall be reduced in the proportion which the number of such male citizens shall bear to the whole number of male citizens twenty-one years of age in such State.

Section 3. No person shall be a Senator or Representative in Congress, or elector of President and Vice President, or hold any office, civil or military, under the United States, or under any State, who, having previously taken an oath, as a member of Congress, or as an officer of the United States, or as a member of any State legislature, or as an executive or judicial officer of any State, to support the Constitution of the United States, shall have engaged in insurrection or rebellion against the same, or given aid or comfort to the enemies thereof. But Congress may by a vote of two-thirds of each House, remove such disability.

Section 4. The validity of the public debt of the United States, authorized by law, including debts incurred for payment of pensions and bounties for services in suppressing insurrection or rebellion, shall not be questioned. But neither the United States nor any State shall assume or pay any debt or obligation incurred in aid of insurrection or rebellion against the United States, or any claim for the loss or emancipation of any slave; but all such debts, obligations and claims shall be held illegal and void.

Section 5. The Congress shall have power to enforce, by appropriate legislation, the provisions of this article.

AMENDMENT 15 [Ratified February 3, 1870]
Section 1. The right of citizens of the United States to vote shall not be denied or abridged by the United States or by any State on account of race, color, or previous condition of servitude.

Section 2. The Congress shall have power to enforce this article by appropriate legislation.

AMENDMENT 16 [Ratified February 3, 1913]
The Congress shall have power to lay and collect taxes on incomes, from whatever source derived, without apportionment among the several States, and without regard to any census or enumeration.

AMENDMENT 17 [Ratified April 8, 1913]
The Senate of the United States shall be composed of two Senators from each State, elected by the people thereof for six years; and each Senator shall have one vote. The electors in each State shall have the qualifications requisite for electors of the most numerous branch of the State legislatures.

When vacancies happen in the representation of any State in the Senate, the executive authority of such State shall issue writs of election to fill such vacancies: *Provided,* That the legislature of any State may empower the executive thereof to make temporary appointments until the people fill the vacancies by election as the legislature may direct.

This amendment shall not be so construed as to affect the election or term of any Senator chosen before it becomes valid as part of the Constitution.

AMENDMENT 18 [Ratified January 16, 1919]

Section 1. After one year from the ratification of this article the manufacture, sale, or transportation of intoxicating liquors within, the importation thereof into, or the exportation thereof from the United States and all territory subject to the jurisdiction thereof for beverage purposes is hereby prohibited.

Section 2. The Congress and the several States shall have concurrent power to enforce this article by appropriate legislation.

Section 3. This article shall be inoperative unless it shall have been ratified as an amendment to the Constitution by the legislatures of the several States, as provided in the Constitution, within seven years from the date of the submission hereof to the States by the Congress.

AMENDMENT 19 [Ratified August 18, 1920]

The right of citizens of the United States to vote shall not be denied or abridged by the United States or by any State on account of sex.

Congress shall have power to enforce this article by appropriate legislation.

AMENDMENT 20 [Ratified January 23, 1933]

Section 1. The terms of the President and Vice President shall end at noon on the 20th day of January, and the terms of Senators and Representatives at noon on the 3rd day of January, of the years in which such terms would have ended if this article had not been ratified; and the terms of their successors shall then begin.

Section 2. The Congress shall assemble at least once in every year, and such meeting shall begin at noon on the 3d day of January, unless they shall by law appoint a different day.

Section 3. If, at the time fixed for the beginning of the term of the President, the President elect shall have died, the Vice President elect shall become President. If a President shall not have been chosen before the time fixed for the beginning of his term, or if the President elect shall have failed to qualify, then the Vice President elect shall act as President until a President shall have qualified; and the Congress may by law provide for the case wherein neither a President elect nor a Vice President elect shall have qualified, declaring who shall then act as President, or the manner in which one who is to act shall be selected, and such person shall act accordingly until a President or Vice President shall have qualified.

Section 4. The Congress may by law provide for the case of the death of any of the persons from whom the House of Representatives may choose a President whenever the right of choice shall have devolved upon them, and for the case of the death of any of the persons from whom the Senate may choose a Vice President whenever the right of choice shall have devolved upon them.

Section 5. Sections 1 and 2 shall take effect on the 15th day of October following the ratification of this article.

Section 6. This article shall be inoperative unless it shall have been ratified as an amendment to the Constitution by the legislatures of three-fourths of the several States within seven years from the date of its submission.

AMENDMENT 21 [Ratified December 5, 1933]

Section 1. The eighteenth article of amendment to the Constitution of the United States is hereby repealed.

Section 2. The transportation or importation into any State, Territory, or possession of the United States for delivery or use therein of intoxicating liquors, in violation of the laws thereof, is hereby prohibited.

Section 3. This article shall be inoperative unless it shall have been ratified as an amendment to the Constitution by conventions in the several States, as provided in the Constitution, within seven years from the date of the submission hereof to the States by the Congress.

AMENDMENT 22 [Ratified February 27, 1951]

Section 1. No person shall be elected to the office of the President more than twice, and no person who has held the office of President, or acted as President, for more than two years of a term to which some other person was elected President shall be elected to the office of the President more than once. But this Article shall not apply to any person holding the office of President when this Article was proposed by the Congress, and shall not prevent any person who may be holding the office of President, or acting as President, during the term within which this Article becomes operative from holding the office of President or acting as President during the remainder of such term.

Section 2. This article shall be inoperative unless it shall have been ratified as an amendment to the Constitution by the legislatures of three-fourths of the several States within seven years from the date of its submission to the States by the Congress.

AMENDMENT 23 [Ratified March 29, 1961]

Section 1. The District constituting the seat of Government of the United States shall appoint in such manner as the Congress may direct:

A number of electors of President and Vice President equal to the whole number of Senators and Representatives in Congress to which the District would be entitled if it were a State, but in no event more than the least populous State; they shall be in addition to those appointed by the States, but they shall be considered, for the purposes of the election of President and Vice President, to be electors appointed by a State; and they shall meet in the District and perform such duties as provided by the twelfth article of amendment.

Section 2. The Congress shall have power to enforce this article by appropriate legislation.

AMENDMENT 24 [Ratified January 23, 1964]

Section 1. The right of citizens of the United States to vote in any primary or other election for President or Vice President, for electors for President or Vice President, or for Senator or Representative in Congress, shall not be denied or abridged by the United States or any State by reason of failure to pay any poll tax or other tax.

Section 2. The Congress shall have power to enforce this article by appropriate legislation.

AMENDMENT 25 [Ratified February 10, 1967]

Section 1. In case of the removal of the President from office or of his death or resignation, the Vice President shall become President.

Section 2. Whenever there is a vacancy in the office of the Vice President, the President shall nominate a Vice President who shall take office upon confirmation by a majority vote of both Houses of Congress.

Section 3. Whenever the President transmits to the President pro tempore of the Senate and the Speaker of the House of Representatives his written declaration that he is unable to discharge the powers and duties of his office, and until he transmits to them a written declaration to the contrary, such powers and duties shall be discharged by the Vice President as Acting President.

Section 4. Whenever the Vice President and a majority of either the principal officers of the executive departments or of such other body as Congress may by law provide, transmit to the President pro tempore of the Senate and the Speaker of the House of Representatives their written declaration that the President is unable to discharge the powers and duties of his office, the Vice President shall immediately assume the powers and duties of the office as Acting President.

Thereafter, when the President transmits to the President pro tempore of the Senate and the Speaker of the House of Representatives his written declaration that no inability exists, he shall resume the powers and duties of his office unless the Vice President and a majority of either the principal officers of the executive department or of such other body as Congress may by law provide, transmit within four days to the President pro tempore of the Senate and the Speaker of the House of Representatives their written declaration that the President is unable to discharge the powers and duties of his office. Thereupon Congress shall decide the issue, assembling within forty-eight hours for that purpose if not in session. If the Congress, within twenty-one days after receipt of the latter written declaration, or, if Congress is not in session, within twenty-one days after Congress is required to assemble, determines by two-thirds vote of both Houses that the President is unable to discharge the powers and duties of his office, the Vice President shall continue to discharge the same as Acting President; otherwise, the President shall resume the powers and duties of his office.

AMENDMENT 26 [Ratified June 30, 1971]

Section 1. The right of citizens of the United States, who are eighteen years of age or older, to vote shall not be denied or abridged by the United States or by any State on account of age.

Section 2. The Congress shall have the power to enforce this article by appropriate legislation.

Index

Abortion, 245, 246
Abzug, B., 180
Adams, J., 82, 181, 182, 240
Advertising, 30, 120–123, 138–140, 142. *See also* Media
Agnew, S., 181, 183, 206
  resignation of, 5, 134, 184
  speeches by, 130
Albert, C., 227, 228
Alienation, 6. *See also* Powerlessness
Allen, J., 220
American Bankers association, 285
American Bar Association, 287
American Civil Liberties Union, 299
American Communist party, 105, 107
Americans For Constitutional Action, 91
Americans for Democratic Action, 27, 91
American Independent party, 98, 106, 109
American Labor party, 107
American Medical Association, 84, 284, 285, 287
American Nazi party, 105
American Petroleum Institute, 285
American Political Science Association, 113
Anti-Ballistic Missile program, 61
Anti-Federalist party, 108
Anti-Mason party, 105
Appropriations, 162, 166, 204, 206

Baker, C., 292
Bank Secrecy Act, 246
Barber, J. D., 155–156, 190, 191n
Barkley, A., 222
Bayh, B., 216
Beard, C., 239, 268n
Berenson, B., 173
Bernstein, C., 131, 147n
Black Caucus, 95
Black, H., 248, 257
Blackmun, H., 247
Blaine, J. C., 106, 226, 279
Brandeis, L., 257, 258, 265
Brewster, D., 230
Bricker, J., 167
Bryce, J., 93, 98, 115n, 152
Buckley, J., 106
Budget, 157, 187
  military, 37
Bureaucracy
  politics of, 41–43
  and the presidency, 157–160
Burger, W., 246, 247, 248, 265
Burns, J. M., 189, 192n
Byrd, R., 232, 234n

Cabinet, 157, 175–177, 181
Cable television, 290
Calhoun, J. C., 183
Cambodia, 162, 168, 188, 209, 252

Campaign financing, 22, 61, 140–146, 230,287
Campaign Reform Law (1974), 145
Cannon, J., 226
Capitalism, 26, 35–36, 108
Celler, E., 221, 222
Census Bureau, 66–67
Center for Public Financing of Elections, 145
Central Intelligence Agency (CIA), 5, 42, 169, 209, 230
Chancellor, J., 130
Chase, S., 249
Chavez, C., 297
Checks and balances, 41, 186
China, Nixon and, 124, 166
Chisholm, S., 194, 204, 215, 232, 233n
Civil Aeronautics Board (CAB), 158, 159, 263
Civil Rights Act (1957), 219
Civil Rights Act (1964), 219, 299
Civil War, 57, 102, 171, 189, 244
Cleveland, G., 102, 209, 279
Cloture, 219, 220, 232
Commager, H. S., 189, 192n
Committee for the Reelection of the President (CREEP), 144, 203
Common Cause, 287, 288
Commoner, B., 23
Congress, 17, 27, 34, 37, 59–60, 81, 87–88, 106, 152, 157, 160, 161, 162, 166, 167, 177, 185, 186, 187, 189, 192–232
committees of, 197, 198, 213–221
elected positions in, 226–229
investigating by, 201–204
law-making in, 197–199
reform of, 194, 196, 213
and Supreme Court, 249–250
Connally, J., 144, 177
Conservative party, 106
Constituent
  awareness, 75
  mail, 200–201
  -service function, 201
Constitution, 81, 82, 104, 108, 153, 157, 161, 167, 168, 181, 185, 197, 206, 207, 208, 248, 253
  amending, 210–211, 250
Constitutional Convention, 239
Constitutional Union party, 106
Consumer Protection Agency, 287
Coolidge, C., 153, 155, 250
Corporation
  executive, 19, 20
  largest, 24, 25
Corrupt Practices Act (1925), 142, 144
Corruption in politics, 3, 143, 230
  See also Watergate
Council of Economic Advisers, 157
Court packing, 245, 249
Courts of appeals, 262–263
Cross-pressures, 70, 124

Dahl, R., 31, 32, 33, 36, 38, 43, 44, 45
Dawson, R. E., 50, 78n
Dean, J., 203
Death penalty, 251
Delaney, J., 279
Dellums, R., 170, 279
Democracy, defined, 273–274
Democratic party, 85, 86–103, 108, 110–114, 284
  convention (1968), 85
  and Republican party, 88–92
Democratic-Republican party, 82
Democrats for Nixon, 122, 144
Demonstration, 154–155, 296, 297, 298
Direct action, 296–299
  boycott, 296–298
  nonviolent action, 297
  sit-in, 296–299
Dixiecrat party, 105
Domestic Council, 159
Domhoff, G. W., 27, 43, 44
Dominican Republic, 168
Douglas, W. O., 171, 208, 248, 249, 252, 258, 265
Draft, legality of, 252
Durkin, J., 279
Dye, T. R., 29

Eagleton, T., 170, 183
Ehrlichmann, J., 178, 180, 262
Eisenhower, D. D., 103, 155, 166, 167, 175, 180, 250, 260
Election, 29, 30, 74
  congressional, 59–60
  presidential, 277
  as ritual, 72
  turnout, 59, 67
Elections Commission, 145
Elite *See also* Pluralist Theory and Ruling Elite Theory
  accountability of, 37–38
  competition among, 33–35
  concept of, 17
  interlocking of, 20, 25
  multiple, 32–33
  political, 16–43
Enemies list, 180
Energy crisis, 23
Ervin, S., 202, 206, 215
Executive agreement, 166, 167, 207
Executive privilege, 239, 261

Fairness doctrine, 289
Family, political influence of, 46, 48–50
Farm-Labor party, 106
Federal Bureau of Investigation, 42
Federal Communications Commission, 42, 144, 159, 263, 293
Federal district courts, 262
Federal Election Campaign Act (1971), 144, 145, 203
Federalist party, 82, 102, 108

National Congress of Parents and
 Teachers, 286
National emergency, and President,
 168
National Labor Relations Act, 245
National Opinion Research Center,
 64
National Rifle Association, 285, 286
National security, 143, 252
National Security Agency, 169
National Security Council, 159, 181
National Welfare Rights
 Organization, 284
Nationalization, of industry, 26, 98
Neustadt, R., 188, 190, 191n
New Deal, 26, 244, 245, 248, 249, 266
New Left, 8
New York Times, 61, 131, 132
Nimmo, D., 127, 147n
Nixon, R. M., 34, 35, 59, 61, 75, 90, 95,
 103, 109, 140, 144, 147n, 153–155,
 160, 162, 164–167, 177–184, 188,
 189, 203, 206, 207, 209, 239, 261,
 262, 268n, 273, 279
 administration of, 20, 22, 129, 228,
  231
 and amnesty, 171
 associates of, 5
 and Cabinet, 175
 and Cambodia, 252
 and China, 124
 Democrats for, 122, 144
 and impeachment, 76, 172, 188
 -Kennedy debates, 139
 pardon of, 171
 reelection campaign, 22, 142, 143,
  287
 resignation of, 5, 134
 and Supreme Court, 172, 246, 247,
  250, 259, 260
 United States of America v., 238
 and Vietnam War, 93, 169, 170
Nuclear Test Ban Treaty, 187

Office of Management and Budget,
 157, 205
Opinion leader, 55, 125
Original jurisdiction and Supreme
 Court, 253
Owens, W., 231

Packaging, of candidates, 120–123,
 135–140. *See also* Media
Packard, C., 20
Packard, V., 6, 7, 15, 120, 147n
Padover, S. K., 168, 191n
Participation, in politics, 46–77,
 272–300
 and media, 132
 non-, 38
 obstacles to, 66–73
Party loyalty, 114, 125–126
Patman, W., 96, 225
Peace Corps, 187
Peace and Freedom party, 109
Peer groups, and political opinion,
 46, 53–54

Pentagon, 21, 22
 mentality, 169
 Papers, 5, 62, 132, 246
Percy, C., 97
Petris, N., 283
Pierce, F., 167
Playboy, 128
Puralist theory, 16, 31–39, 40, 161,
 187, 276, 284
Poage, W. R., 96, 225
Pocket veto, 162
Policy-making, 117, 160–162
Political party, 29, 81–114
 as channel for action, 85–86
 and conflict, 88
 dominance, 99–103
 fragmentation within, 93–97
 group support of, 90–91
 organization, 94
 system, 83
 volunteers, 87
Politics
 defined, 10–12
 learning about, 47–58
 participation in, 46–77
Populist party, 106, 110
Powell, L., 247
Power
 political, 9, 10–12, 16–43, 81, 272
 presidential, evaluated, 185–190
Powerlessness, 8, 9, 71–73, 278
Presidency, 17, 37, 106, 152–190
 and bureaucracy, 157–160
 and Congress, 87–88, 160–162
 duties of, 156–172
 imperial, 185–190
 insulation of, 173, 179
 and the military, 167–171
 performance of, 154–156
 and Supreme Court, 171–172, 250,
  258–260
President
 personality of (Barber Study), 154–156
Prewitt, K., 50, 78n
Price, M., 226
Price, R., 135
Progressive party (1912), 105, 106
Progressive party (1924), 106, 110
Progressive party (1948), 98
Prohibition party, 84, 105
Proportional representation, 107, 111
Proxmire, W., 20, 44
Public Citizen, 287

Ramparts, 128
Rand, C. T., 23, 44
Rayburn, S., 227
Reagan, R., 3
Recall, 294, 295
Reed, T., 226
Reedy, G., 172, 190, 191n
Referendum, 294, 295
Registration requirements, 67–68
Rehnquist, W., 247
Republican party, 85, 86–103, 108,
 110–114, 165, 284

 and Democratic party, 88–92
Residence requirements, 67–68, 278
Reston, J., 131, 147n
Riegle, D., 217, 222, 231, 233, 234n
Riesman, D., 56, 79n
Rivers, M., 218
Rockefeller, D., 25
Rockefeller, N., 25, 27, 121, 184, 207
Rodino, P., 203
Romney, G., 20
Roosevelt, F. D., 26, 103, 153, 155,
 165, 168, 170, 171, 180, 186, 243,
 245, 248, 249
Roosevelt, T., 98, 106, 153
Rosenberg, M., 69, 79n
Ross, R., 267, 268n
Rossiter, C., 89, 99, 115n, 116n, 160,
 164, 190, 191n
Ruling-elite theory, 16, 18–31, 39–40,
 72, 73, 88, 128, 161, 169, 176, 177,
 188, 198, 212, 232, 237, 241, 248,
 278, 279, 284, 288, 291

Sahl, M., 164
Schlesinger, A., 178, 180, 188, 189,
 190, 191n, 192n
Schwartz, C. L., 27
School, political influence of, 46,
 50–53
Scott, H., 228
Secrecy, 42, 230
Securities and Exchange
 Commission, 159
Selective processes, 123–125
Senate, 60, 87, 141, 142, 167, 172, 175,
 186
 Appropriations Committee, 205,
  216, 217
 Budget Committee, 205
 Finance Committee, 205
 Foreign Relations Committee, 207
 Watergate Committee, 202, 203, 204
Seniority, in Congress, 96, 114, 196,
 197, 213, 221–226, 229, 230, 232,
 287
Sevareid, E., 140
Sherrill, R., 80n, 224, 234n, 268n, 297,
 302n
Sierra Club, 34, 293
Sirica, J., 238, 261, 262
Slavery, 244
Socialist party, 106
Socialist-Labor party, 104
Sorauf, F., 82, 83, 91, 94, 115n
Special interest group, 217, 229, 230,
 232
State courts, 263–264
State Department, 166, 167, 169
Stevens, J. P., 258
Stevenson, A., 123, 139
Stone, B., 267, 268n
Stone, H., 245
Stone, W. C., 142
Stouffer, S., 63, 64
Strum, P., 179, 190, 191n
Students for a Democratic Society, 65